BRUT FORCE

The further, staggering adventures
of a professional wine buyer.

Peter Stafford-Bow

Cover design by Patrick Latimer Illustration
www.PatrickLatimer.co.za

www.PeterStaffordBow.com
@PonceDuVin

Acorn Independent Press Ltd
82 Southwark Bridge Road
London
SEI 0AS

To Curly, with more love.
"Yep. Still smells like wine…"

Chapter One

A Short Guide to Winemaking

High summer. The laziest part of August. That short interval when the British weather, much to its surprise, rolls up its sleeves and has a shot at being Mediterranean. Of course, farmers and other wise observers know this is the beginning of the end. The brilliant sunshine and the hum of fat, satisfied bees mark the stalling of the sun's progress, the next equinox now much closer than the last. But, as I lay in my Little Chalfont garden, a bottle of crisp Aligoté relaxing in the ice bucket beside me, it was easy to dream of endless, carefree afternoons in the French countryside.

You might think that a flight of fancy too far. Buckinghamshire is a long way from Burgundy, after all. But I had company. An immigrant, who had put down roots in a soil far from home, bringing a dash of continental glamour to our Home Counties garden. A grapevine. In Little Chalfont! A Pinot Noir, no less, that most exquisite yet fickle of God's fruits. I lay dozing in my favourite spot, my head against her trunk, just a cushion between us, the ground slightly raised where she met the earth. Her limbs, lithe but strong, spread above me, supporting a canopy of green hands, shading me and her young, precious fruit from the summer sun.

"*Veraison*, man. That's my new favourite word."

Fistule descended the metal steps outside the flat, a smoking bong in one hand, a well-thumbed copy of Skelton's *Viticulture* in the other and a slim volume of *The Sayings of The Buddha* poking from his waistband. As chief composter, pot plant tenderer and house environmentalist, it had fallen to Fistule to nurture our vine through its early years. He'd taken to the task with organic gusto, training new growth in spring, pruning back in winter, even sowing autumn cover crops of barley, clover and vetch.

"Your wisdom grows by the day, Fistule," I said, eyes closed.

Was there a man as innocent, as close to nature, as passionate in his embrace of its herbs and produce as dear Fistule? If there were, I had yet to meet him. For Fistule was a creature in love with the soil, at one with the seasons, dewy-eyed in the face of Mother Nature's works, whether ripening grape, stray daisy or orphaned hedgehog.

And was there a fouler contrast than that of Fistule's gentle fertility and the black secret lying just feet beneath my little garden plot? I doubt it. For I have experienced much in my short but exciting life, from the fragrance of desert flowers after rain in the Namib, to the odour of an over-ripe durian in a Chiang Mai tuk-tuk, but even I struggle to conceive of a more deplorable comparison than Fistule's purity and the unmentionable obscenity lurking below us.

Again, you might think I exaggerate. If some horror did indeed lie mere feet beneath my lounging spot, how could I lie there so nonchalantly, dreaming of baguettes stuffed with jambon, of runny cheese and French fancies? The answer is: quite easily. For one adjusts to even the vilest of memories and, besides, I was attached to our little garden. Planting a vine is a statement of intent, even defiance. It says this is my ground, my earth, my little patch of paradise, and woe betide anyone who dare try and take it.

But forgive me, I'm running ahead of myself. I don't wish to distract you from the bucolic scene on that fine summer's day, the lazy, warm air barely moving the leaves, the rich perfume of the soil, and that wonderful white wine doziness, halfway between reverie and dreams.

"I'm trying to identify the soil type, man. Do you think it's chalk?"

"For sure, Fistule. We're on the edge of the Chilterns. Don't you remember when we excavated the garden during your composting toilet project? The soil was full of chalky lumps. Broken masonry too, probably from when they built the car park."

Our vine had grown vigorously over the past few seasons, soaking up the sun in the microclimate of our communal garden. And now, in late, high summer, her grapes were indeed undergoing *veraison*, the pale berries transforming into plumper, darker fruit.

Fistule crouched, took a draw on his bong and consulted *Viticulture*. "So, it's a mixed soil. Chalk with a substratum of car park rubble."

Not just chalk and rubble, I thought to myself. There was an incident from my past too, an episode that should have been allowed to decay and vanish, but which, against all laws of justice and nature, lived on, casting a shadow I couldn't quite shake.

"I couldn't *give* the grapes away last year," said Fistule. He, of course, knew nothing of that terrible episode. "People didn't like the pips. It broke my heart. I made some into jam, but it was too bitty. Ended up composting most of it."

"It's Pinot Noir, Fistule. A wine grape. Bred for its juice, not for the fruit bowl."

"Wodin tried to make wine from it two years ago. Tasted disgusting, man."

"That's because he made it in a dirty old tub in our kitchen and kept sticking his finger in to taste it. You can't home-brew grapes in a bucket, open to every passing wild yeast spore, not to mention whatever dodgy bacteria are currently resident on Wodin's fingers. You've got to have sterile equipment and controlled conditions."

"I'm going to feed them to the birds this year. As nature gives, I shall return." Fistule took another drag on the bong, which bubbled in approval.

Time for a refill of my own. I rolled on to my side and reached for the ice bucket. As I withdrew the bottle, my hand grazed the vine's trunk and I felt a small, sharp pain. A tiny sliver of wood had impaled itself in the back of my hand. I refilled my glass then tweezered out the splinter with the tips of my nails. As I pinched the skin either side of the puncture, a small bead of blood grew in its place.

Vine roots travel deep, especially in stony soil, on their relentless search for water and nutrients. They would have found the two men years ago, contorted in their shallow resting place, the roots growing round or through them as they colonised the guilty earth beneath.

***

The fire roared in the grate. In London now, a cosy, buzzing pub in St James's, right in the centre of the great city. Jenny withdrew her lips from mine and ruffled my hair.

"Leave the punters alone, will you, Jenny? You'll get me done for running a bawdy house." Tom Hawkins, legendary wine merchant, storyteller, dealmaker and pub landlord, set down his tankard of wine and wiped a sleeve across his grey-pink beard.

"I was only saying hello to Felix," sulked Jenny. "He's our best-looking customer and I haven't seen him for a week."

"It's really no trouble at all," I said.

"I'm sure it isn't. But she's got work to do, haven't you, Jenny?"

Jenny made a face and topped up Tom's tankard with wine, before skipping back behind the bar.

"Listen, Felix. I've got a little quiz for you. You'll love this."

Old Hawkins liked riddles. He drew his chair closer and pointed at me. Several of the shorter fingers on his hand were very short indeed, the top halves lost decades ago in some ancient misadventure. They wiggled slightly, like impatient chipolatas, the ends smooth and pink.

"If you get it right, I'll sell you that shipment of Chilean Merlot at half price. You get it wrong, I won't. All right?"

I nodded, but I knew it was a trick. Hawkins hadn't got where he was today by selling million-bottle orders of Merlot to supermarket buyers at below cost.

"Right. Answer this: what is the closest winery to where we're sitting?"

"The closest winery to this pub?" We were sitting in the Flag and Parrot, the finest pub in St James's, for the very good reason that the beer was free. Not to everyone of course, just to those admired by or useful to the pub's owner. I was, I'm flattered to say, one of that lucky group, on account of my job as Head of Wine at Gatesave, England's largest supermarket chain. And the beer was free to Tom Hawkins too, of course, for the very good reason that he *was* the owner.

"The closest winery to where we're *sitting*." Hawkins stabbed one of his few full-length fingers on the table and lifted the tankard back to his beard.

"We're right in the centre of London. So, it's either in the Chilterns," I mused, "or, more likely, south of here, somewhere in Kent or Surrey."

Hawkins smiled behind the tankard and took a long draught.

"Perhaps Denbies, near Dorking?" I guessed. "Or Château Spott-Hythe, in Pluckley?"

"Is that your final answer?"

"Yes, Château Spott-Hythe."

"Ha!" Hawkins slapped the table. "You're miles off."

"Denbies then?"

"No. Follow me." Hawkins stood and walked behind the bar. He beckoned and disappeared through a doorway. I followed him through and down a set of stone steps. To the left lay an archway and a room piled high with barrels on metal racks, a busy thicket of pipes sucking and snaking up to the ceiling, feeding the beer pumps in the saloon bar above.

"Not in there, this way. I've converted the old cellar."

We continued down a gentle slope, the moist stone flags glistening under a line of bulbs strung along the ceiling. The air cooled and the laughter from the pub quietened to a gentle hum.

"Ready?"

Hawkins flicked a switch, there was a soft buzz and the room glowed into life.

"Wow."

As wineries go, it wasn't a big one. Four steel tanks stood along one side of the room while a wall of wooden barrels, three rows high, lined the other. A small grape press and bottling line, still under a blanket of plastic wrap, lay at the far end. Everything was brand new and untouched.

"This is London's first and only urban winery," said Hawkins, proudly.

"Very impressive. Where do you intend to source the grapes? Covent Garden market?"

"Don't be silly, I'm doing this properly. Some Syrah from France, some Nebbiolo from Italy. We'll ship the grapes fresh from the harvest, in chilled containers, press them here, do a bit of oak ageing, then bottle to order. One hundred quid a pop."

"One hundred pounds a bottle! That's a bit rich."

"We ain't making rubbish here, Felix. This'll be proper kit. One hundred pound's small change for some of my punters. Bankers, hedgies, you know the type. We'll do some personalised labels, all that sort of stuff. It'll be lovely."

"Nice." I suddenly had a bright idea of my own. "I've got a little quiz for *you* now. What's the closest Pinot Noir vineyard to where we're standing?"

"Probably your mates down at Château Spott-Hythe. There's a couple of vineyards closer to town but no-one growing Pinot."

"Wrong!" I beamed. "I planted a Pinot Noir vine in my garden in Little Chalfont a few years ago, just twenty miles from here."

Hawkins laughed. "A pot plant doesn't count as a vineyard, you soft sod."

"You'd be surprised. It was five years old when we planted it and that was in the mid-nineties. It's a mini vineyard, our own little *clos*. It produces a terrific yield."

"Lousy fruit, I bet. You can't grow Pinot Noir in a garden. It'll be diseased, over-watered, green-tasting."

"You might think so, but the leaves are healthy, no curling or funny colours. It's growing on stony soil, south facing, protected on two sides by a fence. The fruit tastes rich, the berries are dark and tight. I've been wondering how good a wine it might make."

A vision of the vine appeared before me, her branches rising, slender canes waving, imploring me not to waste another vintage of that sweet, luscious fruit.

"You want me to buy a handful of grapes and ferment a Pinot Noir for you? Sounds a bit of a faff to be honest. I'll pass."

"I'll give you the fruit for free. Most of it goes to waste anyway, no-one wants to eat little grapes full of pips." I don't know why I was suddenly so eager, but the idea really appealed. What a fantastic idea, to make my own wine! What a jape. Oh, I'd look back on this moment with a carefree laugh, no doubt about it.

"Felix, I like the idea of making a Pinot, don't get me wrong. But you've only got a couple of vines. I can't just muck about with a few bunches, I'd need to make a full barrel's worth."

"Last year we picked three hundred bunches."

"That's impressive from a garden vine, but still a long way short of a barrel. You need a third of a tonne of grapes to make a barrique of good wine. That's a couple of thousand bunches."

I thought of the vine's stump rising from the earth, her beckoning branches, heavy with fruit. Wasting food was a sin. And I might be many things, but I'm not a sinner. An idiot, perhaps. A naïve, unperceptive fool, who would bring disaster upon himself for no reason other than a whim and a giggle, but not a sinner, oh no.

"Don't suppose you have any very small barrels?"

Hawkins snorted. Then he looked up, snapped his mutilated fingers and beamed. "Yes, I do!" He marched back to the beer cellar and returned carrying a small cask on his shoulder.

"This is a demi-rundlet, a seven-gallon beer barrel. I use it to serve red plonk when we have a big group in. It holds about forty bottles' worth. That might do the job."

"Fantastic. We're in business!" *Château Felix-Hart*, I thought to myself, *the finest wine known to humanity*.

11

"I'm doing you a big favour here, Felix. I'm only up for it because we're in testing phase." Hawkins placed the demi-rundlet atop a larger barrel and gave it a slap. "I might be suggesting you buy another container of Chilean Merlot, by way of thanks. Come on, let's go back upstairs."

We returned to the passageway and Hawkins flicked the light switch, plunging us into near-darkness.

"When's harvest time in Little Chalfont?" he asked, as we climbed the stairs and emerged into the warmth and light of the pub.

"Middle of October, I reckon. Fruit should be nice and ripe by then."

"Who's nice and ripe?" asked Jenny, over her shoulder, as she finished serving a customer. She turned, took hold of the front of my shirt and stood on tiptoes. "Goodbye kiss, please."

"Listen, Felix," said Hawkins, as I was bidding Jenny farewell. "Make sure those grapes are clean. No rotten bunches, no leaves, twigs, squirrels or bloody badgers, all right? If you deliver me a load of crap, it's straight in the bin."

Jenny released me and I straightened my collar.

"Understood. Nice clean bunches, I promise."

***

A month after my chat with Hawkins, and blessed with a warm, dry autumn, my two flatmates and I stood solemnly before the vine, ready to begin the harvest. Fistule had invested in a special fruit-picking apron, while Wodin wore his usual tie-dyed T-shirt and a green sarong, his long hair tied back in a ponytail. I'd opened a smart bottle of Morey-Saint Denis, out of respect, and handed them each a glass.

"To the vintage," I said.

"The vintage!" We raised our glasses. The wine caught the low autumn sun and shone a brilliant ruby, dancing with strange, dark shapes. I stared, fascinated, realising my outstretched glass was at eye level and that I was viewing the vine through the liquid. I closed one eye and brought the glass closer. Blood red leaves sprouted from a black trunk, the branches swimming as the curved glass refracted them into writhing serpents.

I saw a man dressed in black, a knife in his hand, flailing, stumbling, sinking. "*Cazzo!*" he hissed.

I jumped, whipping the glass aside and slopping a half-inch of wine over the rim. But the vine was green and motionless, no sign of any men with knives, and the only red was the grapes themselves, tight globes of juice, begging to be picked. A cold sweat prickled my back. I wondered whether Fistule had slipped magic mushrooms into my earlier cup of tea. He had a habit of doing that on prestigious occasions.

"You spilt your wine, Felix," said Wodin. "You ok?"

"Of course, I'm just... making an offering to the vine." I took a long sip of the Burgundy. It was excellent, which calmed me a little.

We got down to business, separating into our specialist roles. Fistule harvested the hanging grapes, detaching each bunch with a loving snip from his marijuana secateurs. Wodin carried the bunches to the sorting table, removing any stray leaves, and I carried out a final check, cutting off any split or mouldy grapes. I laid the bunches flat in the plastic vegetable crates I'd borrowed from the local Gatesave depot, taking care not to crush and damage our precious crop. Then we loaded Wodin's pickup and raced into London to deliver the vintage by nightfall.

We parked in the courtyard of the Flag and Parrot and formed a conveyor belt, passing the crates of grapes to one another and down through the barrel hatch into the pub cellar. There, Hawkins's winemaker inspected the harvest, tugging at his goatee as he prodded and turned the bunches, checking for rot or dried fruit. Every so often, he pulled off a grape and tasted it, before swallowing it down, pips and all. He even bit off a piece of stem, chewing the green twig and frowning.

"I'll be blowed," he muttered. "The fruit's riper than a Barossa jam tart, but your stems are tender as new rosemary."

"That's a good thing, I assume?"

The winemaker ignored me and began tipping the contents of each crate into a large metal trough.

"I'm going to do whole-bunch fermentation. No destemming. We'll get a bit of carbonic maceration going first."

Now, I knew this was pretty cutting-edge stuff, proper beards-and-sandals, non-interventionist winemaking. I felt a little pang of pride that a professional had rated my haul of rustic berries worthy of such treatment. The winemaker emptied the final crate into the tank, pushed the grapes down with a wooden paddle, and placed a lid over the vessel.

"I do declare that London's first Pinot Noir vintage is undergoing fermentation," said Hawkins from behind his pewter tankard. "That's got to be worth a celebration."

He turned to the upturned barrel beside him, on which sat a bottle of Champagne and a short, thick sword. I'd seen Hawkins do this a few times, it was his party trick. He took a few seconds to stuff his irregularly shaped hand into the sabre's guard, swearing under his breath, then grasped the Champagne by its base.

"Thought we'd open a nice Blanc de Noirs in tribute!"

I moved back a few feet. Hawkins had been drinking all day and I'd always felt his low finger-count was a poor advertisement for his swordsmanship. He scraped the back of the blade up and down the bottle a couple of times then, with a loud "Hoy!", skimmed the sabre up the bottle and bumped it against the lip. The bottle made a loud clink and the neck remained completely intact.

"Oh, for God's sake!" moaned Hawkins and thumped the bottle back down on the barrel, whereupon it exploded with a deafening bang. A spray of Champagne and broken glass filled the room and I closed my eyes as pieces of bottle ricocheted off the steel tanks.

"Everyone still got their eyes?" called Hawkins.

"You are officially bloody barred from your own pub, Hawkins," growled the winemaker, gently dabbing his face with his apron.

"Ah, shut up, Bruce," said Hawkins, "must have been a faulty one." He peered at the barrel and triumphantly lifted the only recognisable remnant of the bottle, an inch-tall piece of the base.

"Waste not, want not. Cheers!" Hawkins took a sip from the jagged stump, screwed up his face and spat a piece of glass on to the floor.

"Glad we got the grapes in the press before you started celebrating," said the winemaker. "I don't think ground glass is an approved additive under EU law."

"Bugger the EU," growled Hawkins. "How long are you keeping it on the skins?"

"We'll give it two weeks. I'll add a tiny bit of sulphur but otherwise keep it completely natural."

"Is it organic, man?" called Fistule, from underneath one of the tanks.

"You tell me," replied the winemaker. "If the grapes are organic, so is the wine."

"Those grapes are totally organic; I guarantee it."

"Well, there you go. We've got very little volume here, so we may as well try something special. I'll leave it on the lees through to malo, keep the filtration really gentle, no fining, nitro blanket…"

"Woah! Malo, nitro… what's that in English, man?"

"It means he's not going to muck it about, Fistule. It'll be as natural a wine as possible."

"Cool, man. So when's it ready?"

"I'll rack it into barrel next month. It's going to age faster in that funny little cask." The winemaker nodded at the demi-rundlet balanced atop the wall of larger barrels. "We'll taste it every few months to check it's not spoiled but it's up to you really. Give it a year. Two if you like."

"Oh man! We have to wait over a year?"

"Good things come to those who wait, Fistule. There's plenty to drink in the meantime," I said.

And thus, the first vintage of my Little Chalfont Pinot Noir was born. And if I'd known then what I know now, I'd have opened the tank's valves that very second, drained the juice on to the cellar floor, taken old man Hawkins's sabre and slashed that little barrel into a thousand pieces.

Chapter Two

Millennium Fever

The earth spins about its axis. It orbits the sun, each circuit driving the seasons and the vintage. The moon, in turn, circles the earth, tugging the tides to and fro, and all are part of a wider mechanism, an incredible watch, slowly running down. Two years after my Little Chalfont harvest, as the celestial clock ticked to autumn and the northern vines gave up their fruit once more, there were machinations afoot at Gatesave.

Our CEO had been unceremoniously sacked just a few weeks earlier, following the eighth successive quarter of declining sales. The final straw had been the unravelling of the company's bold expansion into the up-and-coming Moldovan retail market, which had proved to be a very long way from upping, let alone coming, and the resulting power vacuum was strong enough to make your ears pop. The top role had been filled, on an interim basis, by the Director of Commerce, a deeply unpleasant man who had spent thirty years rising through the ranks from his ever-so-humble start as a Saturday boy at Gatesave's Crawley branch.

The Director of Commerce, in a little conceit on his acronym, liked to be referred to as 'The Doc'. He felt it gave him an air of learning and professionalism, despite it being widely known that his academic career had peaked at Crawley Sixth Form College with a diploma in hotel management. Behind his back, he was known as The Dick, for no reason other than gratuitous disrespect.

Tapping away at my laptop, I sensed the buzz of conversation quieten. I glanced up. The Dick was meandering his way across the trading floor, easing his way between the banks of desks, lingering for an occasional exchange of words with an attractive female colleague. The Dick himself, however, was not an attractive man. He was wide-hipped with fleshy limbs, his pudgy face invariably painted with a smirk. His hair was combed into an uncomfortable side parting, as though he'd been hard-groomed for church by a severe nanny.

I observed his approach out of the corner of my eye. Every so often, he would pass a senior manager and pause, fixing them with a mean little grin. I knew what that expression meant. It said its wearer was in a position to alter, quite dramatically, the employment status of anyone or anything that displeased him.

The Dick glanced over and my eyes flicked back to my screen, slightly too late. It looked worryingly likely that his destination was the wine team. What the hell did he want with me? Our department's sales performance had been good this year, at least compared to the rest of the business, so I wasn't too badly exposed. I prayed it would be a short interaction.

Sure enough, with revolting slowness, The Dick eased into our little cluster of desks, smiling down at the junior members of the team like an over-familiar scout master. He turned through 180 degrees and docked himself next to my laptop, the desk making a quiet, heartfelt moan as it took the strain of his behind. I looked up and rubbed my hands, an eager, businesslike smile upon my face. But The Dick was staring down at my neighbour, the attractive young fruit juice buyer, who I had poached from Merryfield Superstores just last month.

"That's a lovely dress," he said. My colleague smiled, awkwardly. I felt a flush of anger, the type a young bachelor gorilla must feel when paid a visit by the leader of the troop, the ageing, mangy but still-powerful silverback.

"I hope Hart here's taking care of you?" he oiled, without looking at me.

I was filled with an overwhelming urge to bend, grab the man's ankles and lift them high over his head, sending him rolling backwards over the table and on to the floor. Then I imagined beating him methodically with a stout bamboo cane as he cowered, gibbering, on the carpet, each strike accompanied by a blood-curdling Kendo battle shout.

But I'm a professional, so I took a deep breath and, zen-like, allowed my anger to subside. I did, however, continue to rub my hands, faster and faster, until The Dick could no longer ignore the whisper of hot palm flesh just inches behind his right ear.

He turned to me, scowling, and I beamed back like an unhinged puppy.

"Like-for-like sales up four percent, sir!"

The Dick glowered. I was safe though, senior enough to be taken seriously but too junior to be a real threat. The Dick raised his head, his face easing into a humourless smile as he addressed the floor.

"Is Hart still pretending that wine is too complicated a department to be managed by anyone but himself?"

No-one answered.

"It *is* very complicated, sir, you're right, and if I have failed at making it appear simple then I take full responsibility for that," I said.

The Dick turned back to me, his smirk fading. His eyes narrowed as he tried to work out whether he'd been contradicted.

"I have very little time for complexity, Hart. Simplicity is my watchword, first, second and third." He raised his head and addressed the rest of the team. "Fourth, fifth and sixth!" he added, idiotically.

"That's sage advice, sir," I lied.

"How much Champagne do we have?" The smugness was back. I glanced at my logistics controller.

"Claire, can you give us the current stock position please? I think it's around 2.5 million…"

"Not enough."

I paused. "Not enough, sir? That's a pretty heavy stockholding, around forty percent up on last year, and last January we had to…"

"Not enough." He said it quietly now, there was a dangerous tone to his voice.

"Right, sir. But it's nearly October, so we're pretty tight for shipping more stock. I'm not sure whether…"

"Not. Enough." The whole floor was quiet now and my cheeks were flushing. Why the hell did he want even more Champagne? Ok, it was three months until Christmas and one week more until New Year's Eve. And not just any old New Year's Eve, it was Millennium Eve, the night before the year 2000. Everyone knew it would be a big party night but, for the love of Bacchus, there's only so much England can drink, and our depots were already bursting at the seams.

"I was at a very impressive presentation at the Institute of Directors last week, hosted by one of our largest suppliers, Paris-Blois International," smiled The Dick, as though he'd just been inducted into the Knights Templar by the Duke of Buggering Richmond. My heart sank. "And they showed us the customer insight data they've commissioned on how people intend to spend Millennium Eve. What do you think it said, Hart?"

"I've seen Paris-Blois's presentation, sir. It says that people are going to party. And drink a great deal of Champagne."

"That's right, Hart. And do you know what else it said? There was an extra section to the presentation, you see, that wasn't shown to buyers and junior management."

I bet there was, I thought. A special section for credulous directors, whose idea of a decisive commercial decision was choosing which shade of ivory best suited the new boardroom.

"Did it suggest there was an extra big discount for any retailers who placed another order?"

"Careful, Hart," said The Dick, quietly. "You think you're pretty hot stuff, don't you? Running the wine team, swanning around with that Minstrels of Wine badge on your lapel…" He raised his voice so the surrounding tables could hear. "The presentation explained that buyers across the wine industry are risk-averse. That they have failed to grasp the opportunity offered by this once-in-a-lifetime event. And that retailers' shelves are likely to be bare a week before Millennium Eve."

He turned back to me. "Does that sound like good retailing to you?"

"No, it doesn't, sir." I was referring to the gullible buffoon's naivety, of course, rather than the unlikely scenario of empty shelves, but a touch of ambiguity was clearly in order.

"After the event, their Sales Director, Pierre Boulle, took me to one side and said *you* had been particularly intransigent when asked to place further orders. I assured him we would address the situation. It's a good job someone's looking out for our customers' interests, isn't it, Hart?"

Ah, Monsieur Boulle. The most conniving, double-crossing, groin-oiling executive to ever grace the board of a multi-national luxury goods conglomerate. So, he was the one whispering sweet porkies in the ear of my dear, half-witted Director of Commerce. What a surprise.

"I appreciate your input, sir."

"Paris-Blois are holding a trade event in Epernay on Monday. Last orders for Christmas, you might call it. I suggest you book a train to France and get yourself down there. And don't come back until you've doubled our stockholding."

I nearly choked. "Doubled, sir? That's ridiculous! We'll be overstocked for a year!" Much too late, I realised I'd overstepped the mark.

A wide, angry smile bloomed on The Dick's face. "I do find it *fascinating* how much effort we expend in letting down our customers! Just think how much easier it could be if we decided to help them, to make their shopping experience a pleasure, rather than exerting ourselves so *vigorously* to make their life frustrating." He stared at me, wildly, his smile threatening to coil around his head and consume it whole.

Sweet-talker I may be, but I knew no sugary words would extricate me from this mauling. My mere presence was the problem and rapid flight the only solution. I pushed myself away from my desk with a mighty heave, transforming my chair into a horizontal ejector seat, the wheels propelling me backwards until my journey was arrested by collision with an innocent bystander. I leapt to my feet.

"You're right sir, of course!" I shouted. "I shall book the next available train, immediately." I strode away purposefully and hid in a toilet cubicle until the coast was clear.

***

Twenty-four hours later, I had cleared security at Waterloo International and was boarding the Eurostar to Paris. It was Saturday morning, so there were two whole days until Paris-Blois's Monday trade event, but after my bruising encounter with The Dick, I fancied a night's recuperation in Paris before taking a lazy Sunday train on to Epernay.

After Paris, the only half-bright spot on the trip would be Sandra. Our relationship dated back to my first days as a wine buyer at Gatesave, where she had been my opponent – and tutor – in the fierce world of national account management. She had been a harsh mistress, still was in fact, but I forgave that. For Sandra was as beautiful as she was ruthless and, despite our rather problematic relationship, it was a perverse thrill to see such a professional in action.

We had both moved up the corporate ladder since then, me to Gatesave's Head of Wine, her to Paris-Blois's UK Sales Director. We tangled less frequently over the negotiation table these days, now that she had a team of account managers, and I a team of buyers, to handle day-to-day business. But that hadn't loosened our bond. Quite the opposite.

With a flurry of whistles and shouts, the conductors slammed shut the heavy doors and the train hummed free of the station. My carriage was only half-full, mainly young lovers heading to Paris for a vigorous weekend, some older couples, probably with the same idea, and a few French businessmen on their way home, perusing *Le Figaro* over paper cups of espresso.

The seat opposite was empty. I stretched my legs and composed a text message to Sandra, asking why her boss,

Pierre Boulle, the very same man who had persuaded The Dick of my incompetence, was manipulating us into buying more Champagne than any supermarket could possibly sell in one season. To my surprise, she answered straight away.

Stay with me Sun night at Maison Flavigny. We need to talk.

Now, that sounded exciting. Maison Flavigny was one of the most beautiful châteaux in the Champagne region, the ancestral home of the founders of Champagne Beaufort. The aristocratic owners had fallen on hard times by the early 1990s and had been forced to sell up. The highest bidders were, of course, Paris-Blois International, who acquired the old château along with the Champagne brand, its vineyards and cellars. They now used the estate as a high-class entertainment venue for top clients, senior management and miscellaneous bigwigs.

It wasn't clear, however, why Sandra was inviting *me* to stay. I was important, of course – that's to say, Gatesave was a large customer for Paris-Blois's Champagne brands – but I knew my place and it was unusual for a supermarket middle manager to be lathered with this level of hospitality. What did Sandra want? A night of vigorous lovemaking, perhaps?

Now, it's important I don't give you the wrong impression of our relationship. Romantic it was not. And physically, it had never progressed beyond a peck on the cheek, more's the pity. True, there was plenty of sardonic flirting, though it was likely Sandra used that solely for manipulation. But who knows, perhaps her icy professionalism had crumbled and she wanted to slip in a little tryst before the start of the working week. It was unlikely, but one should always be prepared for the unexpected.

My phone vibrated again. *You'll have own bedroom obvs.*

That was a shame. But probably for the best. I thought back to the last time I'd seen her. It was a launch party for some decadent new jewellery line, Paris-Blois's latest initiative to part the world's high-net-worths from their excess cash. Sandra had called me a few days earlier. "I need a partner for the launch party and you make good eye-candy, Felix. Dust off your dinner suit and meet me Thursday night at the London Silver Vaults."

It had been a fairly dull evening. You might wonder why I bothered. But, as I have hinted, Sandra and I had a complicated professional relationship and, for reasons that will become clear, I was obliged to do as I was told. I've mentioned her looks already, I know, but allow me to elaborate. You see, her beauty alone would be reason enough to do as bidden, just for the opportunity to bask in her glow. Sandra's hair was long and blond, and her skin was so flawless it shone. A face so well-proportioned you couldn't help but stare, those firm cheekbones, perfect nose, lips. I'm a simple man with base urges, so it would be disingenuous not to mention her toned limbs, her prominent, firm curves and the way she knew exactly what every part of her fabulous body was doing.

That night, at the jewellery launch, she had worn one of the pieces, a shimmering mat of diamonds covering her chest so completely that it required no clothing beneath. A cascade of cold, sparkling white, clasped tight at her neck then rushing down over her skin, forced outwards over the push of her breasts, then pouring over the falls, where it split into dozens of strings of dangling gems.

I'd been finding it impossible to shake the image. Not a night had passed without her invading my sleep, that long, black skirt around her lower half and the cascade of gems just covering the rest. The daylight hours were no protection either. I'd be sitting in some dreary meeting, the Head of Frozen Desserts talking earnestly about the disappointing impact of the unseasonably warm autumn on ice cream sales, and suddenly I'd be back in the Silver Vaults, the silent crowd watching Sandra glitter beneath the spotlights, the mat of diamonds moving, slowly, from side to side.

I woke, dozily, feeling like a muffled coat-hook. We were stationary, the window framing a stretch of cold concrete. For a second I thought we'd arrived in Paris, but the floodlit platform was quiet and only a couple of my fellow passengers were on their feet. It was the Lille stop, another hour to go.

So, what did Sandra want? As I've mentioned, our professional relationship was complicated. I was her customer, true, but Paris-Blois was a huge, global organisation, far larger even than Gatesave. So, even if our buyer-seller relationship had been a conventional one, the balance of power would have lain some distance in Paris-Blois's favour.

And our business relationship was *far* from conventional. I was, I regret to say, the victim of a most foul blackmail. A couple of years ago, through a fiendish and unsportsmanlike trick (for which I retain enormous respect; it's just a shame I'm on the sharp end of it) I had rashly revealed a couple of secrets regarding my early career to some of Sandra's associates.

We've all done the odd thing we regret, of course, and who's to say everything in this world slots neatly into black or white? But my misdemeanours had strayed just a little too far into the dark grey and there was one particular incident that now hung over me, concerning the premature death of two Italian gentlemen, now at rest a few feet beneath my Little Chalfont garden.

The Eurostar's engines hummed back to life and the unimpressive suburbs of Lille made way for the grey winter flatness of the Pas-de-Calais countryside. I thought of Sandra again. To date, my duties had been light, borderline enjoyable even, usually acting as her companion at some Paris-Blois-sponsored event, whether a tennis tournament, polo match or the opening of some overpriced handbag-and-belt shop. The only real downside was that, as Sandra's official guest, I wasn't permitted to chase after every demanding young woman who flashed me their come-hither eyes, much to my and their disappointment.

On my arrival in Paris, I banished all thoughts of corporate responsibilities, checking into my usual hotel next to the Jardin Villemin before setting out to tour some favourite haunts along the Canal Saint-Martin. Being a sociable type, it didn't take long to make a few friends, and we were soon bumping our way towards the river in a wine-lubricated join-the-dots, veering into The Marais for a spot of *drôle-et-jolie* and, when that venerable district started to run out of steam, out east to Belleville.

As the sky lightened, I found a willing tutor, a language student, with whom I practiced my French through the early hours until Sunday morning. The sun was high over the trees surrounding Père Lachaise before she declared herself satisfied with my progress, whereupon I was dismissed, exhausted but wiser. I returned to my untouched hotel room to freshen up, grab my bags and catch the early afternoon train to Epernay.

Chapter Three

Maison Flavigny

"*Maison Flavigny, merci.*"

The man considered me for a moment and, as French taxi drivers do, made a mental calculation as to whether my offer of business threatened to compromise his next mealtime. Unable to find an excuse to turn me away, he shrugged and nodded to the back seat.

"*Vous êtes un aristocrate?*" he asked, smirking at his own joke.

"*Évidemment, monsieur,*" I replied. He gave a catarrh-lubricated growl, which I chose to translate as an appreciative chuckle.

The car was grubby, the upholstery pitted with cigarette burns and unpleasant-looking stains in a variety of greys. I located the seatbelt, which was completely immobile and, on closer inspection, appeared to have been stapled at multiple points to the back of the seat. The driver accelerated away from the station without indicating, joining the highway with the confidence of a man untroubled by the whims of fate.

After a nauseous half-hour skirting the vine-combed slopes of the Côte des Blancs, we passed through a small wood and suddenly Maison Flavigny was upon us. It appeared like a thunderclap, as though the quiet waltz of the vineyards had been interrupted by a great brass fanfare. Two dreamy, turreted towers sat either side of the building's vast façade, and I could feel the château threatening to suck us from the road and up the carriage drive by the sheer force of its beauty.

"*Maison Flavigny,*" announced the driver, rather unnecessarily. He turned on to the gravel driveway and accelerated towards the house at a velocity that suggested an attempt at the French land speed record.

As the distance between taxi and château contracted, Maison Flavigny's awesome scale became clear. The wings of the house, which from a distance looked flush with the façade, appeared to unfold and envelope us, like some great white bird of prey. The main body of the château towered above us, the entrance lying atop a flight of stone steps as wide as the building itself. At the end of the driveway, a fountain the size of a large roundabout tinkled prettily. My driver swung his car around it like an angry toddler taking a disappointing Christmas present for its first test-drive and performed an emergency stop.

"*Maison Flavigny*," he spat, in case the impact of my head with the rear of his passenger seat had caused me temporary amnesia. I extricated myself from the car and handed him a one hundred franc note.

"*C'est combien?*"

The answer, presumably, was exactly one hundred francs, because he drove away without answering or giving me any change, leaving a cloud of fine grit in the air and a prominent set of tracks in the immaculate gravel.

As I wiped the dirt from my eyes, I heard the crunch of footsteps. I turned to see a short, wizened man with a garden rake.

"*Bonsoir monsieur!*" I called.

The man screwed up his face and began viciously raking the gravel close to my feet. Not wanting to distract an artisan at work, I lifted my bag and trotted up the steps.

The front door was open and I stepped into a mosaic-tiled foyer, empty except for three pairs of immaculate wellington boots and a brass elephant's foot holding several Champagne Beaufort-branded umbrellas. I passed through the inner door and entered a large and beautiful reception room. A line of satin-upholstered chairs stretched the length of one wall and a chandelier glittered from the ceiling, reminding me, excitingly, of Sandra's diamond chest-piece. A long, marble-topped table dominated the room's centre and upon it stood an empty china vase. Everything looked very expensive and utterly unsoiled.

A well-groomed young woman, entirely at home among the unaffordable furnishings, appeared through a door.

"*Bonsoir*. Felix Hart," I said, extending a hand.

"Yes. I guessed you were," she said, in French-accented English. She smiled and took my hand, gently squeezing the ends of my fingers. "Shall I show you where you are sleeping?"

I followed her up a sweeping set of stairs, our movements silent on the thick carpet. I'd dressed smartly, a proper jacket and shoes, and carried a neat leather case rather than my usual, more practical, canvas bag. I was glad I'd done so. A poorly dressed man wandering these corridors might well be accused of being some sort of tradesman or, worse still, the wrong class of burglar. The French notice these things and, in my experience, tend to negotiate harder if they feel an opponent has disrespected them by dressing shabbily.

But the real crime would have been to disrespect Maison Flavigny itself. I could feel the château, the very building, demanding tribute, as if her owners were of secondary importance, their feeble, mercenary activities paling against her majesty.

"You're in the Green Room," said the woman, opening a door, one of half a dozen along the corridor. I followed her into the bedroom, which was indeed decorated like a tribute to some woodland nymph. A four-poster bed with green satin sheets and cushions lay in the centre, while the wallpaper was patterned with dancing emerald leaves. A jade dressing table sat before the full-length window, framing an impressive view of the front gardens. I spotted the groundsman, far below, still raking over the mutilation wrought upon his carriage drive.

"There is no TV, no internet, sorry," said the woman, smiling.

"Guests have to make their own fun, do they?"

"Yes. You are welcome to join the other visitors in the lounge. It is well stocked with Paris-Blois's finest wines and spirits. You are having dinner with Sandra tonight? 7 p.m.?" She expressed it as a question, but it was clearly an instruction.

"Where's Sandra staying? Is she next door?"

The woman smiled again. "She said you would ask that. She is on a different floor. It is an informal dinner so will be served in the lounge, not the dining room. But please wear a tie."

She paused, hands behind her back, and twisted her body slightly from side to side. "Do you have a tie?"

"Yes, I do."

"Good. *À bientôt.*" She walked quickly out of the room, her heels noiseless on the carpet.

It was just after six o'clock and there was little to do in the room beyond leaping up and down on the bed or painting my face with the wide array of Paris-Blois cosmetics lining the dresser. I decided my time might be better spent exploring the château, so I complemented my jacket with a smart tie and retraced my steps to the ground floor. A little intuition led me towards the back of the house, then the clink of glasses guided me the rest of the way.

The lounge was as well appointed as the rest of the château. I spotted Sandra as soon as I entered, tucked away in an alcove, alone at a table for two. A pair of male guests sat in armchairs, reading newspapers, and there was a short bar in the corner, its polished shelves snug with golden liquids – Scotch, Bourbon, Cognac, all from the Paris-Blois stable. A guest leant on the bar, murmuring to the waiter. *Time for an aperitif*, I decided. I padded across the carpet.

"*Bonsoir. Gin-tonic, s'il vous plaît.*"

The barman rattled three ice cubes into my glass and, out of the corner of my eye, I saw Sandra rise. She was dressed entirely in black – a skirt with high heels, a polo jumper under a short jacket – the only colour a gold brooch on one lapel and her blond ponytail, which flashed from side to side as she approached.

"Glad to see you've taken care of yourself," she said, addressing my drink. She placed each of her hands on my biceps and leant forward, kissing me on both cheeks. A professional manoeuvre. Completely natural to the rest of the room, but engineered to prevent any unwelcome lunging, which I suspect is the kind of thing women as attractive as Sandra have to put up with all the time. Being a gentleman, of course, I had no intention of lunging, at least not without an unambiguous invitation.

"I did say seven o'clock, but I'm happy to eat now; an early night suits me." She linked her arm with mine and guided me back to her table. There was no mistaking the hot jealousy from the other men as they watched us cross the room. "I have a lot of work to do ahead of tomorrow's trade tasting," she added, possibly to dispel any notion she might be proposing recreational activity.

"Fine by me."

"Oh, don't forget to leave a message in the visitors' book." She nudged me toward a broad leather file lying open on a cabinet. "Your boss enjoyed his time here last week, by the way." Sandra turned back a few pages and pointed. Sure enough, there was his vain, over-large scrawl:

Manifique! Steve 'The Doc' Pendle.

"I see his French is as elegant as his signature," I said.

"You should have more respect for your senior colleagues, Felix."

I turned back to today's page and, with a flourish, dashed off a quick line.

Le plus beau. Rien ne se rapproche. F.H. x

Sandra looked at the page and smiled. Maybe the little kiss was a bit much, but I've always been the affectionate type. She took the fountain pen and replaced the top. "Very nice. Thank you." She nodded to the table. "The food here is excellent, but the main kitchen's closed on Sunday evening. You should order the entrecôte. Without waiting for a reply, she gave the barman a quick wave and held up two fingers.

"You and your boss have done an excellent selling job on my esteemed Head of Commerce, Sandra. How many nights in Maison Flavigny did that take?"

"Just one. Plus a night in Paris." She gave a thin smile.

"Including his wife, I suppose. Or someone else?"

"Careful, Felix. It's not nice to start rumours."

Sandra gestured to the table and we took our seats.

31

"Let's talk business then," I said. "I've been ordered here to buy several containers of Champagne that I don't want or need. If I buy them, I'm unlikely to reorder for another twelve months. And that's if I'm not fired for poor cash flow management in the meantime."

Sandra ignored me.

"I don't understand why it's in your interest to overstock me, unless Paris-Blois is suddenly desperately short of cash. Are you?"

Sandra smiled. "You'll be the one short of cash if you continue to defy your director's instructions. Why do you doubt his judgement? And mine, for that matter?"

"We've already shipped four million bottles of Champagne. I'm now expected to buy another four million that I don't need."

"So buy them. And sell them. That's what supermarkets do, isn't it?"

"*Et à boire, madame?*" asked the barman, offering Sandra a heavy-looking book, the leather cover bearing a tiny, gold-embossed Paris-Blois logo.

"We'll have the most expensive claret on the list please," I said.

"Not the *most* expensive but the '82 Margaux will be fine." Sandra smiled at the waiter, whose eyes widened in surprise, then narrowed as he glanced at me.

Well, I thought, *that's a turn up. This may well be the final buying trip of my career, but at least I'll be ending it in style.*

"Why shouldn't I give my number one account a treat when business is going so well?" Sandra said, leaning back and adjusting her ponytail.

I could think of an even better treat, I mused, distracted by the contours of her polo neck, though the '82 Margaux would do for now. But, figure-hugging knitwear and vintage claret aside, I hadn't got to the bottom of the idiotic commercial position I'd been forced into.

"That's more Champagne than we sold in the entire previous year. You're telling me we're going to sell, in one night, an entire year's worth of Champagne?"

"Why not?"

"Look," I said. I took a pen from my pocket and turned over the menu card. "Gatesave has a thirty percent market share of the take-home Champagne market. That suggests, if we sell everything and maintain our normal market share, the United Kingdom will consume twenty-seven million bottles of Champagne in one night. At home. That doesn't even include all the Champagne sold in pubs, clubs and bars."

Sandra shrugged. "Our forecasts say that's what's going to happen."

I was scribbling faster now. "Population of the United Kingdom, sixty million. Those of drinking age, around forty million. Take off five million for Methodists, Muslims, Mormons and Quakers, ten percent for those who choose not to indulge in alcohol due to an unadventurous or delicate nature, another ten percent for those unable to lift their own glass due to disease or incapacity, then a million more for the emergency services, long-distance lorry drivers, oil rig workers, prisoners and lunatics in straightjackets. That's twenty-seven million, give or take."

Sandra giggled. "You're *so* numerate, Felix. No wonder you're a top buyer. You make arithmetic a spectator sport."

Head of Buying, I wanted to say. But I knew she was playing with me.

"A bottle each. You're saying every single drinker in Britain will neck a whole bottle of Champagne, at home, on New Year's Eve. In addition to all the wine, beer and spirits they've bought. And before they even go out." I shook my head. "I'll be fired in January if I order all that."

"And you'll be fired in December if you don't," said Sandra. "So let's go for the longer-term plan, shall we? We're releasing our next vintage several months early, so trade buyers can ship the stock before Millennium Eve. You can taste it tomorrow. You'll need to be quick though, we have most of the world's major buyers at the auction. You don't want to be leaving empty-handed, do you?"

"So, you've intimidated, bribed and cajoled every large retailer into buying far more stock than they can possibly sell. Well, I'm only a humble Head of Buying but I think that's a recipe for a very nasty cash-crunch in the New Year, when no-one's ordering any Champagne."

Sandra shrugged.

"Which is inconvenient, maybe even slightly painful for you," I continued, as Paris-Blois's plan slowly dawned on me. "But extremely unpleasant, possibly terminal, for most of your less profitable competitors."

The steaks arrived, accompanied by thin French fries. I frowned. I've always preferred the more voluptuous, English style of chip.

"*Bon appétit*." Sandra pushed the fries aside and sliced into her entrecôte.

The waiter reappeared, sporting a sleek decanter and an 'aren't I clever?' expression, and poured each of us a glass of Margaux.

"Cheers," I said. We touched glasses, but she didn't reply. The wine was magnificent.

"Why did you invite me here this evening?" I'd resigned myself to the conclusion it wasn't for a night of bedroom gymnastics. And I was fairly sure it wasn't for my witty repartee either. And given that they are, by some distance, my premier skills, I was pretty stumped.

"I need you to do a job for me."

I tried to recall which sponsorship-heavy events were coming up. "Japanese Grand Prix?"

"No. Something a lot more involved than just accompanying me somewhere. I need you to attend a wine tasting."

I took another deep mouthful of the Margaux. "I can do that."

"It's an important wine tasting. A high-profile, competitive blind. Professionals only." She'd stopped eating now and had placed her cutlery on the plate. She was serious, no hint of a smile. I felt the first tiny stirring of fear in my stomach. I wasn't sure why. On the face of it, a wine tasting sounded like nice work, particularly if it was a lineup of posh old claret or Burgundy. But my intuition's pretty good, particularly when it's warning me that my hide might be at risk.

"Do you know Lord Flashman?" she asked.

"Not personally. I know who he is, obviously." Lord Flashman was a fabulously wealthy aristocrat, the owner of Basildon House – the largest palace in London after the Queen's own pad – and he was reputed to possess the finest wine collection in England.

"Flashman is planning to hold a competition to determine whether Burgundy still produces the world's finest Pinot Noir, or whether it has been usurped by Pinot from some other part of the world."

"Sounds quite fun."

"There's nothing fun about it. Paris-Blois have been informed that our top Burgundy, Domaine Henri-Leroy, will be in the competition."

"Ah. So it's yours to lose."

For the past decade, Domaine Henri-Leroy had held the record as the planet's most expensive wine, thanks to consistently stellar scores in *American Goblet*, the world's highest profile wine magazine, and the insatiable thirst of the Russian and Chinese super-rich.

"Indeed," said Sandra. "A poor showing by Domaine Henri-Leroy would be a... suboptimal outcome."

I'll say. There'd be some big, quivering, sulky lips in the Paris-Blois boardroom if their ludicrously overpriced Burgundy ended up being spanked by some cheeky Oregonian upstart. I smiled and lifted my glass, making a little prayer to the gods that it should come to pass.

"In the interests of fairness, each participating winery is permitted to send a judge to the competition, though not a paid employee. We've decided to send you. You're a Minstrel of Wine, highly respected, and you're not an employee of Paris-Blois International."

Not an employee, no. But on the bloody hook to them, that's for sure.

"Ok. So I just taste the wines and… what? You want me to try and recognise yours and give it the highest score?"

A cold smile. "There's a bit more to it than that. All you need to know right now is that it's very important and you need to not mess it up." My stomach gave another little lurch and I necked a soothing half-glass of '82 Margaux to settle it.

"Pierre wants to see you tomorrow evening after the trade event. At our offices on the Avenue de Champagne."

Oh, does he indeed? Pierre Boulle, of course, was Sandra's boss, the European Sales Director for Paris-Blois International and one of my very least favourite people. Pain in the *derrière* didn't get close. The man was a foaming Gallic sociopath, a copper-bottomed arsehole and an all-star, sphincter-clenching blowhard.

"I'll see you in the morning, Felix. Enjoy the wine." Sandra dropped her napkin over the uneaten portion of her steak, pushed back her chair and walked out.

The waiter floated over and, painfully slowly, nosed the spout of the decanter towards my empty glass, a turd-smelling expression on his face.

"I'll take it from here, *garçon*," I said, snatching the jug's handle. The man grimaced and crept away sideways, like an insulted crab, keeping one eye on me as he withdrew.

I poured until my glass was recklessly full and took it for a tour of the room. The other guests had departed. I perused the bar, taking in the fine spirits, then gave the door of the built-in humidor a little tug. To my delight, it popped open and a breeze of cool, rich tobacco washed over me. Glancing around to check I really was alone, I lifted a fistful of Cuban cigars and dropped them into my jacket pocket, the little tubes giving a pleasing rattle as they knocked together.

My mood improved and I spotted the guest book. Taking another deep draught of wine, I turned the page back to the previous week.

Manifique! Steve 'The Doc' Pendle.

What kind of arse gives himself a nickname like that? Who did he think he was, an army medic in a prisoner-of-war camp?

A professional wrestler? His handwriting was a scrawl, in places the ink hadn't even properly marked the page, leaving just a white indentation. The Doc had either been drunk or didn't know how to use a fountain pen. *Probably both*, I mused. I removed the pen top and leaned over the page. The central 'o' in Doc was only half-formed and I placed a little dot over the top, creating a rather attractive cursive 'i'. There was also plenty of space to insert a 'k' at the end of the word. I blew at the page and admired my handiwork. I was feeling much better as I hummed my way back to my bedroom, glass in one hand, decanter in the other.

I swept the cushions off the bed and hung up my suit. I was fiddling with the window, cigar in mouth, trying to work out how to open it, when there was a double tap on the door. For a second, I wondered if it was Sandra, suddenly overcome with guilt at blackmailing me and begging to make amends. Then I realised it was probably the waiter, demanding return of his decanter and Havanas. Well, if he wanted a tobacco suppository he'd come to the right room. I flung open the door, wearing just my boxer shorts and the cigar, to find the young lady concierge from earlier that afternoon, holding a clipboard.

"Sandra wanted me to check that everything was ok with your room, Mr Hart," she said, addressing my bare chest and maintaining an impressively professional expression. "She said you sometimes can be very difficult." She slipped inside and pushed the door shut.

"No need to worry, *madame*," I assured her. "I promise I'm very easy."

Chapter Four

Champagne O'clock

The next day was bright but cold, a sign of winter's imminent victory over the dull damp of autumn. A Paris-Blois courtesy car whisked me into Epernay, to the Avenue de Champagne, that impossibly grand boulevard lined with the headquarters of the world's sparkling wine elite.

The grandest *Maison* of all, of course, was that of Paris-Blois's flagship, Champagne Louis Beaufort. Most of the architecture was obscured behind a two-storey-high wall, upon which had been hung the name of the brand, almost tastefully, in six-feet-high bronze calligraphy. My car slowed, nosed onto the pavement and paused before the entrance, a triumphal arch framing a huge pair of wrought iron gates. They opened slowly, without any obvious human intervention, and the car bumped onto the cobbles, coming to a stop next to a sign stating '*Visiteur VIP*'.

"*Merci*," I said. My driver didn't reply. A smartly dressed guard stepped forward and opened the car door; this time my *merci* was acknowledged with a brief nod. I grabbed my leather case and entered the headquarters of Champagne Beaufort.

I was directed into a large conference room. The winter sun streamed through the skylights, projecting bright shapes high onto the wall. Chairs had been laid out in neat lines, a thin layer of cushion topping each seat. I'd arrived early but a couple of dozen people were already present, some seated alone, others standing and whispering in small knots. A long table lay at the front of the room, ranks of Champagne flutes packing its surface like glass soldiers on parade.

I took a seat around ten rows back, near the rear. I've never been one for sitting at the front of class, and I watched as the room filled up with buyers from various supermarkets, restaurant chains and wine merchants. I spotted a familiar figure: a pale, slight man, around my age, his face haughty and instantly dislikeable. It was Benedict, the Champagne buyer from Merryfield Superstores, Gatesave's great rival. His eyes flicked around the room, attempting to identify someone who didn't despise him. He saw me and, unwisely, strode over.

"So, Felix, it appears even the mighty Gatesave are forced to pay homage to Paris-Blois?"

"Your frilly underpants are showing, Benedict." I nodded at his trousers and he looked down for a split-second before tutting and glaring back at me. "I'm here to get a sense of who's prepared for the millennium and who isn't," I said. "I suspect you're in the latter camp?"

"Actually, we're in very good shape. Just here for a little top-up."

"Really? I heard you were in a flat panic and in need of several million bottles."

"Who told you that?" he demanded, flushing. It appeared that Paris-Blois had done as good a selling job on Merryfield's clueless directors as they had on mine.

"You just did."

Benedict reddened further. "Well, I hope you don't get priced out when the bidding starts," he said. "You may be the bigger supermarket, but we sell just as much Champagne as you. We have a more affluent customer base, you see."

"You really are terribly important, Benedict. If only everyone was as aware of that as you."

"In fact," continued Benedict, "we're expecting to overtake you in Champagne sales this year. We have a few surprises up our sleeve."

"A half-price Champagne offer in November, I assume?"

Benedict's eyes bulged. "No, not necessarily," he said, swallowing.

"Well, it's very kind of you to give me so much warning, Benedict. I'll be sure to put on a little promotion of my own the week before. Good luck with the festive season."

He stalked off and I scanned the room once more. There was Sandra, standing at the front, talking to a male colleague. By now, all the seats were filled and several dozen people stood at the back of the room. A good turnout. Clearly, no-one wanted to be stranded, shelves empty, for the night of Millennium Eve.

The audience quietened as the Head Winemaker for Champagne Beaufort strode into the room. He was young and handsome, with lush, collar-length hair, as though he'd just stepped out of a grooming commercial. He greeted Sandra, putting an over-familiar arm around her as they kissed, and whispered in her ear. She laughed but I was pleased to see that she pulled herself free. He shook hands with a couple more Paris-Blois executives and took up a position facing the audience, who fell silent.

"A big welcome, everyone, to this very special, exceptional event at Champagne Beaufort," he began, his heavy French accent sending a shiver of excitement through the room's more easily pleased English speakers.

"The biggest, most special, most incredible night is coming. I talk, of course, about the Millennium Eve, when all the peoples of the world come together, in love." I sighed, loudly enough for the rapt young woman beside me to turn, sharply, and frown.

"In love for each other. And in love, of course, for the greatest drink known to mankind." In one smooth movement, the Head Winemaker swept his hand down, grasped the slim glass before him and raised it above his head. "Champagne!"

The room burst into applause, allowing me to sigh more deeply without attracting further disapproval. When the clapping had subsided, he ran his hand through his hair and continued. "At the request of our dear customers, we have convoked this meeting to give you a final opportunity to improve your stock position of Champagne Louis Beaufort."

He stood to one side and a ceiling-mounted projector hummed to life, shining a huge Paris-Blois logo onto the wall.

The logo faded, to be replaced by the image of a wizened old man labouring over a rack of Champagne bottles in a dim cellar.

"Artisanal, traditional, respectful," murmured the Head Winemaker. We were treated to a dozen more slides of mist-wreathed vineyards and cobwebbed caves piled high with ageing bottles, all accompanied by gushing, heavily accented commentary. Then, with the click of a mouse, the romance was gone and the wall shone with a businesslike grid of numbers.

"And now, to the main event. The first lot is five hundred thousand bottles of Champagne Louis Beaufort Brut. My colleague here will conduct the auction." The Head Winemaker waved at a smartly suited older man. "But, before we start, you must know what you are buying, of course. You will not be disappointed!"

Half a dozen young women, each holding an open magnum of Louis Beaufort, marched to the table of glasses, surrounded it and began to fill the flutes with short bursts of Champagne, the foam rising up each glass and subsiding just as it reached the rim. When every flute had been charged, the servers lifted their trays and glided along the rows of supplicants, each of whom plucked a flute as they passed.

"We have released the vintage six months early, so our customers can be sure their favourite Champagne is available." *And to be sure you make a bloody killing*, I thought. I did a little mental calculation, working out the cash-flow benefit in releasing several million bottles of Champagne six months early. *Enough to fund a few Grand Prix sponsorships*, I mused, *that's for sure*.

An earnest-looking young man raised his hand. "Why are you releasing the vintage so early? Surely, in such a young wine, there is a loss of complexity and depth when you compromise on maturity?"

A few heads turned to check the source of the challenge. Who was this impertinent man, daring to challenge the Head Winemaker's artistry, his intuition, his flowing locks?

"No, no, no," laughed the Head Winemaker, humourlessly, as he made a swiping machete gesture with his hand. "You do not understand the style we strive for." He raised a glass. "I travel a lot. A lot," he repeated, nodding at the front row, who nodded in return. "Last month, I was in New York, in the clubs, and I hear everywhere 'We want fresh. We want a fresh style.' And I am just back from Shanghai, incredible place, such a big market, really buzzing. And what are people saying? 'We want...' Yes?"

"Fresh!" parroted a few members of the audience.

"Exactly! The fresh style!" The audience nodded to one another and smiled.

"They want. *The fresh style*," he repeated. The easily led, which appeared to include most of the room, were with him now, nodding confidently as though they too had just popped into Mr Chang's wine bar on Shanghai High Street to find a billion consumers hurling steamed dumplings at the sommelier and screaming for a lighter, less complex Champagne.

"Fresh! Fresh! I hope that answers your question!" barked the Head Winemaker. The impudent challenger, silenced, stared at his shoes.

"You will be amazed by this new expression," he continued. "So poised, so fresh, so... yes, sexy!"

The cork taint hit me as soon as I lifted my glass. I brought it a little closer, but it was a proper minger, smelling like damp chipboard wrapped in a month-old dishcloth. I raised my hand. The Head Winemaker ignored me, but Sandra looked over.

"Ladies and gentlemen," called the auctioneer. "I am starting the bidding for five hundred thousand bottles at seventy francs per bottle, ex-cellar Epernay."

"No bids in Euros please, I cannot yet do the maths," smirked the Head Winemaker, to guffaws from the crowd. "Maybe next year."

"Seventy francs, yes!" yelped a prissy voice from the front of the room. It was Benedict. He stood and turned to the audience, face shining like a school swot about to be awarded his first gold star of the day.

Sandra raised her eyebrows, still looking at me. "Corked," I mouthed, making a cut-throat gesture with my fingers. She glanced at the Head Winemaker, still basking in the glow from the audience.

"It's certainly a fresh style, if you like fresh cork," piped up the earnest man, emboldened once more. A murmur rose from the audience and a few members waved their glasses at the waitresses. Sandra whispered to the Head Winemaker, who froze, then made a face like a man attempting to pass a large stool in a railway station toilet, in the knowledge his train is about to depart. The noise from the audience increased. The Head Winemaker stared, appalled, at the empty magnums of Champagne.

"Is… impossible. It is… the fresh style," he stammered.

I stood and raised my hand, focussed on the auctioneer. "*Monsieur!*" I called. The man looked over, as did most of the audience. "I like the style. Seventy-one francs."

The room erupted in laughter. Benedict leapt up and down with glee. "I know where I *won't* be doing my Champagne shopping this Christmas!" he howled.

The auctioneer looked at the Head Winemaker then back to me. He nodded then addressed the audience, though he could barely be heard over the laughter. "Any advance? *Non?*" He looked to another man sitting at a desk at the side of the room and nodded once more. "Seventy-one francs to the gentleman." The desk-bound man made a note in his ledger. *Good*, I thought, *that's over ten percent of my requirement bagged, at a better price than I'd dared hope.*

Sandra stepped forward and the audience quietened. *Beauty silences faster than threats*, I thought to myself. She rewarded the crowd's submission with her smile.

"Ladies and gentlemen, please accept our apologies for this little technical issue. There is clearly a problem with our sample magnums. They were hand-filled and there must have been a fault with the corks. No other bottles will be affected. The stock you're bidding for has not even been disgorged, of course."

A murmur rose from the audience and a few people glanced at me. "In fact, I think Mr Hart may have obtained something of a bargain." Sandra smiled at me, though rather coldly.

"Mr Hart said he likes the corked style!" shouted Benedict, but no-one laughed.

I stood and held my glass up to the light. "I was referring to the underlying quality," I called back. "It's perfectly obvious the wine is tainted, but equally obvious it was due to an isolated cork batch. In fact, I believe the quality of this *cuvée* may be quite exceptional. I think, however, I'll try another sample before I bid again."

At this, the audience laughed good-naturedly and several joined in a call of 'new samples please'. Then I spotted a man in the front row, among the Paris-Blois executives. He'd turned to stare at me but there was no ambiguity there, the look was pure hatred. It was Pierre Boulle, Sandra's boss, and the entire reason I'd been forced into this absurd charade in the first place. Despite my generous intervention in their fiasco of an auction, I suspected our afternoon meeting would not be a jolly one.

The waitresses returned along the rows, collecting the tainted glasses on their trays, and the Head Winemaker regained his voice. "Ladies and gentlemen, please give us ten minutes, we will have more Champagne for you, very quickly." The volume of chatter rose and I retook my seat. The woman who had frowned at me earlier was now much friendlier. "How arrogant that the Head Winemaker didn't even taste his wines before pouring! But very strange they were all corked. Every single magnum! I've never seen that before." Nor had I, but before I could reply, a hand touched my arm. It was Sandra.

"Mr Hart, sorry to interrupt, the auctioneer would like a quick word."

I followed her to the man seated at the desk. Sandra placed her hand on my shoulder and whispered in my ear.

"That was embarrassing, thank you for your help." Before I could reply, she continued: "Rather than taking up your day bidding against the rest of the trade, I'm willing to offer you an option on another three million, at eighty francs per bottle. A generous offer."

"How about seventy-one francs?" I replied.

"How about eighty francs, Felix? And how about you stop being a dick? This crowd will bid most of the lots up way above one hundred, especially now that idiot Benedict's been given free rein with Merryfield's procurement budget."

"Eighty francs it is then."

"Good." She nodded to the man, who made a note in his ledger. "You're free to have lunch at La Briquetterie, it's on me. But don't drink too much, we have our meeting with Pierre at four o'clock."

La Briquetterie, in the nearby village of Vinay, is one of the Champagne region's finest restaurants. I was off like a shot, a Paris-Blois chauffeur whisking me out of Epernay and right to the *hostellerie*'s door, whereupon I gorged myself on foie gras, escargot and rare steak. I wouldn't say I drank *too* much, I erred on the side of quality rather than quantity, but a bottle of Vintage Krug and a fantastic red Coteaux Champenois later, I confess I was quite pleasantly bladdered. The car returned me to Champagne Beaufort's headquarters just before four, and a flunky led me upstairs to a large boardroom.

As the door opened, I heard an angry voice. It was Boulle.

"It was no accident! That's the third time this year! Find out who's doing it!"

Boulle stood in the corner, his back to the room, shouting into a mobile phone. Sandra sat at the glass boardroom table, her face grim. As I entered, she nodded to a seat at the end of the table. I sank into it, enjoying the way the pneumatics gently took my weight. I gave the leather arms a squeeze. *This must be a jolly expensive chair*, I thought. The little bulge in my jacket pocket reminded me of my leaving present from the restaurant. I fished out the napkin and unfolded it carefully on the table, revealing three exquisite petit fours. Well, two were exquisite, one had squashed slightly, leaking a delicious-looking brown treacle onto the linen. I scooped it up with two fingers. Salted caramel. Absolutely delicious.

I sighed contentedly and pushed my shoulders back. The seat tipped, much faster than I expected, and I was forced to grab the chair's arms and quickly extend my legs, by way of balance. As I declined to a horizontal position, the tips of my shoes collided firmly with the underneath of the glass tabletop, which emitted a splendidly loud chime.

Both my companions jumped, Pierre Boulle whirling round in shock. "What ze hell is ze preek doing?" he shouted, holding the phone to his chest and pointing at me. I thrust my head forward a few times, to persuade the chair to return to a more conventional position, but it appeared to be locked in relaxation mode, and I only succeeded in banging the tips of my shoes repeatedly against the underneath of the table, like a crazed gong-slave at the Burmese royal court.

"For Christ's sake, stop doing zat!" screamed Boulle.

I lifted my head slightly. "Sorry," I gargled. The salted chocolate had caused me to salivate quite generously and, in my horizontal position, there was a clear danger of drowning in a slurry of caramel and repeating red wine. Sandra walked over and pushed some hidden lever, returning me to a more orthodox position.

"Thank you," I said, once I'd swallowed the rest of the mouthful. Sandra didn't reply. I gazed at the two remaining petit fours, wondering which to address next.

"*Alors!* You! Idiot!" said Boulle, pointing the phone at me.

"How can I help?" I asked.

"You fancy yourself as a connoisseur, *non*?"

"Well, that's for others to judge," I said. "Though I am, as you know, a Minstrel of Wine."

"Yes," sneered Boulle. "I am aware. Well then, *Ménestrel*. Judge this!"

Chapter Five

The Judgement of Basildon

A flunky appeared beside me and set down a glass, a great bulbous thing holding a small measure of red wine. I wriggled to the edge of my seat and grasped the stem, giving the wine a swirl. As I poked my nose into the bowl, I was greeted by a luscious fog of plum and leather. It was a Pinot Noir, a good one, fuller bodied than the Coteaux Champenois I'd polished off over lunch. I took a sip. Gorgeous. Not particularly mature, still brooding, but perfumed and poised. Top class Burgundy.

"That's a very fine wine," I said.

"It's the finest. The finest wine of all," snapped Boulle.

"If you say so."

Boulle placed a bottle on the table, the label facing me. Domaine Henri-Leroy. My eyes widened. I returned to the glass and took another sip.

"I do say so," said Boulle. "And so do three hundred years of history. And the world's greatest sommeliers, wine merchants, journalists…"

I finished the glass. "Well, you can add me to their number. It's jolly good. Is there any more?"

A reasonable request but, rather rudely, no-one responded.

"As I told you last night," said Sandra, "there's a competitive Pinot Noir tasting planned in London, in which Domaine Henri-Leroy is obliged to participate. It is a mischievous initiative, of course, designed to embarrass us."

"Why must people do this?" said Boulle, rubbing his hand over his forehead. "Disrespect history in this way, set vignerons against one another, disrupt the harmony of the world?"

I didn't have a good answer for that, so I remained silent. I stretched for the open bottle, which turned out to have been placed just out of my reach, possibly deliberately. Pierre scowled then waved his hand, and the flunky crept over to refill my glass with another tiny measure.

"The tasting is the idea of Sir Francis Walsham and Lord Flashman," continued Sandra, "and will take place at Basildon House, in the centre of London."

Now, that *was* interesting, in a winey kind of way. Sir Francis Walsham was a Francophile, a lover of Bordeaux and Burgundy, and the owner of Le Grain d'Or, London's most venerable wine merchant. Lord Flashman, on the other hand, was an evangelist for New World wines, *his* cellars were rumoured to contain the world's finest collection of non-European wine. They were both swaggering braggarts, of course, especially Flashman. But he was a member of the House of Lords and owned Basildon House, the largest residence in London after Buckingham Palace, so you could hardly blame him.

"The tasting will pit six French Pinot Noirs, all Burgundies, against six Pinots from other countries. Sir Francis Walsham has picked the French wines, Lord Flashman will pick the non-French. They have placed a wager as to whether the wines of Burgundy will triumph over those from outside France."

"What's the stake?" I swallowed the wine. It was absolutely marvellous. I turned and waved my glass at the flunky, who grimaced and tiptoed over.

"It is a gentleman's bet," said Sandra.

"Probably to choose who buggers who in the bathroom of the House of Lords," muttered Boulle.

"Yes, Walsham and Flashman have nothing at stake, except their pride. But we, as you know, have a lot at stake. The news of the competition will be announced tomorrow, it is to be called The Judgement of Basildon, after the venue. We expect significant press interest, not just from the wine trade but the wider media too. They do like to take a pop at the French."

"Why don't you just refuse to take part? Say it's beneath you."

"We will be seen as cowards!" Boulle slammed a copy of *American Goblet* on the table and stalked off to the far end of the room. A small yellow post-it had been stuck, helpfully, next to one of the headlines.

Henri-Leroy: A tarnished lily?

I tried to focus on the article. The words danced around, making me feel a little dizzy, so I placed my fingers over my eyes for a few seconds, hoping that when I removed them the letters would have slowed to a gentler waltz. When I did, I was surprised to find the entire magazine had disappeared.

"It's vanished!" I shouted, in genuine surprise.

I looked up to see Sandra standing next to me, the magazine in her hands. She was reading aloud.

"...one asks whether the ownership of Henri-Leroy by Paris-Blois International has prioritised earthly matters over the heavenly."

"The journalist is an arse-ole!" shouted Boulle, from the other side of the room.

"The allegation, Felix, is that we are more concerned with the profit margins of Domaine Henri-Leroy than with the quality of the wine. We did initially dismiss the request, flat refused to take part. But the world's highest profile wine journalists are already aware of the tasting and it became clear we would be traduced throughout the world of wine if we failed to participate. The editor of *American Goblet* stated he would refuse to review our wine in next year's vintage guide if we pulled out. The Russians and Chinese use *American Goblet* as their bible for what to buy and we can't afford not to be in it."

"Oh dear," I commiserated. My glass was empty and I waggled it behind my head, hoping the flunky was paying attention.

"We do not, however, intend to lose this competition. It would deal a huge blow to the pre-eminence of Burgundy and damage the reputation of Domaine Henri-Leroy. We will not permit this to happen to our most profitable wine."

"You said you wanted me to be a judge?" I peered at the tiny smear of wine that had been deposited in my glass and turned to the flunky. "Could you pour me a grown-up's measure, please? I'm here to study Domaine Henri-Leroy in intense, forensic detail. How can I do that if you're only prepared to lightly paint the bottom of my glass?"

Sandra sighed and gestured at my goblet, which was filled, with excruciating slowness, to a slightly higher level. I downed the wine and replaced it on the table, flicked the rim and nodded to the flunky once more, who shuddered with irritation.

"The tasting will take place at Basildon House, just a stone's throw from the cellars of Walsham's shop, Le Grain d'Or. There will be twenty tasting judges, a mixture of winemakers, journalists and merchants. The attendee list and the methodology for the tasting are secret but Walsham has poor IT security and it was quite straightforward to gain possession of the plans and the names of the attendees."

This was starting to sound like less of a wine tasting and more of a conspiracy. I've never been much of a fan of conspiracies, at least not when I'm on the bottom rung of one.

"Our initial plan was to approach enough of the attendees and persuade them of the benefits of voting for the status quo. We're confident our wine is the best, of course, but it would be reckless to leave things to chance."

I wondered what toolkit of persuasion Sandra and her boss had in mind. Money? Sex? Blackmail? I had no problem with the first two, but the reminder of blackmail lowered my spirits slightly.

"The problem is that this is a blind tasting." Sandra paused and looked at me, possibly to check I was paying attention.

"Can't you just bribe one of the serving staff into telling you which wine is yours and tip the wink to your tame tasters? Surely that's well within your capabilities?"

Sandra gave a thin smile. "It's not just a blind tasting, Felix. It's a *double* blind. Lord Flashman has procured the services of a retired Detective Inspector, a consultant who advises casinos on fraud prevention. This man has drawn up a preparation process on which he has staked his forty-year career in Scotland Yard. He has declared the methodology unsubvertable."

"How inconvenient," I said, tapping the rim of my empty glass and catching the eye of the flunky.

"There are two separate decanting stages before the tasting. No one present for the first stage is permitted to be present at the second stage. We have a good understanding of the plans for the first stage, thanks to our compromising of Le Grain d'Or's email server."

"Jolly good," I said, draining the glass. I started to feel a touch of sympathy for Domaine Henri-Leroy. The wine was excellent, but you can't stand still these days, not for a second. If you do, some bugger's going to be right up your backside before you know it, whether you like it or not.

"Are you listening, you preek?" shouted Boulle, rather interrupting my reverie.

I let the question hang, mainly because I was still swilling the last mouthful around my gums. I gave Boulle a thumbs up, which he took unnecessarily badly.

"Sandra, this guy? *Serieusement?*" He stared at me, then turned to Sandra and shook his head. A bit rude, I thought, given I was the one doing *them* a favour.

Sandra looked at me and spoke more slowly.

"Listen, Felix. This is important. There are twelve wines in the tasting. Each of the twelve will be poured into a decanter etched with a number, in the cellars of Le Grain d'Or on St James's Street. The only people present will be Walsham and his most trusted assistant. The number of each decanter is decided only at the last second, by drawing lots."

"Ok, twelve numbered decanters. I get it."

"Walsham will lock the decanters in a large wooden chest, which will be transported, by horse-drawn carriage, the couple of hundred yards to Basildon House. The progress of the chest will be watched, every step of the way, by the assembled media."

"Walsham 'imself will be sitting on the chest, looking like a prize ponce," added Boulle. I nodded in sympathy.

"When the chest arrives at Basildon House, Walsham will hand it over, with the key, to Lord Flashman. It will be carried to the cellars, to be unlocked by Flashman and his cellar master, all overseen by the retired Detective Inspector. There, the contents of each decanter will be transferred to a *second* set of serving vessels, each of which are etched with an identifying mark. This second code is, once again, chosen by drawing lots. This means the identity of the final serving vessel is unknown to Walsham or anyone else present at the scene of the first decanting."

"Are you keeping up?" barked Boulle.

"Yes. No one person sees any wine in both its original bottle and its final serving decanter."

"Exactly," said Sandra. "The identity of the wines will only become known after the event, by going through the process in reverse."

"So, you're shafted." I made a circular motion with my empty glass in the direction of the flunky. "You can't track the contents of your Domaine Henri-Leroy from its bottle to the first decanter and on to the second."

"Yes, Felix. That's right."

"So… you'll have to bribe the Inspector. Of course, that's what you've done. He probably approached you!"

"Yes, that would be the obvious solution. But we have experience of this man. A couple of years ago one of our operatives negotiated an understanding with him over a different matter in Atlantic City. The details are unimportant. He appeared to go along with our plan, only for it to turn out he'd been communicating with the authorities all along. Our operative is now in prison and will be for some time. Our Inspector appears to set great store by his incorruptibility."

"Self-righteous arse-ole!" muttered Boulle.

"So, what's the trick? Secret cameras? You can't be bribing Lord Flashman and Sir Francis Walsham. That would render their wager rather pointless. And I don't think either of them need the money. Interesting," I mused, stroking my chin.

"We didn't invite you here to drink a bottle of Henri-Leroy and shoot the breeze, Hart!" snapped Boulle.

Sure enough, the bottle was empty, save a few millimetres of sediment in the base. The flunky lifted it and crept out of the room.

"Felix. Paris-Blois doesn't want to take part in this silly charade, but we did obtain one concession. I mentioned that we're permitted to nominate one of the tasters and that you are our nominee."

It dawned on me that I might be playing an unpleasantly central role in this little game. Tasting a dozen of the finest Pinots in the world in the surroundings of a Lord's private palace, the world's media baying outside, sounded quite fun. But there was always a sting in the tail where my obligations to Paris-Blois were concerned and, drunk as I was, it sounded like a bum deal.

"I'm very flattered, Sandra, Monsieur Boulle, but I must decline. I'm sure you can find a more worthy candidate."

"It's not a request, Hart! We're *ordering* you! *Crétin!*" Boulle folded his arms and glared at me.

"Sorry, old chap. You can't make me. I'm out."

Sandra opened a file and removed a piece of paper. It was a photograph. She pushed it towards me. "You don't know her. But you knew her son." I peered at the picture. A hard-faced, determined-looking woman in a headscarf, looking straight at the camera, no attempt at a smile. Behind her, rugged hills.

"Somewhere in the Calabrian countryside, a mother grieves for her missing boy. She was born into violence, a culture of vendetta. When she was widowed, two decades ago, four men died as she avenged her husband's murder. Can you imagine how she might go about answering the death of her son?"

Boulle placed his hands on the table and leaned towards me, smiling. "She is a very important businesswoman, Hart. Our office in Reggio Calabria tells us she is inconsolable. 'Tell me who has taken my boy,' she says to everyone. 'Just give me a name.'"

"No-one in Italy knows the name of the guilty party," said Sandra. "A tiny number outside Italy do, however. Three of them are in this room."

"It was an accident," I said, quietly. My mouth was dry. Another drop of Henri-Leroy would have gone down very well.

"We're just requesting that you attend a wine tasting, Felix. Is that too much to ask?"

What a conniving bunch of sods, I thought. But an encounter with a grieving *'Ndràngheta* matriarch from the blood-soaked badlands of Calabria, backed up by an army of young hoodlums begging to avenge her pain, wasn't my idea of a fun date.

"Good. So it's settled. Now, I want you to concentrate." Sandra placed a glass of water before me. I gulped it down.

"Sir Francis Walsham's most trusted assistant is a young man by the name of Percy Woods. He is passionate about fine Burgundy, but he lacks the means to properly indulge his passion. Grand Cru Burgundy is a most expensive habit. Paris-Blois is a generous sponsor of young talent, however, and we have provided him with funds to allow him to pursue his interest. An informal educational scholarship, you might say. Just last week we funded an all-expenses-paid trip to Burgundy, including first class travel, a suite at a château just outside Beaune, and meals at a series of Michelin-starred restaurants. Our only request was that he make a generous purchase of our top Burgundies and prioritise us over our competitors on Le Grain d'Or's wine list."

"Sounds like standard practice from your lot," I said.

"Indeed. Unfortunately, to an outsider, this might look a touch like bribery, and Walsham, his employer, is a stickler for integrity. And so, just yesterday, one of our sales team explained to young Percy Woods that we require a little more from him."

"Some help with a forthcoming tasting, perhaps."

"That's right. Specifically, the identifying number of the initial decanter into which Domaine Henri-Leroy is to be poured. He was unwilling to comply, of course, but it was pointed out that Walsham might take a dim view of his most trusted assistant taking hospitality in exchange for inflated orders. Imagine a copy of the letter, conveying our thanks for the generous order and trusting that he enjoyed his wonderful trip, making its way into the upstanding Walsham's hands. Not quite illegal but, shall we say, *awkward* to explain."

I thought back over the past couple of years and the number of free meals, junkets and jollies I'd accepted. I quickly gave up. Completely compromised. No point in turning over a new leaf now.

"Young Percy Woods and his boss, Walsham, will be the only two present at the initial decanting. Walsham's helpers take possession of the chest only when it has been locked. While the wines are being loaded on to the horse-drawn carriage, one of our operatives will obtain the number corresponding to Domaine Henri-Leroy from the newly co-operative Percy Woods. This will be conveyed to you on a small piece of paper."

"Sounds risky. Can't you just text it to me?"

"Our retired Detective Inspector has an inconvenient distrust of cell phones. The tasting judges are required to surrender all electronic devices before the initial decanting has even begun."

"If they've confiscated our phones, they're not likely to allow someone to just saunter up with a cheat sheet, are they? I assume we're all locked in a cellar somewhere in the bowels of Basildon House?"

"Right and wrong. They certainly won't allow you judges to mingle with the public, you'll be under the watchful eyes of our Inspector and Lord Flashman's servants. You won't, however, be locked in a cellar. You will be in plain sight, out in the open, in front of the media and public who have come to witness the spectacle. That way everyone can see you aren't being briefed. You will be confined with the rest of the tasting judges in a little roped-off area, right outside the gates of Basildon House. You will observe the approach of the carriage, then be instructed to follow the locked chest inside. You will then take your places around the table in the grand dining room, while the chest descends to the cellars underneath Basildon House for the second decanting."

Sandra unfolded a large piece of paper, smoothing it flat on the table. It was a map of the area between Green Park and

Piccadilly Circus, the heart of St James's, showing the location of Le Grain d'Or and Basildon House.

"We obtained this map from Walsham's email account." She pointed to a small square shaded pink, labelled 'judge assembly point'. "You are to stand on the outside of the group of your fellow tasters, precisely here." She made a little cross with a pencil in the corner of the pink square. "You're tall, so it will be polite of you to stand at the rear of your group, facing the approaching carriage but with your back to Green Park. It is important that no-one stands behind you. Understand? Stay alert but don't look around or act in a suspicious manner. Our operative will pass you the number corresponding to the decanter of Domaine Henri-Leroy."

I refilled my water glass and drank it, which cleared my head a little. "But that number is useless on its own. I'll need the corresponding code on the second decanter."

"Yes. And that's our problem. Unfortunately, we are not aware of the arrangements for the second decanting. The details have been kept separate, deliberately, from the first stage. Flashman is a member of the House of Lords, his server utilises a government firewall and we have not been able to compromise his encrypted email account. After the locked chest descends to the cellars of Basildon House, we're in the dark. We don't even know how the second set of decanters will be marked. All we know is that the second decanting will be handled by Lord Flashman himself, aided by his cellar master, under the watchful eye of the Inspector."

"Sounds like you've got some more work to do then. I assume you'll let me know when you've worked it all out." I stretched. "Thank you for the wine. I'm sure it will win anyway, it's showing very well."

"You're the one with work to do, *putain!*" hissed Boulle. He stalked out of the room. I didn't like the sound of that.

"You're going to be killed if you screw this up," said Sandra, quietly.

How the hell was I going to get out of this mess? I needed to do a runner, but where to? Sandra had perched on the corner of the boardroom table as she'd flattened the map. She was just an arm's length away, one leg tucked behind the other. I gazed at her legs, sheathed in black. She'd kicked off one shoe and the top of her foot rubbed, slowly, against her calf. She had an amazing figure. I'd need another identity – a fake passport, bank account, driver's licence. I followed the fabric higher, up and over her knees. Unfortunately, I'd failed to cultivate friendships with any top counterfeiters, so obtaining fake documents was going to be tricky. *Shapely*, I mused. The word could have been invented to describe Sandra. Her skirt had ridden up far enough to expose a couple of palms' worth of thigh, firm and smooth under her tights.

"Did you hear what I said?"

"Yes. You're going to kill me."

"Exactly." She sighed and filled my water glass. "Deservedly so, if you don't pay attention."

"I am paying attention. Even if I identify your wine, I can't direct the result all by myself."

"Yes, you can. We've approached several of the judges and, through a variety of means, have kindled their enthusiasm for preserving Domaine Henri-Leroy's status as the finest Pinot in the world. Their identity is not your concern. But their helpful scores will tip the result firmly in our favour."

"I don't understand. How will they know which wine is yours?"

"Because you'll tell them. By the start of the tasting you, and you alone, will be aware which decanter contains Domaine Henri-Leroy. Once the tasting has begun, you will communicate this to our collaborating judges by lifting the correct glass and stating a pre-agreed phrase. You are to say: 'The wines are quite open; they have clearly been aerated.' Our judges will be expecting this, though they're unaware who else is working with us."

"What if we're forbidden to speak? It's very bad form to talk during a competitive tasting."

"You're a very badly behaved young man. No-one will be surprised at you blurting out a stupid comment." She smiled, not unamusedly.

"Rules are rules. They might cancel the entire tasting."

"After all the trouble they've gone to? I think that's unlikely."

All very clever, I thought. *Except for one glaring problem.* "Your plan is useless without the codes for the second decanters. It all sounds rather half-baked, to be honest. I can't see how it's going to work at all."

Half-baked or not, my stomach was churning quite thoroughly. I hadn't a clue how to get out of this one, apart from a sprint to the door and a life working as a goat-herder in the Massif Central.

"We have a lead. But you're going to have to do the heavy lifting." My heart sank. "Lord Flashman's cellar master. We've done our research, made a few subtle approaches, dangled a few tasty incentives, but this member of Flashman's staff appears to value their integrity more highly than most. We've nearly exhausted our options."

"Oh dear," I said, hoping that might scupper the whole adventure. "I'm sure you'll find something. We chaps all have our soft spots." Please God, let him be a fanatical monk, eschewing money, sex, power, glory and all that Uncle Tom Cobley has to offer.

"Not a he, Felix. A she."

Sandra placed another photo on the desk and my eyes widened. A young woman with fierce eyes stared back, tousled dark hair surrounding a slim, smooth face, a slight smile at one corner of her mouth. I felt the familiar rush of blood down below.

"I thought you'd like her. Lord Flashman's cellar master is a young woman by the name of Lily Tremaine. She doubles as his personal wine buyer."

"Interesting," I said.

"She's attending our annual fine Burgundy tasting on Thursday in Vougeot. It's all above board, just a little piece of corporate PR we run each year for fine wine merchants and sommeliers. You're going too. Your Eurostar and TGV tickets are here." She handed me an envelope.

"We understand that Ms Tremaine intends to take the Minstrels of Wine examination. I suggest you scrub up and kindle a beautiful friendship. Find a way to obtain those decanter identification numbers, Felix. I'm sure she'd appreciate a tip or two from a qualified Minstrel."

I took another look at the photo, then slid the envelope into my jacket.

"If she's receptive, I'd be delighted to give her a few pointers."

Chapter Six

Deep Burgundy

Sadly, there was no time for my usual, overnight warm-up in Paris. After a sleepy glide on the Eurostar, I endured a rude, ten-minute rattle on the Metro, shaking me awake as it clattered beneath the capital to Gare de Lyon. I had no intention, however, of spending the next leg of my trip in the company of a frigid cheese baguette, and certainly not when Paris-Blois were paying, so I'd reserved a table at Le Train Bleu, leaving a civilised interval before my connection to Dijon. An hour or so later, splendidly fortified by a lunch of duck and Mercurey, my TGV was roaring through the countryside to Burgundy.

It was gone six o'clock, cold and dark, as the taxi dropped me at my final destination – a grand, medieval château on the outskirts of Vougeot. I was obliged to walk the final hundred yards, the only route into the castle a broad, wooden walkway over a long-empty moat, our friendlier era having replaced its waters with a carpet of grass. I pulled my coat around me and walked quickly, my shoes slipping slightly on the frost sparkling the boards. I passed through the main gate into a courtyard where a footman, warming his hands before a flaming brazier, bowed and gestured to a doorway.

I pushed aside a thick curtain and entered a large, high-ceilinged room, full of people, the air warm and thick after the brutal chill outside. I removed my coat, which was whisked away by another footman. The light was low, the bare stone walls softened by several huge, hanging tapestries, each illuminated by discreet little bulbs embedded in the floor. A pair of iron chandeliers, festooned with candles, spluttered overhead. I was a little late, the tasting had been underway for an hour already, so the room's mood had moved from academic rigour to a more sociable buzz.

Of course, the venue was completely unsuitable for a serious wine tasting. Professional sampling sessions are supposed to be conducted in neutral-coloured surroundings with white linen and plenty of natural light. But this was a Paris-Blois PR event, designed to shock and awe, so here we were, in a castle in the French countryside, supping the finest wines known to mankind, by candlelight. I didn't see anyone complaining. I suspected the complaining types hadn't been invited.

Three sides of the room were lined with tasting tables, behind which, every couple of yards, stood a Paris-Blois sommelier chaperoning a decanter of Burgundy's finest. I passed slowly along the row of tables, allowing a sommelier to pour me a small measure of something expensive, which I swirled, sniffed and tasted. I removed my notebook and scribbled a few poetic adjectives, exchanged conspiratorial nods with the sommelier, then peered over my glass at my fellow attendees. I counted around one hundred, slightly more men than women, though I was pleased to see the women were less likely to be of pensionable age. Most of the tasters were deep in discussion with the sommeliers behind the tables. Which was Lily Tremaine? I knew I'd recognise that face in an instant. Tall and slim, Sandra had said. I moved slowly along the tasting bench, holding my glass before the next pourer.

"*Gevrey-Chambertin, Monsieur.*"

"*Merci.*"

I buried my nose in the glass and moved slowly to the centre of the room, my notebook before me but my eyes searching left and right. Tall and slim, dark hair. There were several possible candidates but the dim light and the constantly moving crowd made it difficult to focus.

"Muscular, precocious, probably needs food," said a woman's voice.

I wheeled round, nose still in glass, the wine sloshing against my nostrils. A plump, friendly-looking woman, twenty years my senior, gazed with delight at my wine-moistened face. As I extracted my handkerchief and dabbed the excess Gevrey-Chambertin from my nose, she looked down and pretended to read from her tasting notes.

"Closed at the start but a hard finish. Wouldn't you agree?" She swayed slightly.

"Quite forward, rather lush," I replied, extending a supportive hand, part-affectionate, part-structural, as she tilted alarmingly to one side.

"*Madame. Vous devez goûter le Musigny!*" A young sommelier took the woman by the arm and, with a courteous nod to me, steered her towards a newly filled decanter. *Thank goodness for that*, I thought. *It's nice to be admired but I have serious business to attend to*. I drifted to the other side of the room, sipping as I moved. I realised my search required a more systematic approach. I inserted myself into the scrum surrounding a tasting table and held out my glass, taking in the faces as they sniffed and scribbled their notes. Satisfied none of the group fitted Lily's description, and my glass charged with Nuits-Saint-Georges, I moved along the row of tables.

I merged seamlessly into the next knot of guests, a bunch of middle-aged wine merchants, hotly discussing the merits of three competing vintages. Nothing to detain me there. Behind them, a young, studious woman, writing earnest notes on a clipboard. Too short and mousy to be my target. Further on, a man and woman talking in low voices, her back to me. Tall, slim, long dark hair. This might be her. As I edged closer, I could hear the man speaking French. The woman laughed and replied, in French, with a German inflection. That didn't sound right; my target was English. She turned to refill her glass and caught my eye. Attractive, for sure, but not Lily Tremaine.

I sidled up to the next table, ready for a refill. Two Pommards to choose from. An elderly man held two glasses, sniffing from one to the other. His younger companion leaned right over his glass, swirling it continuously, as though trying to conjure a genie from the depths. I slipped between them and presented my own glass to the *garçon* for a pour.

"Well, I think they are exquisite," said the older man. "You can smell the land, the *terroir*." He sounded hurt, as though the other man had offended him. I took a sniff then a sip. The wine was incredible, black fruit in a polished iron grip. What would a bottle of this cost on whichever London wine list these chaps curated? Hundreds of pounds. Perhaps a thousand. *Let's make the best of it while it's still free*, I thought, finishing the glass.

"It doesn't get much better than that," I agreed.

The younger man snorted into his glass. I didn't like the tone of the snort, sounded a little contemptuous for my liking. His head was still bowed right over his glass, nose nearly touching the little whirlpool of red he'd spun.

"My young friend doesn't like the wines," sighed the older man. "Evidently, they are no longer in fashion with the youth."

"Given the prices these wines fetch, I'd suggest they're very much in fashion," I said, feeling like a cynical old pro.

"If sleeping with the dead is your thing, I suppose they're in fashion." I turned back. The younger man had a disconcertingly high, musical voice. Mocking too, which raised a little flush of pique in my normally calm and even manner. *You'd better watch your tone, you little squit*, I thought. *I don't care if you're chief bottle washer at the high court of master sommeliers, you'll be talking at an even higher pitch once I've introduced my knee to your bollocks.*

Then he lifted his head from the glass and looked at me and I blushed Burgundy-red. There would be no knees meeting bollocks, that was for sure. It was Lily Tremaine. She wore a man's dinner suit, white shirt and bow tie but there was no mistaking those fierce eyes, the strong cheekbones and that little smile at one corner of her mouth, the same as in Sandra's photograph. Her long dark hair was tied to the side and tucked beneath her jacket collar.

"So, do you sleep with the dead?"

"Not to my knowledge," I said.

"Well, that's good," she replied. "I'm not saying corpses can't be beautiful but they're more suited to canvas than the palate, don't you think?" She paused. "If you *do* think, that is?" She smiled and raised her eyebrows.

I hoped the low light disguised my red face, not to mention the disconcerting rush of blood down below. I wondered how I'd mistaken her for a man just seconds ago. She was indeed tall, nearly my height, but her dinner suit was a slim cut, showing off her lithe figure and long legs. Her white shirt was a woman's, tailored to follow the contours of her chest.

"That's very philosophical," I said. "If these wines are dead, how do you intend to bring them back to life? With your charm?"

There was a little flash from her eyes. She was still smiling, though there was a competitive edge to her expression, as though she was about to challenge me to a wrestle. *Not the worst thing that could happen*, I thought, with a rush of excitement.

"Let me show you how to bring wine to life," she said and took my glass, pouring the rest of the Pommard into the spittoon. The *garçon* closed his eyes and grimaced.

"I say, I would have drunk that!" declared the older man. Lily leaned past me and kissed him on the cheek.

"Sorry, Charles, I shouldn't have wasted it. Thank you so much for the tutorial, I do appreciate it!"

The old man, still holding a glass in each hand, beamed like a lighthouse. I could swear his white hair actually flashed silver.

Lily led me to the corner of the room where a bored-looking man stood before a decanter of pale red wine. His face lit up when he saw Lily. I peered at the empty bottle alongside the decanter. It was labelled Fleurie.

"You've brought me to the Beaujolais stand at the world's most exclusive Burgundy tasting? You know how to show a chap a good time, don't you?"

"What's the best wine you've ever tasted? And don't tell me it's any of these corpses here, or that's the end of our conversation."

Well, this was a question to answer well, that's for sure.

"It was a Shiraz, made by Wikus van Blerk, the South African legend," I replied. "I drank it in the Karoo, on the way to see his mountain vineyard outside Prince Albert. He was passionate about African *terroir* and the cycles of nature. He was a lunatic, too. You'd have got on well."

Lily stared at me. "You've met Wikus van Blerk? How? He… doesn't receive visitors."

"Not usually. But he did receive me. He even sold me some of his wines. First time they'd seen the shores of Europe."

"Ah, I know who you are. You're Felix Hart; you run the buying team at Gatesave."

"Yes, that's me. You have me at a disadvantage though," I lied.

"You're also the devil."

"Oh," I said. "That's a bit strong. I don't have horns." That was only half a lie. I was so attracted to her I was starting to feel faint.

"I mean you *work* for the devil. Gatesave. How did you get invited here, for Christ's sake? You guys don't sell fine wine."

"We do sell a little, actually, in our more upmarket stores." And who are you to talk about dodgy employers, I nearly said, given that you work for Lord Flashman of Notting Hill, a politician and aristocrat to boot. But I didn't. I had to play innocent. "So, which virtuous institution do you work for? Mother Theresa's all-lepers-welcome wine and tapas bar?"

"That's moderately offensive," she said, "but moderately amusing too. I work for a private individual. As their cellar manager."

"Someone very rich then."

"Yes." She turned to the man behind the decanter and winked. "Your *other* wine, Pierre." She held out both glasses.

The man bent down and lifted an unmarked bottle from beneath the table. He poured a measure into each glass. The wine was red but with an unusual brightness, as though lit from within. Lily handed me my glass.

"Now, taste it."

I smelled it first. The aroma was loud, vibrant, unrestrained. Unusual, I thought, but I'd smelt plenty of funky, off-beat wines before, so I wasn't discouraged. Then I tasted it. At first, I thought my tongue has been tasered. The wine literally fizzed around my palate. I tried to say, 'there's something wrong', but the wine wouldn't let me; it seemed to be wringing my taste buds, making my mouth physically juice up, the very opposite of the drying effect you feel with normal, astringent wines. And then, suddenly, shockingly, there was something else, a clarity of taste I'd never experienced, a sharpness that told you the wine was alive, that it was tasting you.

"What is it?" My mouth tasted of balsamic vinegar and mango, of coal and flint.

"It's life. You're tasting the living."

"How do you…?"

"How do you make a wine like that? It's what you *don't* do, not what you do."

"So, what *don't* you do?"

"You don't work for the devil, that's what."

This was, by some distance, the strangest conversation I'd had at a wine tasting. And that wine had staggered my senses, knocked them from their axis. "Why do you keep mentioning the devil? Are you religious? Or some kind of organic communist?"

"We'll talk about it later."

"Later when?" A vague memory of Sandra broke through, exhorting me to find a solution.

"Later tonight. In bed."

I was somewhat lost for words, but it felt, suddenly, as though things were going my way. Lily raised her eyebrows. "We are going to bed together, aren't we?"

I focussed and recovered my wits. I wasn't sure whether to thank the wine or my own repartee. Either way, things were looking up.

"Yes. Obviously."

***

I crept to the window and scratched my fingernails against the glass to clear a spy-hole, sending curls of frost floating to the stone floor. I guessed it was a little before 6 a.m. The sky was still countryside dark, the stars iced pinpoints against the black. Illuminated by a window far below, the frost-coated grass of the moat glowed, like a pale ghost.

"Get back in here."

She didn't need to ask; I was already on my way back to the four-poster, my feet almost burning with the chill from the stone flags. Central heating clearly wasn't a priority at Vougeot castle.

"Christ! You're like an icicle," she gasped as I slipped back in.

A little later and much warmer, it was time to attend to my mission.

"So, you know that I work for the devil, whatever that means. Who's this rich person *you* work for?"

"He's a member of the House of Lords."

"Fancy that. You're used to living in castles then?"

"Not castles. But I do work in a palace. Basildon House."

I did my most convincing double take, quite difficult when you're sandwiched between a heavy layer of blankets and a lithe woman.

"You work for Lord Flashman! That's impressive. I'm attending his fancy Pinot Noir tasting three months from now."

"You're a taster at The Judgement of Basildon? Well, well, what an honour," she said.

"You're a hard one to please, aren't you?"

"You're not doing too badly. But I am when it comes to wine, yes. And the thought of all those old farts pontificating about which wine's superior to another, as though you can boil everything down to a single score... so boring! Pathetic, in fact."

"There should be some pretty impressive wines in the lineup."

"There are some pretty bloody dull wines there too. All that ultra-premium Burgundy from Sir Francis Walsham's little shop. Nothing scoring less than ninety-eight points in *American Goblet* magazine. Dull, dull, dull."

Lily started to move against me in a way that was anything but dull. I realised I was running out of time.

"The competition's all about French Burgundy versus the rest of the world," I said. "It must be your job to help Lord Flashman select the Pinots from the other countries."

"Maybe it is. But I've signed a legal contract swearing not to disclose anything about the tasting. Especially not to one of the bloody judges." Her movements suggested the conversation needed to be placed on pause. Just enough time for one killer fact.

"I'm a guest of Paris-Blois International," I said.

"Oh my God!" she gasped. There was a lot going on and it wasn't immediately clear whether it was an exclamation of excitement or disgust. But a few minutes later, when she'd caught her breath, she picked the conversation up where we'd left it.

"You're Paris-Blois's representative at The Judgement of Basildon? You really *do* work for the devil!"

"They're only a wine company. Well, a bit more than wine."

"They're not *only* a wine company. They're everything that's wrong with the world of wine. Take that top cuvée of theirs, Domaine Henri-Leroy."

"Come on, you can't say that's a bad wine." I reminisced, for a second, over my boozy afternoon in Epernay. Then I remembered Sandra's threats and Boulle's hateful face, and my spirits fell a little.

"It's a technically proficient wine, sure," replied Lily, "but they're notorious for their use of pesticides, spraying filth all over their vineyards, poisoning the wildlife, the workers. Disgusting."

"Who doesn't do a bit of spraying? Can't blame them for wanting to keep the mould away from those valuable grapes."

"A bit of spraying? Listen. One of my friends is a winemaker on a neighbouring estate. They want to produce clean, organic wines. Living wines. But they can't because Domaine Henri-Leroy are so careless with their spraying. Clouds of their filthy pesticide drift onto their neighbours' land, month in, month out. The entire village is so poisoned no-one can even apply for organic status. They're disgusting!"

She pushed me off, clearly upset. I'd misread that one. Looked like I was soiled goods now, as sullied as an over-fertilised vineyard. I was glad I hadn't owned up to being Paris-Blois's man yesterday evening. I'd have been spending last night alone for sure.

"I didn't know they were so badly behaved. Sorry."

"Whatever."

This was bad news. After a promising start, I'd completely alienated my key contact. And then, in a flash of brilliance that quite took me by surprise, it came to me.

"So, why don't we cause a little upset?"

"What do you mean?" she said, sulkily.

"You're helping Lord Flashman set up the wines for the competition. If you tell me which one is Domaine Henri-Leroy, I could give it really poor marks."

She turned back to me and snorted. "Why would you do that?"

"To make amends for working for the devil. And because I don't want us to finish badly."

"You idiot," she said. But there was a hint of affection in the insult. "You've no idea about the tasting. There's an old copper, a retired Scotland Yard Inspector, who's created unbreakable security around the whole event. Even Lord Flashman and I don't know which wine is which."

"I know. You'll receive a locked chest full of numbered decanters. Your job is to pour each into a new serving vessel with a different code, so it's a double blind."

Lily was silent for a while. "There are only supposed to be five people who know the process," she said. "Me, Lord Flashman, Sir Francis Walsham, Walsham's assistant and the Inspector. So how the *hell* do you know that?"

"Because I'm working for Paris-Blois. And they've hacked Walsham's email account, so they know the process."

"You're kidding me? What a bunch of freaks. They've gone to all that trouble just to win a wine tasting?"

"There's a lot of money at stake."

"Of course there is. They have to win, don't they? So they can ensure Henri-Leroy remains the most expensive wine in the world."

"Then help them lose."

Lily moved her face close to mine.

"I don't trust you. Why the hell should you want to make them lose? They've employed you to help them win. And anyway, you can't cheat. You don't know which wine corresponds to which decanter."

"I have to make them lose. I know what they're like. If I help them win and take my payment, they're bound to blackmail me. They did exactly that to Walsham's assistant. That's how they'll know the decanter number for Domaine Henri-Leroy. They're going to communicate it to me just before the tasting."

"Oh my God," she said softly. "They've blackmailed poor Percy Woods?"

"Yes. He accepted some overly rich hospitality last month and has just been presented with his first bill, much to his distress."

"Silly Percy."

"Indeed. But not silly Felix. Hence my intention to make them lose. And lose badly."

"Why didn't you just tell them to piss off when they approached you? Why have you gone along with it?"

"To be honest, I really fancy my contact at Paris-Blois. She's rather gorgeous. I was hoping to get some action before I sell them down the river."

"Oh my GOD!" shouted Lily. "You're, like, the worst person in the world!" She howled with laughter then drew close again. "But there are twenty tasters. Your bad score alone isn't enough to sink Domaine Henri-Leroy."

"There are another six tasters ready to follow my lead," I said. "I just have to say a special phrase while holding the glass containing Henri-Leroy. Obviously, I'll lift the wrong glass as I say it, so another wine gets the inflated points. And I'll give Henri-Leroy a really stinking score into the bargain."

"Tell me you're joking? A third of the bloody judges are already nobbled? Unbelievable." She shook her head then nibbled my ear. "What's the magic phrase then?"

"The wines are quite open; they have clearly been aerated."

"How boring."

"I think that's the point. Will you help me?"

"Yes, I'll help you. You're cleverer than you look, you know." She climbed astride me.

It had been a close thing, but I was feeling very clever indeed. Which, with hindsight, showed what a staggeringly stupid sod I really was.

Chapter Seven

Dinner Dance

London is justly famous for its gentlemen's clubs. If your idea of a good time is a wood-panelled room scattered with snoozing ex-military types, or a private lounge stuffed with stockbrokers gargling mediocre Rioja, the city is your oyster. All boast a prestigious waiting list, a wad of arcane rules and a low-tempo stab at culinary competence. But there is no institution in that city, nor indeed in all of Christendom, with as daunting a barrier to entry, as astonishing an archive of mysteries, or as magnificently stocked a cellar, as the Worshipful Institute of the Minstrels of Wine.

And so, it was with a sense of humility that I stood upon a table in the Salon de Dijon, one of the many watering holes dotted about the vast, ten-storey Minstrels Hall, and uncorked my third Burgundy of the night.

"*Vive la Bourgogne!*" I shouted, at the top of my voice. A roar of approval erupted around me.

It was the 13th November, and the five hundred and twenty-fifth anniversary of the Battle of Héricourt. There was a tradition that a serious Burgundy drinking session should take place in the Salon de Dijon on the anniversary of all the famous battles of the Burgundian Wars. The tradition was still in its early days – in fact it was I who had invented it a couple of months after my graduation as a Minstrel – but it had been enthusiastically supported by the merrier elements within the Institute's membership.

"*Ménestrel Hart! Voulez-vous descendre, s'il vous plaît!*" screamed the bar manager, clearly unimpressed by my confident use of the furniture.

I raised my hands in a gesture of submission and hurled myself onto the heads of my fellow revellers, who held me aloft for a few seconds before we collapsed to the ground.

"Charles the Bold is on his arse again!" shouted a historically literate and rather drunk Minstrel.

I clambered to my feet. I didn't want to be barred from the Salon de Dijon again. Last time I was suspended for three months and I'd been forced to miss the anniversary of the Battle of Nancy. That had been a shame. For the followers of *La Société de Guerre Bourguignonne*, as I had christened our historical think-tank, the Nancy re-enactment was the biggest night of the year.

"*Alors! La Bataille d'Héricourt est terminée!*" screamed the manager. "*Nous sommes fermés!*"

Our crowd staggered out of the Salon de Dijon into the third-floor hallway and considered our options. On the opposite side of the hall lay the Salon de Bordeaux, a larger but more sedate restaurant favoured by the duller, more mercantile wing of the Institute. It was also the only area where Minstrels were permitted to entertain guests, so one was expected to observe a degree of decorum. I wasn't averse to a long, claret-soaked dinner every so often, but this wasn't the time for earnest talk of shipping rates and vintage yields. We needed a less formal setting. Given our hearty mood and the associated likelihood of being barred from most of the other bars in Minstrels Hall, that meant a hike up to the tenth floor and the open-air La Terraza Asada. Aside from being the most tolerant drinking emporium in the building, La Terraza had the advantage of being the only bar in Minstrels Hall that allowed you to bring your own bottle.

"Last one to the top gets the Gamay," sang one of the more competitive of our crowd, and she raced up the stone staircase, long hair streaming behind her, an uncorked bottle of Burgundy in each hand.

We burst onto the terrace, panting and giggling. The cool October air had discouraged the less well-insulated of the Minstrels' membership from venturing out of their cosier nooks and crannies, and our arrival tripled the population of La Terraza. Four large charcoal grills dominated each side of the terrace, each sporting the national flag of the four great barbequing nations: Argentina, South Africa, Australia and the United States. In summer, all four would be roaring, ribs, steaks and sausages fizzing and spraying explosive puffs of juice, perfuming the night air with Cajun spice and Worcestershire Sauce. But tonight, the only action was from the Argentinian *asada*, its glowing coals roasting a fine-looking collection of lamb on the bone.

The autumn air calmed us a little and we broke into smaller groups, four of us colonising one of the stone tables close to the grill. We'd each salvaged a bottle of good Burgundy from downstairs, so we lined up our haul, waved for a lamb steak and settled down for a good al fresco Pinot session.

"So, Felix," said one of our group, "your two years is nearly up! Which House will it be?"

That was the question. For those Minstrels approaching the second-year anniversary of their graduation – a group which included yours truly – a fateful decision loomed. On the fifth of January, two years and a day after the harrowing tasting exam that had marked our entry to the ranks of the Minstrels, I and my fellow second-years would be obliged to choose which of the four Minstrel Houses to join.

The Houses were the foundation stones of the Minstrels of Wine, clubs within the club. Over the two thousand-plus years of the Institute's existence, various Houses had risen and fallen, some merging, some banned, others simply evaporating into irrelevance. There were currently four, each with a very different ethos and style. Membership brought a delightful collection of perks – each House had its own private bars, restaurants and lodgings inside Minstrels Hall. Being an enthusiast for late-hours gallivanting, I frequently found myself using Minstrels Hall as a base for overnight stays when I'd missed the last train back to Little Chalfont. As a fledgling Minstrel, however, I was limited to the first-floor lodgings, where the rooms were little more than broom cupboards, with space for just a single bed and a basin.

The privilege of staying in the exclusive House quarters would be a pleasant step up.

The decision was binding. Once you'd joined one House you couldn't change your mind and flit off to another, unless your House was dissolved or subsumed. But that hadn't happened for well over two hundred years and the four existing Houses all had large, stable memberships.

Of course, you weren't expected to just guess which of the four you might like to join. In the six-month run-up to decision day, each of the four Houses put on a series of dinners and meetings, so potential recruits could work out whether they'd fit in. I'd already attended a few, for research purposes, not that I've ever needed much of an excuse to jump into a wine-soaked jolly.

Just last week, House Mercantilist, the largest of the four, had held a sumptuous dinner in the Great Hall, and a fabulously decadent session it was too, with suckling pigs rotating on spits and First Growth claret sloshing into goblets. The Mercantilists' membership was dominated by successful men and women of commerce, rather like myself, though the male membership significantly outnumbered the female, which put me off a little. The Mercantilists was the House of choice for Port shippers, Burgundian négociants, the Bordelais and the Champenois – all the aristocratic, old-school regions who had dominated the world of wine for centuries. The owners and managers of great European estates would clink crystal with distributors from New York, Hong Kong and Tokyo, all merrily swilling from the most well-appointed cellar since Louis XIV's Versailles. The world of retail was represented too, prestigious wine merchants and auctioneers, plums in mouth, joined in more recent years by the powerful selectors for chains of casual dining restaurants and, of course, the carnivorous supermarket wine buyers. As a red-meat-eating supermarket operative myself, you might think House Mercantilist just my bag, but I found the atmosphere stuffy. There was far too much talk of deals, acquisitions, shipments and trades, and nowhere near enough cheering, singing, footsie and giggles for my liking.

To my embarrassment, House Mercantilist actively courted my membership. I would be standing at the bar of the Salon de Dijon, sniffing a pot of Pinot and minding my own business, and a dark-suited type would sidle up, dropping heavy hints that membership of House Mercantilist would do wonders for my career. Now, I'm as ambitious as the next greasy pole-climber but given that most of my working hours were spent in the company of winemakers bearing gifts, I felt little need to spend my social hours in the company of the same. So, I politely declined their approaches, much to their chagrin, explaining that my passion lay in the study of wine and the history of the Institute itself, and that I was thinking of joining one of the more academic Houses.

This, you won't be surprised to hear, was complete cockwash. I had no more desire to study the history of wine than I did to place my knackers in a basket press. If I'd been the type to pore over ancient Greek shipping routes or aspire to translate the *Naturalis Historia* into Cyrillic, the obvious choice would be to join House Archivist. This venerable House, founded by some toga-wearing troublemaker a couple of millennia ago, was the repository of all the research carried out by the Worshipful Institute since its foundation back in darkest God-knows-when BC, when the Persians exported wine on magic carpets and dinosaurs roamed the Napa Valley. As you can tell, history isn't really my strong point, unless it involves celebrating the anniversary of a medieval battle with a well-oiled banquet, preferably ending with a rousing chorus of 'One Mint Julep' and a wrestle in the hay.

But, in fairness to House Archivist, they did know their amphora from their arseholes. The previous month, we prospective candidates had been given a tour of their museum, and a bloody impressive collection of statues, scrolls and knick-knacks it was too. Minstrels Hall descends at least five floors below ground level, most of which is reserved for the exclusive use of House Archivist, and deep in the Institute's bowels they store a vast library of wine, some of it astonishingly ancient. The Provost, the fiercely intelligent Ms Jacinda Rougegorgefils, had led us second-year graduates on a whirlwind tour of the reserved floors to whet the appetite of the historians among us. We were whisked past glass cases containing Dom Perignon's diaries, vine-growing manuals in Latin and Greek, and ancient wine vessels from Georgia. By far the most striking object was a bronze statue of Dionysus, some twenty feet high, rescued from the sack of Constantinople centuries ago. He stood, naked as the day he was born, six-pack and todger on full display, heavy goblet in one hand and a great trailing bunch of grapes in the other, guarding a large steel door with a fearsome set of locks.

"The tour ends here, I'm afraid," smiled Ms Rougegorgefils, patting the statue's chap affectionately. "Dionysus guards the closed section of our archive, which is available only to selected members of House Archivist."

Unsurprisingly, rumours regarding the contents of the closed archive ranged from the eyebrow-raising to the buttock-clenching. It was generally accepted that the fire-and-bomb-proof rooms contained astonishingly rare wines, including second century Aglianico from Mount Falernus and fortified Shiraz from Persia. The Fort Knox-like security doors hinted at historical treasures too, the most impressive alleged to be a priceless iconostasis, a solid silver screen dismantled and spirited from the basilica in Constantinople in 1205 AD, just hours ahead of an army of drunken, rioting crusaders. The archive was also believed to contain an amphora from the last wine shipment to sail from Pompeii before the eruption of Mount Vesuvius, a branch from the first vine planted by the Romans in the Rhone Valley and original bricks from the wine bar at the first Olympic Games.

Beyond that, members of House Archivist remained tight-lipped, so speculation regarding their secret inventory ran riot. An acquaintance – who was *not* a member of House Archivist – swore that on his own tour, a decade ago, he'd seen a collection of ancient Greek decanters shaped like erect phalluses, cast in solid gold. And at one particularly well lubricated banquet, the ancient Minstrel sitting next to me claimed he'd sneaked into the closed archive in the 1950s, before the high security door was installed, and discovered a collection of mummified remains, including Basil the Great's finger, a minotaur's foreskin and Hitler's lost bollock.

Now, I'm as fascinated by embalmed genitalia as the next person, but I knew House Archivist wasn't for me. The dinner held for prospective members a few weeks earlier was pleasant enough, starting as it did with a one-hundred-strong vertical tasting of Châteauneuf-du-Pape, featuring wines dating back to the nineteenth century, followed by a fabulous feast of roast goose and tender baby goat. But, as the drunken conversation degenerated into games of 'Guess the Pope' and the more boisterous Archivists hurled Latin insults at one another, I was pleased to find I was out of my intellectual depth.

Nor did I fancy membership of the slightly alarmingly named House Terroirist. Named after the French concept of *terroir*, which translates roughly as 'a sense of place', this rather earnest House attracted the more serious merchants, winemakers and grape growers, particularly the practitioners of organic and biodynamic viticulture. It had a reputation as something of a cult and there were even tales of anarchist splinter groups, dedicated to the overthrow of modern agriculture. The Terroirists enjoyed an uneasy relationship with House Mercantilist, which they considered a cartel of corrupt capitalist mercenaries, which, to be honest, wasn't far off the truth. House Terroirist was also the smallest of the Houses, though in recent years it had become the fastest growing, presumably on account of the renewed fashion, in winemaking circles, for tree hugging and organic manure-throwing. It had a younger and more female membership, which appealed, but ultimately had an air of worthiness that put me off.

I'd made my mind up months ago.

"My friend, it has to be House Hedonist," I replied, pouring a healthy glass of very moreish Fixin.

"House Hedonist. Of course! What other House could Minstrel Hart *possibly* join?"

He was right, there was no other option. House Hedonist was everything I looked for in an educational institution; I'd even read up on their history. The most ancient House by far,

House Hedonist had been founded by Aristippus of Cyrene, a philosopher, sports fan and pupil of Socrates no less, back in the days when horses were wooden and Paris was a chap with an eye for a bit of Spartan skirt. Unlike most philosophers, who tended to over-analyse one's purpose in life and indulge in unproductive hand-wringing, Aristippus had quickly come to the conclusion that the only sensible path was that of luxury, feasting and fornication.

Back in those days, the Institute was based in Athens. Upon his arrival in the city, being a fan of the vine and a bit of a party animal, Aristippus immediately joined the Minstrels. According to the archives, he fell out with the more po-faced of his contemporaries, especially dull old Plato, and put his beliefs into action by founding House Hedonist. He established the annual cycle of feasts at the Institute, marking him out as a jolly good egg, though on the minus side he was also responsible for the fearsome entrance exam, now known as *La Vendange*.

Two thousand years later, House Hedonist still held the best parties, drawing its membership from the jollier ranks of sommeliers, journalists, winemakers and wandering bards. It boasted an even split of men and women, which as a feminist I consider extremely important, and sported no fewer than four private bars and restaurants including one, named *La Stanza Spumante*, sited in the centre of a huge Jacuzzi. To be frank, I was at a loss to understand why the entire Institute's membership didn't join House Hedonist two years after graduation. Some people take life too damn seriously, I suppose. Not a mistake I intended to make.

Chapter Eight

Lightly Oaked

My desktop phone chirped.

"'Allo, Felix. How was Christmas trade?"

It was Tom Hawkins. He never bothered to give his name, there was no mistaking Hawkins's throaty pirate's drawl. I swivelled my chair away from my desk and faced the window, taking in the damp London view. Outside, six storeys down, the cold, grey Thames crept by.

"Not bad, Tom. Champagne stock's a touch heavy but hopefully it'll sell over New Year. How's life?"

"Surviving, just," Hawkins guffawed, before dissolving into a series of coughs, followed by a sigh, a slurp, and the clunk of pewter against wood.

"I'm pleased to hear it. Nice bit of business with the Primitivo, by the way." The previous month, Hawkins had sold me eight containers of a rather tasty Puglian red at an extremely tasty price. The wine had won a gold medal at the International Wine Jamboree and had sold out within a fortnight.

"Nice little winery that. Plenty more in tank too; you should buy another load. Anyway, listen." There was another pause, slurp and clunk. "Your Pinot, it's done."

For a second, I was confused. I hadn't agreed any Pinot shipments with Hawkins.

"You should come down the pub and taste it."

Of course, my Little Chalfont Pinot! That silly miniature cask, the demi-rundlet of garden grape juice we'd harvested. I'd forgotten all about it. It must have been barrel-ageing in Hawkins's cellar for a good couple of years now.

"I assume it's only fit for fish and chips?"

"Come and have a butcher's, Felix."

So, straight after work, I caught the tube, rattling beneath London's frozen streets to St James's. As I ducked into the Flag and Parrot, one of the barmaids beckoned me over, lifted the bar hatch and waved me down the steps to the cellar. I could hear Hawkins's voice before I reached the underground winery. He was talking to his winemaker. As I pushed the cellar door open, they turned to greet me.

"Felix! Have a taste of this."

The little cask had been placed atop a large upturned barrel, four wooden wedges holding it in place. A white bung protruded from the top.

"Go on, Bruce."

Hawkins's winemaker smoothed his goatee and picked up his 'wine thief' – a long glass pipette, open at both ends, with a short bulge in the middle. "There's only a few dozen bottles' worth here so I don't want to waste it." He worked the bung loose and poked the glass tube a few inches into the demi-rundlet. He placed his thumb over the top and lifted the tube free. The wine thief, true to its name, now held a dark red core of liquid. Three small sherry *copitas* stood alongside the little cask, and the winemaker held the wine thief over each in turn, removing his thumb for a split-second, allowing a short squirt of red to tinkle into each glass.

"Having a big night, are we?" I muttered, peering at the miniscule measures of wine.

"Taste it," said Hawkins.

I held the tiny glass to a nostril first and gave a light sniff. I was expecting a vibrant dose of vinegar, perhaps blended with an undertone of second-hand arse rag. What I wasn't expecting was a symphony of rich red fruit, a genuinely complex bouquet, wrapped in wisps of smoke and perfume.

"Good God, it smells of wine!" I exclaimed.

"Thank you," said the winemaker. "I do try."

"Taste it," repeated Hawkins, grinning now.

There was barely a cat's lick of wine in the glass, so I necked the lot, drawing my breath through the liquid as it washed over my palate. It was astonishing. For a second, I wondered whether it might be the finest wine I had ever tasted. There was a richness that was nearly obscene, more of a texture than a flavour. It felt as though a gossamer-silk sheet, soaked in sweetest cassis and plum, had been placed over my tongue, before melting in a mist of wildly expensive, seasoned leather.

"What… what the hell have you done to it?" I said.

"He ain't done nothing to it," said Hawkins.

"Minimal intervention," declared the winemaker. "I sampled it every three months or so, just to check it hadn't spoiled. For the first year, it was quite closed; didn't taste of anything much. Then last year, it started to open out, first the fruit, then… well, you've tasted it."

"It's young but already tastes like a five- or ten-year-old Burgundy," said Hawkins. "You could pass that off as a Grand Cru if you were dodgy. Which I'm not," he added.

"I'd like to take all the credit," said the winemaker, "but that fruit you harvested, it's incredible. Must be an amazing little microclimate. South facing, you said?"

It was indeed south facing. Protected from prevailing winds by the fence bordering Little Chalfont municipal car park, planted on a pile of rubble and the remains of a composting toilet. And that's not all that lay beneath the vine… Sandra's photograph of the Calabrian widow flitted through my mind and I gave a little shiver. Harvested from a historic Buckinghamshire estate, situated over a shallow grave on the edge of a council car park. Not the most romantic back label.

"We should bottle it a-sap. Can't risk it oxidising in that little barrel," said Hawkins.

"We'll have to do it by hand. Won't take long. I'll use the pump syphon, nice and gently. Just need a helper to keep the nitro-sparge handy. We'll purge the ambient ullage, keep the oxygen away from it." The winemaker stroked his tuft of beard, approvingly.

"Well, gentlemen, purge away," I said. I hoped I'd have a chance to taste the wine again. "I assume I get a couple of bottles by way of payment for the grapes?"

"Don't bloody want much do you?" said Hawkins, good-naturedly. "Don't worry, we'll bung you a couple of bottles. We'll give it three months to settle down post-bottling. Reckon I might win a few bets with this one," he added, chuckling to himself.

I thought of the vine once more, her snaking limbs embracing the Little Chalfont garden as her own, leaves like jade beneath the summer sun.

Win a few bets. What a good idea.

Chapter Nine

Overstocks

"But the worst performance," stated the Director of Commerce to the packed but silent trading floor, "in fact, the worst overstock position I have ever seen, in all my long years in retail, belongs to the wine department."

He gave a smile, a rift of mirthlessness in the doughy hills of his pale, hateful face.

"Perhaps the head of the wine department would like to explain how we find ourselves holding *seventy-two* weeks' worth of Champagne stock on the third of January?" The Director of Commerce looked at me, smiling, eyebrows raised.

Because you ordered me to ship it, you colossal scrotum, I thought.

"Well, we didn't want to run out," I replied, to titters around the room. The Dick's smile shrivelled like a salted slug. "But we have a plan to address the issue," I added, hastily. "In fact, I expect us to be in an acceptable stock position by the end of the month."

This statement, it is fair to say, was a monumental porky. I had no plan and there wasn't a hailstone's chance in Hades of spiriting away our excess Champagne stocks. As Paris-Blois had intended, every retailer was in the same position, bloated with overstocks, depots stuffed fatter than a Macsween haggis. Some had already slashed the price of their Champagne in a vain attempt to stimulate an early January sparkling wine binge.

"How are you going to do that?" said The Dick.

"I'll be telling Paris-Blois International to buy the stock back from us," I said.

This was a spectacularly optimistic proposal, though there was no harm in trying. It would raise a smile from Sandra, at least, and she looked good when she smiled.

"You have a pretty high opinion of your negotiating abilities, don't you, Hart? Well, if that stock isn't cleared by the end of the month, you can find another job. Maybe Paris-Blois will employ you!" A couple of junior toadies guffawed at this and I made a mental note to stumble and spill hot coffee on their groins at some point over the next few days.

Well, here I was in a pretty little pickle. Unsurprisingly, the population of Britain had balked at consuming a metric tonne of fizzy wine each over Millennium Eve, choosing instead to mark the new year with a merely slightly-above-average level of vomit-inducing merriment. The result, as even the most fresh-faced depot operative could have predicted, was a string of warehouses up and down the country full to the gunnels with unsold and unsellable Champagne.

And so, with the air of a man measuring the remainder of his wine career in days rather than decades, I dropped Sandra a note, suggesting we needed to talk about Gatesave's Champagne stock position. To my surprise, she answered promptly, agreeing to meet at a Soho wine bar the following evening.

"My treat. We're quite cash rich at the moment," she smiled, giving me a malicious peck on each cheek.

"I'm sure you are. With your New Year's Eve blitzkrieg behind you, I suppose the war of attrition is now well under way?"

"Indeed. One of our competitors is due to issue a profits warning to the Paris stock exchange tomorrow. A dramatic downturn in predicted earnings for the year ahead, or something to that effect."

"Congratulations, you must be delighted. I'm sure my successor will be just as receptive to your kind hospitality. I imagine they'll be in place by the first week of February."

"Try not to be so melodramatic, Felix. Gatesave won't be firing you anytime soon."

"I think you'll find they will. The Director of Commerce, who you buttered up so beautifully before Christmas, has said so publicly. He blames *me* for our ludicrous Champagne overstocks, of course. So, unless you're willing to take your stock back, you'll be entertaining a new Head of Wine by Valentine's Day."

A bottle of vintage Champagne Beaufort arrived at the table. The waiter directed a stream of golden fizz into our glasses. Sandra lifted her flute and leaned forward. I'd noticed her yellow blouse was unbuttoned a notch or so lower than usual. The V of her shirt widened as she moved closer.

"Oh dear. Cheers anyway." She touched her glass to mine. Sandra didn't do anything, least of all mis-engage a shirt button, without a plan and an end in mind. I took a mouthful of Champagne. Superb. Deep and generous with a firm, delicious peachiness.

"Cheers," I replied. "Maybe I'll put on a huge promotion as a final hurrah, cut the price of your Champagne by three-quarters," I tilted my glass and studied the tiny bubbles. "I could put an ad in the press: 'Champagne Beaufort, now cheaper than Cava'. That should do the trick, shouldn't it? Maybe I'll even keep my job."

"I think my company would consider that an act of war," said Sandra, "but you're not going to do that. You can't afford it."

She was right, of course. Sitting on several million pounds' worth of slow-selling Champagne was a pretty lousy cash-flow strategy. But selling your stock at several million pounds below cost was certifiable lunacy.

"The Director of Commerce suggested Paris-Blois might offer me a job."

"How glib of him. But you already work for me. Why should I need to pay you?"

"I'm not going to be much use to you when I'm fired from Gatesave, am I?"

"No." Sandra took a small sip of Champagne. "We'll buy the Champagne back from you."

I looked up, sharply. "That's a very constructive approach." I didn't believe her for a second. This was either a joke or a trick.

"I mean it. Our CEO has signed it off. We can start uplifting your stock next week. But I need you to do something for me."

Of course she did. And it wouldn't be a small thing either. The idea of Paris-Blois buying back several million pounds' worth of Champagne out of the goodness of their heart was laughable.

"I'm already doing something for you, remember? The Judgement of Basildon."

"Something else. It's two years since you graduated as a Minstrel of Wine, correct?"

"Yes." What on earth did Paris-Blois want with the Minstrels? An inside track on how to pass the entrance exam?

"So, you're about to choose which House to join."

"Yes. Tomorrow night. Surely you don't need me to spy on the Minstrels? What are you hoping to find out? How to get more of Paris-Blois's Burgundies on their in-house wine list?"

"Four employees of Paris-Blois International are Minstrels of Wine already. We have no need for insights into the Institute's procurement policies." She paused as our waiter refilled the glasses. "All four are members of House Mercantilist."

Of course they are, I thought. The dullest House, home to buyers and traders from every corner of the business world. A great writhing orgy of networking and dealmaking. Didn't appeal to me at all. I preferred my orgies clean and pure, unsullied by the grubbiness of commerce.

"That suits us, naturally," she continued. "House Mercantilist is a valuable source of market gossip. We've been less interested in the academic research and strange rituals of the other Houses."

"But you're interested now?"

"Yes. Which House do you intend to join?"

"That's supposed to remain a secret until tomorrow night."

"You intend to join House Hedonist, don't you?"

"What makes you assume that?" My eyes flicked down to the yellow V in Sandra's blouse. That fourth button down was doing a sterling job holding everything together. It was clearly under considerable strain. I felt a pleasant flush of warmth and drained the rest of my Champagne.

"My Minstrel colleagues have told me enough about the four Houses for me to make an educated guess, Felix." She moved a hand to her neck and traced her fingers down the loose buttons. For one wonderful moment, I thought she was going to pop open the fourth, but she pulled the fabric closed and, to my dismay, pushed an unfastened button home with her thumb.

"You're not joining House Hedonist."

I was about to contradict her before I realised what she meant. She wanted me to join a different House, no doubt cosying up to her colleagues in House Mercantilist, fishing for insider titbits over Port and cigars. What a bloody buggeration. Was there any part of my blameless life that this miserable corporation didn't want to ruin?

"I'll join whichever House I like! I'm not interested in your Mercantilist friends. I'd rather sign up to the Women's Institute jam committee."

"I'm sure you would. But then I'd rather not buy back twenty million pounds' worth of Champagne from an incompetently run retailer." She smiled. "And you work for me, remember?"

I remained silent and studied my glass.

"Why are you so set on joining House Hedonist anyway? They spend most of their time eating, drinking and fornicating, from what I hear."

There was little point in responding to such a stupid question. "What can I do that your four Paris-Blois Minstrel colleagues aren't doing already?" I said, lifting my glass.

"Nothing. I don't want you to join House Mercantilist. You're to join House Terroirist."

I paused mid-sip. That *was* a surprise. House Terroirist was the most left-field of the Houses, obsessed with environmentalism, vinous heritage and moonlit chanting. What did Paris-Blois want with that bunch of fruit loops, with their cloudy orange wines and artisanal vermouths?

"House Terroirist…?"

"Yes. That's the House I want you to join. At the Institute's ceremony, tomorrow."

"Why?"

"We believe there is an element within House Terroirist, a criminal element, who are threatening our interests. We've heard they call themselves *Les Malherbes*. We want you to keep an eye on them. You'll be doing everyone a favour. Paris-Blois, the Institute, yourself, all law-abiding members of the wine trade, in fact."

I doubted very much that I'd be doing myself a favour. I suspected the benefit would be almost entirely on Paris-Blois's side. And I didn't like the sound of the criminal element either. I'd had quite enough of mafia conspiracies for a lifetime, though I doubted a bunch of organic grape fanatics could be as malevolent as a Calabrian organised crime syndicate.

Well, hindsight is a wonderful thing. And if I'd been better informed about grape fanatics, organic or otherwise, I'd have sprinted out of the wine bar that very second, hailed a taxi to Heathrow and booked a one-way flight to Kashgar.

Chapter Ten

A New Vintage

It is common, these days, to hear titans of industry boasting of their Harvard MBAs. Other graduates flaunt their Oxford PPE or blush, faux-modestly, as they recall their time at the *École normale supérieure*. And, further back in history, Tang dynasty mandarins, philosopher-kings from Plato's Academy, and Brahman gurus of the most rigorous Vedic schools, all surely succumbed to pangs of pride as they reminisced over the rigour of their student days. But, without doubt, all would fall silent, humbled in awe, before the nerve-shredding intellectual effort, weeping artistry and sheer, superhuman endurance required to tackle the final practical examination of the Worshipful Institute of the Minstrels of Wine.

I sighed, casting my mind back a couple of years to a gentler, more innocent time. It was two years, to the day, since I had swaggered through the front door of the Worshipful Institute, joined my fourteen fellow Initiates in the Great Hall, and embarked upon *La Vendange*, the Minstrels of Wine's legendary practical exam.

Only five of us had survived the tasting, the rest misidentifying one too many wines, or collapsing, comatose, across the exam table. For the failures, the penalty was immediate eviction from the examination hall and humiliation before the massed ranks of the Institute. Some accepted their lot and walked out, heads held high, others crept out, sobbing. Some refused to leave, arguing the toss with the invigilators, even physically resisting their expulsion, until they were carried bodily from Minstrels Hall and ejected into the back alleys of Covent Garden.

And the ordeal hadn't ended with the tasting exam. Those who survived the first round had to contend with *Le Récital*, an obligatory musical performance accompanied by the Minstrels' in-house orchestra. That task had whittled our number from five to three. Just a trio of graduating Minstrels out of the fresh-faced hundreds who aspire each year to don the purple cloak of the vinous elite.

The manager of the Salon de Dijon placed a finger on my empty plate and drew it slowly across the bar towards him. He raised an eyebrow.

"Yes, another slice of Comté and a jug of Savagnin," I replied. *A plate of tangy cheese and a carafe of wine from the wild hills of Jura would be very high on my list of last suppers*, I mused.

"You'll be asleep before *La Vendange* is halfway through," warned the manager. I smiled to myself. That was unlikely. I'd known this was going to be a late night and I'd taken a dose of *Madame Joubert's Lekker Medisyne Trommel* an hour earlier.

Now, you may be unfamiliar with this old Afrikaans folk medicine, for it is known only to a tiny handful of well-travelled, worldly men and women. It was introduced to me by a wise old teacher, many years ago, on the day of my expulsion from school, and it has aided me on many occasions when fatigue, peril or sheer over-indulgence threatened to blunt my usual laser-like focus.

Madame Joubert's tingling warmth had already percolated through my body and I was far more alert than the empty carafe of Savagnin suggested. And so, an hour later and pleasantly buzzed, I joined my fellow Minstrels filing slowly into the Great Hall. On this auspicious day, Minstrels were expected to enter via the Gods' Entrance, emerging high above the theatre's floor. The arena would soon be full and an excited babble filled the hall, for tonight was indeed *La Vendange*, the annual harvest of new blood, and the undisputed highlight of the Minstrels' year.

We descended through the tiers, Minstrels peeling off to the left and right, locating their personal seats. And these were no hard or under-stuffed seats either, for the Minstrels' prestigious rears received the same respect as their palates. Nearly every member had the right to their own generously upholstered, reclining chair, sporting armrests large enough to house an ice bucket and wine glass. I say nearly, because the honour of a personal seat was extended only to those Minstrels who were members of a House. An honour I was mere hours from earning!

The greenest Minstrels of all, the first-year graduates, sat in a row at the front, chattering excitedly. We second-year graduates, known in Institute parlance as '*Secondes*', sat further back, around halfway up the tiered seating, in a special cordoned-off row. This lay right in front of the Invocator's VIP box, known as the *loge*, a slightly raised area surrounded by a palisade of vine-wood posts. It was from the loge that the Invocator and other senior Minstrels observed *La Vendange* and passed judgement.

I joined Valentina and Hugo, my two fellow survivors from that crazy, staggering examination exactly two years ago. Valentina, being a carefree and flirtatious soul, gave me a generous kiss and a squeeze as I took my place. Hugo, being French, did the same. It wasn't often you saw the top nobs up close, so I turned around for a good gawp at the occupants of the loge, resplendent in their purple hoods. I spotted the Provosts of House Archivist and House Mercantilist taking their seats, each bowing to the crimson-robed Invocator before they did so.

While the audience chatted and meandered to their places, the floor of the theatre was a hive of activity. Upon it lay two dozen long, thin tables, running parallel to one another. Each was draped in white linen and separated from its neighbour by a gap of a few feet. A perfectly straight, single row of glasses lined each table from end to end, and an army of workers, wielding bottles and clipboards, filled each glass with a measure of wine. Before each bottle was allowed near the tables, a group of official sniffers nosed a sample, lest it be corked, oxidised or otherwise knackered. Other inspectors, wielding rulers, followed the pourers from glass to glass, checking the levels of wine and occasionally raising a hand if a measure was incorrect. I could see every bottle was identical, each made of dark glass like an old beer bottle, their only distinguishing mark a number scrawled in white ink.

I thought of my part in the forthcoming Judgement of Basildon conspiracy, now just one month away. I wondered whether anyone had ever cheated La Vendange and managed to learn the identity of the wines. The examination was administered by House Hedonist and, unsurprisingly, the methodology by which the wines were selected was a closely guarded secret. It was thought that several wines were in contention for each slot in the exam, and only at the last moment was the final choice made. Some claimed the selection process followed a drawing of straws fashioned from Dom Perignon's favourite vine, others that it included the movement of a pendulum around a magnetised effigy of Dionysus, some even swore it involved the rolling of dice made from the knuckle-bones of Aristippus himself.

The truth was that – aside from the judicious application of performance-enhancing drugs – cheating was well-nigh impossible and would require a conspiracy as large as the Institute itself. And that, as any decent cheat or philosopher could tell you, would rather miss the point.

The preparations were now complete. At the start point lay transparent whites, then the colour deepened as the row of glasses progressed, from watery green through pale straw to gold. Halfway down the table, the colours darkened further, to salmon orange and bubblegum pink, before turning red then near-black in the final few yards. The pourers and inspectors withdrew and a file of bearded men in frock coats, each holding a staff topped with a carved pine cone, entered the room. These were the Institute's in-house guards, responsible for everything from the smooth running of the major festivals to keeping out drunks from the streets of Covent Garden. They took up station around the perimeter of the theatre's floor.

"Did you know they've reduced the number of wines by thirty, to just one hundred and fifty?" asked Hugo.

"Outrageous!" I replied.

"They felt the exam was too difficult," Hugo continued. "No more than six people have passed in each of the last ten years. And only three in ours, obviously. Last year alone, twelve Minstrels died of old age."

Died of morbid obesity aggravated by a fermenting liver more like, I mused, but I could see the Worshipful Institute's problem. Back in the olden days, membership tended to be purchased rather than earned. So long as you could identify the business end of a wine bottle and hadn't been caught fortifying your *gran reserva* with Crimean donkey lubricant, you were in. But in recent decades, the entry criteria had been tightened, slowly but relentlessly. From correctly distinguishing a red from a white, the entrance examination, *La Vendange*, had grown into a tasting extravaganza of Himalayan proportions, scalable only by the vinous few.

The crowd quietened and I leaned forward. The Initiates were arriving! Each wore a blindfold and a black silk mask, symbolising the presence of divine, proscribed knowledge. One by one, with faltering steps, each was led into the hall by their personal guide and positioned at the head of their appointed table. When all the Initiates were in place, the Invocator rose and the orchestra's trumpets sounded a glorious fanfare. The blindfolded candidates jumped in shock and I chuckled, slightly unkindly. I'd done the same two years ago and I was glad they hadn't made the experience any more pleasant. They may have reduced the tasting to a mere hundred and fifty wines, but it was important to maintain *some* standards.

"*Welcome Initiates, on this, the twelfth day of Dionysus!*" called the Invocator.

I turned in my seat. The Invocator was standing, but we were too close to the vine-wood palisade to see anything but his crimson hood and wrinkled face. This would be the third time I'd heard his strange little speech. I doubted it would make any more sense this time around.

"Do you know any of this year's Initiates, Felix?" whispered Valentina.

"A couple," I replied. "There's a wine buyer for one of the big Dutch supermarkets. And another woman I bumped into at a tasting in Burgundy recently."

"Bumped into her, did you?" mocked Valentina, blowing on my neck.

"Yes, just briefly."

"Oh dear. Are you losing your touch, Feel?" She ruffled my hair.

"Stop fiddling with me and pay attention to the show."

"*And may all win, in the manner of Dikaiopolis!*" declared the Invocator, ending his speech with a bang of his staff against the loge's floor.

Each guide removed their candidate's blindfold and the game was on. I focussed on the line of hapless students. As anyone in the wine industry can tell you, the details of *La Vendange* are known only to those who have experienced the exam. All participants swear an oath, the *omertà di vino*, promising to keep the ordeal a secret, on pain of black-balling from any prestigious job in the world of wine. So, rumours aside, this was the first moment the poor boobs had been faced by the sheer horror of their predicament. One hundred and fifty wines! They were required to sniff, taste and swallow each sample – spitting was forbidden on Minstrel property, out of reverence to Dionysus – then whisper the answer to their guide. Five wrong answers and the candidate would be eliminated. A scoreboard displaying the Initiates' names hung helpfully from the ceiling, five blank spaces next to each, ready to record their accumulating mistakes. And they were competing against the clock too. A digital display, suspended next to the scoreboard, began a ninety-minute countdown.

I spotted Lily, my darling conspirator in the Judgement of Basildon, three tables along. She wore her tailored dinner suit and a bow tie, just as she had that night in Burgundy, but you'd have to be a blind dog lost in a London fog to mistake her body for that of a man's. I thought back to that frost-kissed night in the Vougeot château, Lily and I diving under the bedcovers in our freezing room...

Back to the present. The Initiates were well under way; all had tasted the first half-dozen wines and no-one had incurred a penalty, not yet. Most used the standard tasting method: hold the glass by the stem, give a flick of the wrist and send the wine spinning into a tight little whirlpool. Then sniff, pause for thought, and taste.

But Lily had her own technique. She would raise the glass a couple of inches and tilt it, observing the colour at arm's length, as if deciding whether it was worth lifting further. Then she would tap the base of the glass sharply against the tablecloth, as though rousing the sleeping wine, and bring it quickly to her lips, simultaneously taking the aroma through her nose and the liquid into her mouth. She would close her eyes, swallow and whisper to her examiner, who would nod, and so on to the next wine. It was mesmerising. She barely paused to think. There was no doubt, just a tap, sensory immersion and bang, right answer.

The spell was broken by a buzz, followed a couple of seconds later by another. A dozen or so wines in, some Initiates were making mistakes. That was bad news, psychologically, for the fumblers. With only four wrong answers allowed in the entire exam, you had to average over thirty correct wines for every mistake. And it only became harder as the tasting progressed, as palate fatigue and sheer intoxication took their toll.

"The Provosts wish to serve you a carafe from each of their Houses," said a voice. My two companions and I turned to see a bearded guard, staff in one hand, tray of empty glasses in the other, crouching in the walkway between our seats and the loge.

"By tradition, these will be served in order of the foundation date of each House. Each Provost will raise a toast to the founder of their House."

Lordy, what a turn-up. Personal service by the Provost of each House! I hadn't expected that. And by Hugo's breathless "*Non!*", not to mention Valentina's excited tweak of my thigh, my companions hadn't either. A charming little ritual ahead of our final decision on which House to join. Perhaps, a spot of last-minute advertising, to change any wavering Minstrels' minds?

"The Hedonists propose a toast to their founder," said the guard.

Everyone knew Hedonists was the oldest House – or, more precisely, the oldest House still in existence – so it was their turn first. And sure enough, here was Lord Slipcote of Brighton & Hove, Provost of House Hedonist, bowling down the aisle with a decanter of golden wine. He beamed from beneath his shock of white hair and I spotted a couple of dark splash stains on his purple cloak as he drew close.

"Valiant *Secondes*!" he declared. "On this day of Theemeter, I offer you a jar of our House Wine!"

The guard passed him three glasses and he generously over-filled each before handing them out. Then he filled a fourth and chimed it recklessly against each of ours.

"To *Aristippus*!" he said, happily.

The wine was sweet and oxidised, like badly stored Retsina in a Greek taverna.

"Delicious!" I said.

"No, it isn't, it's bloody awful!" replied Lord Slipcote, joyfully. "But it's our House Wine, so get it down you! Anyway, enjoy the rest of *La Vendange*. Looking forward to seeing at least one of you later!"

He winked at Valentina and my heart sank. I knew she intended to join House Hedonist and it drove home how bloody unfair it was that the door to the world's most prestigious feasting and carousing fraternity had been slammed in my face. God knows what kind of initiation ceremony the Hedonists had planned but I was pretty sure that wonderful cocktail dress would be up and over her head before they'd finished the aperitif. Whereas I'd probably be sitting through a lecture on organic viticulture in medieval Alsace. What a miserable disgrace.

We finished the wine and I peered down at the Initiates. Most were around a quarter of the way through and nearly all had at least one cross next to their name on the scoreboard. Some had two and a couple already had three crosses – I couldn't see them surviving long. But Lily still had a clean sheet. What a trooper.

For no good reason, I felt a rush of pride and, as the minutes ticked down, I watched just her, willing her on. I was interrupted, once again, by our guard.

"The Archivists propose a toast to their founder," he said.

"Just three *Secondes*, clearly a low-yielding vintage!" A woman's voice, precise and friendly. It was Ms Rougegorgefils, the Provost of House Archivist. In contrast to Lord Slipcote's spectacular mop of hair, she sported a neat bob. Her cloak, clean and uncreased, lacked his carefree splash-stains too.

"Minstrels Soto, Blanchett and Hart," she smiled. "On this day of Theemeter, I offer you a jar of our House Wine."

Glasses were poured, red wine this time.

"To *Gaius Plinius Secundus*," she declared, nodding to each of us as our glasses met. The wine was definitely a step-up from the last, a deliciously juicy, berry-scented brew. Looks like the Romans had one up on the Greeks when it came to house wine.

"A little taste of Mount Falernum. Not the original vintage, thank goodness." She smiled at Hugo who chortled in return. Some kind of historians' in-joke, clearly. Hugo had always intended to join House Archivist. He was a studious chap, a graduate of the Sorbonne before he drifted into more cerebral pursuits behind Parisian wine bars.

The Provost returned to her seat in the Invocator's loge. I peered down at the Initiates, just as a buzzer sounded and a candidate threw up his hands in despair. A fifth cross appeared next to a name on the suspended screen.

"Mr Bourne has displeased the gods!" declared the Invocator. And so he had. The first eviction. A pair of bearded guards escorted the unfortunate Mr Bourne from the theatre, his dreams of becoming a Minstrel of Wine ground to dust under the wheels of *La Vendange*.

"Not much point in the other Provosts serving us," whispered Valentina. "That's all three of us spoken for, isn't it?"

I made a noncommittal noise. The whole Institute knew I wanted to join House Hedonist, I'd been blabbing about it for months. But only I was aware of my recent, unwelcome change of plan.

"The Terroirists propose a toast to their founder," said the guard. *Here we go*, I thought, *my first encounter with the head of my future House*.

"Room for a little more wine, *Secondes*?" drawled a woman's voice. River Jordaan, the provost of House Terroirist, did not fit the traditional image of a wine trade stalwart. With olive skin and dreadlocks, her black hair threaded with silver, she looked like a cross between the Wild Woman of the Hills and a liberal arts professor from Brooklyn.

Members of House Terroirist were obliged to adopt a *naturae nomine*, or 'name of nature', at some point after initiation. Your *naturae nomine* was supposed to relate to your job, express your passion, or hint at membership of a sect within the House. Some took the names of clouds, trees or soil types, others were rumoured to take the names of pests and weeds – God only knows why – while others named themselves after geographical features. Hence 'River'. I wondered whether anyone had christened themselves 'Swamp', or 'Bog'.

"Any space for an old *Juffer*, Minstrels?" The Provost took the seat to my right and held up an earthenware carafe. "On this day of Theemeter, I offer you a jar of our House Wine."

The guard passed more glasses, which she filled with a cloudy orange liquid.

"To Botwulf of Thanet!" We touched glasses. Given House Terroirist's embrace of all things biodynamic, I took a very small sip, expecting a blend of Sunny Delight and the drippings from a hedgehog's bile duct. But the wine was crisp and vibrant, a touch strange but definitely palatable.

Ms. Jordaan leant in, her face just inches from mine.

"I see you, Minstrel Hart," she said, her grey eyes fixed on mine. I held my breath for a second. I've always been wary of dreadlocks; they're not the easiest hairstyle to keep clean. But she smelt fresh, if slightly earthy, like rain on dry soil.

"Well, I'm right here," I replied, wondering what the hell she meant. Was she very short-sighted? She couldn't possibly know I intended to join House Terroirist, could she? Her skin was smooth and her proximity kindled a little rush of warmth to my belly.

"I see you for what you are, Minstrel Hart," she said, "and I will see you again, later. Farewell for now." She placed her hand on my thigh, which gave me another little rush, and pushed herself to her feet.

"What was that about?" asked Valentina, when the Provost had disappeared safely back into the Invocator's loge.

"Felix is joining House Terroirist, perhaps?" said Hugo.

"Yes. Perhaps," I replied. Hugo and Valentina looked at one another. I had no idea how to explain myself. No-one who knew me would ever believe my passion lay with environmentalism and the cycles of nature. I was a man of velvet and silk, comfort and joy, not organic sackcloth and bloody ashes.

I turned my gaze back to the Initiates' progress. Most were now halfway through the tasting. Four had dropped out and all had incurred penalty points. I looked for Lily. There she was, one of the furthest ahead, through the whites and rosés and well into the reds. The board displayed two crosses against her name. *Keep it up*, I thought, *don't lose your rhythm*. She seemed in good shape; a tap of the glass on the table, a mouthful of wine, a pause, then a whisper to the examiner. A nod. Next wine. A tap, sip, swallow, whisper… suddenly, her examiner's hand shot up and a buzzer sounded. I winced. Third mistake.

"Is she your favourite then, Felix?" asked Valentina.

"You know you're my favourite," I replied, finishing the orange wine.

"Was…" she said, nudging Hugo, who smirked.

We are custodians, not owners of nature, I mused. Who was I to pledge loyalty to just one, when I belonged to all…? I gave my head a shake. Strange thoughts. Was I becoming a philosopher? I hoped not. Speaking French was one thing, to start thinking like a Frenchman quite another. The buzzer sounded again.

"Madame Fillon has sinned against the gods," called the Invocator.

Another one out. More Initiates succumbing to the pressure.

"The Mercantilists propose a toast to their founder," said the guard. The final House of the four.

"Madame. Sirs. An offering from the youngest of the Houses." Nathanial Jägermeister, the provost of House Mercantilist, stood before us, his immaculate gown linked at the neck by a gold chain. He flourished a crystal claret jug. "On this day of Theemeter, I offer you a jar of our House Wine."

The contents of his decanter were, I suspected, the most expensive house wine on the planet. Once we had respectfully raised the toast, "To *Johan sanz Terre!*", my suspicions were confirmed. A mature, Left Bank Bordeaux of immaculate pedigree. Provost Jägermeister said a few words, puffing up the magnificence of House Mercantilist, but I paid little attention, losing myself for a while in the glorious wine.

A series of buzzes brought me to my senses. Provost Jägermeister had disappeared and the countdown clock showed we were down to the tasting's final minutes. The Invocator solemnly declaimed the latest victims of *La Vendange* and, with a shock, I saw there were just six Initiates left. Had Lily been evicted during my reverie...? No, there she was, attacking her final few wines. But she was clearly the worse for wear. With one hand she still tapped each glass against the table and brought it to her lips, but her other arm was now wrapped around the shoulders of her examiner. It was difficult to read his exact expression from my perch a dozen rows back, but it appeared to flip between incredulity and excitement, as Lily whispered each answer into his ear. *Clever technique*, I thought to myself. I recalled my own *Vendange* experience two years ago. I'm no lightweight but, by the time I'd reached the final wines, I could barely stand and, as every Initiate knows, spilling just a drop would result in immediate disqualification.

But there was nothing in the rules of *La Vendange* forbidding the molestation of one's examiner or using them as structural support, so long as you didn't attempt to solicit advice. Lily's examiner looked like a sturdy enough chap, I guessed he could take the extra weight. And if he was half the man I was, he'd probably sprouted a staff of his own, every bit as sturdy as those wielded by the bearded guards, as Lily whispered sweet grapes into his ear. The lucky sod. I felt a strong, unfamiliar sensation, like a malicious knuckle screwing into my stomach. I realised, to my astonishment, that it was jealousy.

"Is there any more wine?" I asked the guard.

"Minstrel Hart, you have a reputation as a man of appetite. Pray wait until *Le Récital* and we will quench your thirst."

Another buzz and a fifth cross appeared next to the latest victim. A young woman in a tight gold dress shouted an expletive and hurled her glass to the floor, where it shattered, making her examiner and the nearby Initiates jump. A pair of guards approached, pine cone-topped staffs pointing forward, but the woman turned and, with a toss of her long blonde hair, stalked out of the theatre.

"Ms. Hailsham has sinned against the gods!"

Just five Initiates left. One of them was on his final wine. He tasted and whispered to his examiner. The man nodded solemnly and the room burst into applause. First one home. The Initiate staggered forward, fists raised in triumph, and sank to his knees, wisely keeping his face turned upwards, to suppress the urge to vomit. A chunder during *La Vendange* would be considered a sin against the gods, of course, as serious as the spilling of wine from one's glass, and punished by immediate disqualification.

Lily was nearing the finish line too. She gave her penultimate wine a tap and brought it slowly to her mouth, her other arm locked tightly round her examiner's neck. I could see her shoulders moving up and down as she took long, deep breaths. Then she whispered to the examiner, but his hand shot up – wrong answer! A buzz and a fourth cross against her name. Worse still, the examiner's arm movement had caught her by surprise, knocking her hand from the man's shoulder and causing her to stagger. She toppled backwards, still holding the glass of wine before her, and a huge 'oooh!' rose from the audience.

Lily landed awkwardly on her backside, letting out a scream of pain, but she'd managed to throw her free arm behind her, stopping her from rolling onto her back. She thrust her other arm upwards, still holding the wine, keeping the precious glass as upright as possible, and there it remained, pointing to the roof, the red wine swirling violently but, so far as I could see, unspilled.

The examiner peered down at Lily, checking for splashes of wine on her clothes or the floor. Then he took a step back, face neutral. The audience leapt to their feet and applauded wildly. She was still in the game! Lily carefully placed the glass on the table then climbed to her feet, wincing as she rubbed her lower back. Her examiner made no attempt to help her. She placed both hands on the table and grimaced, recovering her breath. One wine to go. No spare lives. The clock ticked down to the final minute.

Lily lifted the final glass. She was still breathing heavily. With one palm on the table, she banged the glass down hard and brought it straight up to her face, almost hurling the contents into her mouth. She turned to the examiner, grasped his shirt collar with her free hand and pulled his head to hers, panting her answer into his ear. He took a step back, a somewhat shocked expression on his face, straightened his collar, and gave a little nod. The audience burst into applause once more. Lily was home.

Less than thirty seconds on the clock. Two more Initiates scraped in, each down to their final life. But their fifth colleague was too far back and the clock reached zero with half a dozen wines to go. A gong sounded and two guards flanked the unfortunate Initiate, who replaced her glass with a sigh, giving a little round of applause to the four finishers. The audience, still on their feet, gave a rousing ovation in return and, as the unsuccessful Initiate was escorted from the room, Lily and her three successful colleagues embraced one another.

"Monsieur Dubois. Miss Tremaine. Gospodin Sokolov. Frau Arslan. You have pleased the gods!" called the Invocator, banging his staff on the floor, and the audience cheered and whistled.

I sank back into my seat.

"Stone the crows, that was nearly as stressful as doing it for real," I muttered. "Guard! I'll have that drink now please!"

"You'll be serving yourself, Minstrel Hart," he replied. "The Invocator requests your presence in the loge. All *Secondes*, follow me please."

The Invocator himself! Like humble gladiators summoned before Caesar, we stood and followed the guard. I saw the Invocator was back on his feet too.

"And now, *Le Récital*!"

Chapter Eleven

Concerto

At the entrance to the loge stood a staff-wielding guard. As we approached, the man moved aside.

"You may enter the Invocator's loge, *Secondes*."

I stepped through the gap in the vine-wood palisade, praying there was a well-stocked bar inside and that I wouldn't have to make too much small-talk with the Provosts. Valentina and Hugo followed. We climbed half a dozen wooden steps and suddenly there we were in the Invocator's loge, the best view in the house, standing like three prize plums in front of the grand panjandrums of the Minstrels of Wine.

The Invocator sat in the centre upon a throne, crimson-robed, his wizened face smirking like an old ham receiving a lifetime achievement award for outstanding work in youth theatre. The four House Provosts sat to his left, hoods up, their cloaks a plummier shade of purple, while another half-dozen nobs, their dress festooned with gold and silver trim, sat to his right. The two rows behind were occupied by a shower of less senior officers, mere rear-admirals and brigadiers, wedged closer together than their front row chums, all wearing subtly different shades of purple. The effect was disconcerting, like unearthing a box of unfashionable Christmas decorations in the attic of an eccentric and sadly deceased relative.

Well, I thought, *what a wardrobe of delights we have here*.

"Welcome *Secondes*!" said the Invocator, voice low and trembling. "The edict of Melampos is clear. You are to choose your House." He stretched out both arms, as though expecting a hug. Just in time to avoid making an embarrassing faux pas, I realised he was, in fact, gesturing towards a table at the front of the loge. Upon it lay four drinking vessels: a silver dish shaped like a scallop shell, a tall goblet of smoked glass, a simple earthenware cup and a golden chalice, studded with gems. A cup for each House. Helpfully, the crest of each House was displayed behind the relevant ornament, in case any idle second-year Minstrels had failed to learn each House's traditional drinking vessel. *Thank God for that*, I thought.

"Minstrel Soto. Join your House."

Valentina stepped forward and grasped the silver scallop shell with both hands, raised it to her lips and gave a dirty great slurp.

"Wonderful!" exclaimed Lord Slipcote from beneath his hood, a curl of escaping white hair nodding in agreement. "House Hedonist is forever fortified by your presence!"

"Now, Minstrel Blanchett," called the Invocator. "Join *your* House."

Hugo turned and lifted the dark glass goblet, keeping one hand under the base as he took a long, careful draught. *Yes, don't drop it Hugo*, I thought. *It's probably Emperor Hadrian's original bollock-washing beaker.*

"House Archivist is forever fortified by your presence," said Provost Rougegorgefils, bowing slightly from her grand seat.

"And Minstrel Hart. *Your* House?"

I turned to the table and gazed out over the thousand-strong audience, all merrily chatting away beneath us, oblivious to our private little ceremony. The silver scallop shell lay before me, its fanned ribs glittering beneath the wine. There was plenty left, the golden liquid still rippling back and forth after Valentina had disturbed it. I was nearly overcome by the urge to grab it and neck the lot. Why the hell not? Then I'd be a fully paid-up member of House Hedonist and there wasn't a thing Paris-Blois or anyone else could do about it. Other than have me dismembered and hurled from Tower Bridge, of course. There was always that. My eyes moved past House Archivist's smoked glass goblet to House Terroirist's aren't-we-ever-so-humble piece of earthenware. It looked like an egg cup knocked up by an eight-year-old in remedial pottery class, pathetic next to the crown jewel bling of House Mercantilist's chalice.

My options were limited, to say the least. *Oh well, here's to earnest lectures on indigenous Slovenian grape varieties*, I thought. I grasped the earthenware cup. It was heavier than I expected, as though made of granite. The wine was the same as the one Provost Jordaan had poured us earlier, sharp and spritzy, the orange House Wine of the Terroirists. I drained the lot. May as well get my money's worth.

"House Terroirist is forever fortified by your presence," murmured Provost Jordaan, just loudly enough to be heard over the audience.

"One worthy addition each to House Hedonist, House Archivist and House Terroirist," declared the Invocator, rising to his feet. "You are no longer *Secondes* but true members of the Extant Houses. Let the Italian Hand record it thus!"

A bespectacled, red-robed officer to his right leaned over a ledger and scrawled a note.

"And now Minstrels, forgive me, for the Odeion cannot wait." He banged his staff on the ground and began to speak, his voice booming from the speakers surrounding the theatre.

"*And so, via Kadmos of Tyre and Melampos we learn. Oh this Odeion! Hurry, lest Apollo rise too soon...*"

"Please-a, take a seat Minstrels," whispered the Italian Hand, fresh from recording our ascendance. He nodded to three empty chairs tucked at the side of the loge. To my delight, a silver Champagne bucket, containing a bottle of something celebratory, lay on a stand next to each seat.

"A gift from your new Houses on the twelfth of Dionysus, Minstrels," explained the Italian Hand. "Please, Minstrel Hart, you must sit there. And Minstrel Soto, there please." We each took our seats, which were comfortable, though rather less showy than the thrones supporting the Invocator, Provosts and their front row friends.

Valentina pulled her bottle from the iced water. Dom Ruinart Champagne, Blanc de Blancs.

"Wow! My House knows how to celebrate!" she beamed, popping the cork and filling the slim crystal glass proffered by the Italian Hand.

Hugo lifted his bottle, a smart-looking Franciacorta, and poured his own measure of dancing fizz. I grasped mine and pulled it free of the ice. There was no label, just a brown luggage ticket tied around the neck, stating *Grasparossa #430*. The top was secured by a distressed looking cork held in place by a metal staple and a length of dirty twine. *Oh Jesus*, I sighed to myself, *is this to be my lot as a member of House Terroirist? Everyone else parties like it's Dom Perignon's twenty-first birthday while I'm forced to wade through a half-gallon of lentil-infused puddle water?*

I glanced at the head of my new House. Provost Jordaan was observing me, her face neutral. I hoped I hadn't looked too ungrateful, it would have shown poor judgement to offend the House headmistress on day one. I smiled and nodded in thanks, but she didn't respond, just continued to watch me. I unwound the twine and pushed the staple aside, the cork pushing itself into my hand with a hiss, followed by a riot of crimson foam. The Italian Hand passed me a glass and I filled it, a deep red topped by an inch of furious pink bubbles.

"To our third year as Minstrels. Real Minstrels now!" declared Valentina.

I took a deep mouthful and the wine exploded down my throat. Good God, I'd never tasted anything like it; it felt as though a cherry-scented grenade had detonated on my tongue. I spluttered, pink bubbles fizzing from my nose, at which Hugo and Valentina roared with laughter.

"Enjoying your wine, Felix?" she asked, once she'd caught her breath.

I wasn't sure. The fruit was strange, soft and fleshy but with unripe notes too. I held my nose and the bubbles subsided. I realised the orchestra was playing. The sound of a clarinet, sharp and attacking, climbed over the wash of violins. *Le Récital* was under way! I looked to the front of the hall. A man stood on a raised platform in front of the orchestra. I recognised him as the first of the tasters to finish. Dubois, I think his name was. I followed the music with a few artistic elbow movements of my own and was soon a third of a bottle down. The wine started to grow on me, damn peculiar though it was.

And then, with a twiddle and a flourish, Dubois polished off his Mozart. I saluted him by finishing my third glass of the Terroirists' red fizz.

"Minstrel Michel Dubois has pleased the gods!" boomed the Invocator.

It was a standing ovation for Dubois. He'd completed *Le Récital* and was now a fully fledged Minstrel. *Good for him*, I thought. Welcome to the club. Don't drink the water.

"Hope you're not flagging, Feel; we've a long night ahead of us," called Valentina over the applause. I smiled and waved her away. "Look," she pointed, "your friend's up next."

The applause quietened and Lily stepped on to the platform. I felt my chest thump. Her hair was now loose and she had discarded her jacket and bow tie. She brought a small, bulbous vessel to her lips and, accompanied only by a harpsichord, began to play. The music sounded strange and ancient, the metallic plucking of the old keyboard blending with the trill of Lily's own instrument, coarse and bewitching.

"What the hell is she playing?" whispered Hugo. I glanced up at the scoreboard, which now displayed the recital piece of each Initiate.

"Michel Blavet, *Flute Sonata in D minor*, apparently," I replied. Could have been Good King Wenceslas as far as I was concerned. I wasn't really an aficionado of classical music, preferring a stage-dive at the Mean Fiddler over buttock cramp at the Wigmore Hall.

"I can read!" whispered back Hugo. "I mean, on what *instrument* is she playing the flute sonata?"

I saw what he meant. I may have been a philistine but I knew flutes were long, silver and stuck out at the side. This looked like a small, deformed rugby ball with a spout. It was dotted randomly with holes, over which Lily's fingers danced, and she tilted the spout back and forth in her mouth as she played.

"No idea. Is it the dwarf bagpipes?"

"It's a vessel flute, boys. An ocarina," said Valentina. As the only genuine professional musician among us, I took her word for it.

"Is that allowed?" said Hugo.

"I'm not sure," she replied.

I poured another glass of red fizz and watched Lily. She'd never mentioned she played obscure wind instruments, though in truth the subject had never really come up. Her poise was impressive, her slim body tall but relaxed, the seams of her white shirt following the shape of her body from shoulder to waist. You'd never guess she'd just tasted 150 wines. I focussed on the sound. Though coarse, it was far more compelling than a clarinet or flute; it reminded me of nature, of woodland after dark, of ancient, silent vines in winter. I felt a wave of déjà vu wash over me, almost suffocating in its intensity.

The Little Chalfont vine was before me, the wood hard and unyielding, its branches creeping slowly from the trunk, occupying the garden, waiting for spring, then summer, when it would offer its bounty. Red grapes, nearly black, swollen with juice, demanded passage to the winery. To what end? Something dark, with a strong grip; its roots curling around my throat...

I was underwater. I broke the surface and gasped. My glass was empty; I didn't recall finishing, but I refilled, the bottle finding my hand, my eyes fixed on Lily and the trilling of the ocarina as her fingers flickered over the holes. Can a wine taste of soil and air? This did. As a vine's roots search downwards, embracing then drawing life from the earth, her offspring are released, potent and heady.

The wine tasted of blood and rust. The bottle was empty. I could hear the music of the pouring wine slow and stop, replaced by the notes of the harpsichord. There was another sound, a rumble from behind me, voices. I wanted to tell them to quieten down, but I couldn't move my eyes from Lily. She removed the ocarina from her mouth and bowed, holding the instrument out before her. It looked like a heart, sitting in her palm like that, rounded at one end and pointed at the other, the windway and holes like severed veins. The crowd was applauding, louder and louder. I felt something tugging at me.

"Felix, are you all right?" I looked at my arm. Hugo was pulling my sleeve. It dawned on me where I was. Like a great vine uprooting itself, I pushed myself to my feet, joining the crowd in a standing ovation.

I say standing ovation but only half the hall were on their feet. Not only were many still seated, but I even heard the odd boo among the applause. I scanned the crowd to spot the offenders.

"Can you hear those sods booing? That's not on," shouted Valentina over her applause.

"I think she may have broken the rules with that dodgy flute," replied Hugo.

I looked back at the Invocator and his chums. There was a serious discussion under way, much waving of gown-shrouded arms and shuddering of gold-trimmed hoods. It was clear Lily's eccentric interpretation had divided the jury.

"Then we vote!" declared the Invocator. "Italian Hand, please keep tally." The bespectacled man nodded and opened his ledger.

"Provosts first. House Hedonist?"

"I thought it was jolly tuneful and great fun, very much in the tradition of Aristippus," replied Lord Slipcote. "I vote aye." *Good old Hedonists*, I thought.

"House Archivist?"

Provost Rougegorgefils pressed her hands together. "The device and delivery were eccentric, but I am aware of no precept forbidding this. The piece was from the classical cannon, within the specified parameters of duration and, I judge, performed to a sufficient standard of quality. Therefore, I vote aye."

"House Terroirist?"

"A welcome deviation from sclerotic orthodoxy," said Provost Jordaan. "Aye from me." This was going well, three in a row.

"House Mercantilist?"

Nathanial Jägermeister, Provost of House Mercantilist, pursed his lips. "Sorry, a no from me. That instrument is not from the classical tradition. For goodness sake, there are standards to be maintained. If we allow this, they'll be playing sleigh bells and tambourines next year." He shot a filthy glance in my direction. I wondered if he'd voted against my own percussive performance two years ago. Or was he just sore that none of us wished to join his House of gimlet-eyed mercenaries?

"Heads of Chapter. Your votes please. Lisbon?"

"No. This was not correct." Oh dear, I thought, more than one of us has their pants in a twist.

"Venice?"

"No. Against our traditions." *Bollocks to your traditions*, I thought, angrily.

"Constantinople?"

"This was not appropriate for *Le Récital*. A no from me."

Good God, what a bunch of snivelling creeps. What the hell was wrong with these people? That put us four to three against.

"Rome?"

"It must be no, I am sorry."

You stuck up berk, I thought. *No wonder you couldn't keep the barbarians out*.

"Athens?"

The Head of the Athenian Chapter raised his hands and looked to the sky, as though attempting to conjure rain. "I do not understand my fellow Heads of Chapter. What we have seen is the very essence of *La Vendange*, of the Institute itself. An aye from me."

"Well said!" called Provost Jordaan, her dreadlocks bobbing as she nodded. Provost Jägermeister harrumphed and the Heads of Chapter studied their hands.

The Invocator continued to call the names of cities, all of which presumably housed a Chapter, a foreign outpost of the Minstrels of Wine. I knew some Chapters had been around for centuries, millennia even, others less than a hundred years. I tried to keep count of the ayes and noes on my fingers as the Italian Hand marked his ledger.

"Toledo?"

"The young lady shows artistry and passion. An aye from me!" said a heavily accented Spaniard. *Excellent*, I thought. *If I'm counting correctly, we're even again.*

"New York?"

"That instrument reminds me of the fife," whined a pale-looking man from inside his hood, "and I cannot abide marching bands! A firm no from me." Oh dear. Kicked out of West Point for wetting the bed, were you?

"Amsterdam?"

"No." Bastard!

"Stellenbosch?"

"Aye." Hurrah!

"Mendoza?"

"Aye." God bless Argentina!

"What's the score?" whispered Valentina.

"I'm pretty sure we're even again."

The Chapters of Bordeaux and Reims said no but Montpellier and Dijon said yes. A shake of the head from Jerez but a thumbs up from Trier. Napa, Beirut and Tbilisi in favour. Santiago, Mumbai and Adelaide against.

"The Hidden Houses? How do you vote?"

"Aye!" came the cry from an alarming-looking creature on the back row of the loge, his face obscured by a carnival mask. God knows who or what he was hiding from but he'd voted the right way so I wished him all the best.

The Invocator conferred with the Italian Hand.

"Minstrels. The votes are tied. The casting vote is mine." The Invocator rose and approached the three of us. "As our newest-minted House members, what do you have to say?"

"Invocator, I must respectfully point out that ordinary Minstrels do not enjoy voting rights in *La Vendange*!" called Provost Jägermeister.

"Provost, I am well aware of that. I am asking for an opinion, not a vote."

Provost Jägermeister glowered under his hood and the back rows of the loge craned their necks, anxious to hear our half-baked pearls of wisdom. The audience had quietened too, aware that a great cogitation was taking place above them.

"I thought the performance was exquisite," declared Valentina. "The ocarina is difficult to play well and she showed great musicianship."

The Invocator looked at Hugo.

"I'm… not sure," he muttered, "I don't think it had the finesse of a proper instrument."

"Oh, for God's sake, Hugo," muttered Valentina.

"And Minstrel Hart? Who appears to have drunk his entire bottle of Provost Jordaan's wine before we're even halfway through *Le Récital*!"

A wave of tittering emerged from the senior Minstrels and I glanced down at the empty bottle between my feet. I paused, unsure whether I was supposed to justify my rapid drinking or conjure up a suitably approving comment about Lily's performance.

"The wine was good," I said.

The Invocator turned to his colleagues.

"Our Minstrel with the greatest appetite has declared the wine to be good!"

I thought he was making fun of me but no-one laughed this time. Moving his hand to the microphone hidden in the folds of his cloak, the Invocator stepped to the front of the loge and addressed the massed audience.

"Minstrel Lily Tremaine has pleased the gods!"

Chapter Twelve

Initiation

There is little point, unless you are a wine-soaked orchestral fanatic, in dwelling on the final two participants in *Le Récital*. Suffice to say, both Minstrels scraped through, the Turkish Initiate performing an unsettling interpretation of Tárrega's *Capricho Arabe*, accompanying her guitar with a peculiar, though largely tuneful, wailing, and the Russian Initiate executing an aggressive performance of a Thalberg piano concerto, culminating in a punch to the principal violin's chin for poor timekeeping.

I, of course, was far more interested in what was to happen to me. And as the final Initiate received the Minstrels' purple robe over his shoulders, Provost Jordaan rose from her seat, approached my chair and placed her hand on my arm.

"Come, Minstrel Hart. It is time for dinner."

I was delighted to hear it. I needed something substantial to soak up the evening's booze, particularly House Terroirist's bizarre red sparkler. With a farewell wave to Hugo and Valentina, each now in conversation with their own Provosts, I followed Jordaan out of the loge, and together we exited the Great Hall.

The House dinners following *La Vendange* were reputed to be the greatest feasts in the Minstrel calendar. I hadn't experienced one until that point, of course. Initiates who had just passed *La Vendange* were escorted from the hall by a guard of honour, returning home to recover from their ordeal. And immature first-year Minstrels, as Hugo, Valentina and I had been last year, were also expected to leave straight after *Le Récital*. But now, we too were House members, even if my chosen home wasn't exactly my first choice.

The lift deposited us on the tenth floor of the East Wing, an area out of bounds to all but members of House Terroirist. Only around a third of the colossal Minstrels Hall was open to all members – a handful of restaurants and bars, a few conference rooms and guest bedrooms, plus the Great Hall itself, of course. The rest was divided into the realms of the Houses.

The Archivists controlled most of the basement floors, which housed their archives, museums and cellars. The Mercantilists owned most of the North Wing, where they could plot and network to their hearts' content. The Hedonists had possession of much of the South Wing. Their realm housed several bars and restaurants, and their wing's fifth floor, home to a series of bathing chambers and saunas, was a strictly no-clothes area. I could have wept with jealousy.

House Terroirist occupied the uppermost stories of Minstrels Hall, including most of the roof. This was no accident. The Terroirists' philosophy was to be at one with nature and their floors, high above the offices and theatres of London's West End, were lined by terraced balconies, planted with vines and other shrubs, positioned to make the best of England's unreliable sun. Many of their feasts and rituals also took place in the open air. Given that it was early January and bollock-shrinkingly cold, I prayed that tonight's dinner would be an indoor affair.

"It will take an hour or so for the members of the House to assemble. While they do so, let me show you around the Terroirists' realm. We'll start with the Top Garden." Provost Jordaan took my hand, which seemed slightly over-familiar, but after a bottle of her crazy red sparkler I didn't mind at all. She led me to a wide spiral staircase of wrought iron that corkscrewed its way up through the roof. As we climbed, I became aware of Jordaan's perfume; a subtle, herbal smell, like the Mediterranean countryside, with hints of thyme and rosemary.

"The other Houses prefer to close themselves off from the elements, for reasons of privacy, comfort or to protect their archives. We, however, do not."

We emerged onto the roof of Minstrels Hall. I had heard plenty of tales of the Top Garden and its strange ceremonies, though you never really know when you're being told porkies at the Institute, especially after everyone's sunk a few glasses.

A tree, the size of a two-storey house, sat in the centre of the garden, its branches bare against the sky. Glass lanterns hung from the lower boughs, casting their soft orange light on the trunk. The tree was surrounded, at a respectful distance, by a ring of iron pillars supporting a roof of vine-entwined metal trellising. In summer, it must have created a sheltered canopy running the circumference of the garden. In mid-winter, it stood stark and naked, the vine branches frozen around the pillars and struts.

"This is where we eat tonight."

It was bloody freezing. I pulled my cloak around me. Provost Jordaan didn't appear to feel the cold, however, her bare arms smooth and un-goosebumped in the frigid air. That's what a dozen winters pruning vines in the Dolomites does for you, I suppose.

"What do you do when it rains?"

"The same as we do when it doesn't."

Well, I was bloody glad it wasn't raining then. I made a mental note to invest in a waterproof fleece ahead of the next dinner. Jordaan passed through an arch in the trellis and approached the tree, stroking the trunk.

"I trust you'll be attending our next function, the day after tomorrow? The Ritual of Oak and Mistletoe," she said, as if that explained everything.

"I'm pretty sure I'm free," I replied, shivering, making a further mental note to purchase waterproof trousers and fur underpants.

"Good. Let's take a look at one of the balconies, the views from there are excellent." Jordaan opened a heavy gate. We descended a tight stone stairway that opened onto a deep balcony, planted with lavender bushes and dotted with slatted wooden boxes.

"We keep hives on the larger balconies. House Terroirist produces all the honey the Institute needs. A nice tradition,

I think. The bees are clustering right now, keeping their queen warm."

I didn't blame them. I'd prefer to have been clustering myself, rather than freezing under an inadequate purple cloak on a tenth-floor open-air balcony. The view, however, was superb, the dome of St Paul's resplendent among the City of London's towers. Further east, the dark ribbon of the Thames snaked its way through the light-studded Docklands to the black of Rainham Marshes beyond.

"This is a wonderful place to see sunrise," said Jordaan. "But come springtime, don't stand in front of the hives. It does inconvenience the bees."

"That's the last thing I'd want to do."

"Good. That doorway leads to the House lodgings. We have fifty bedrooms for the use of House members. Nicely appointed and very convenient for Terroirists visiting from out of town. All full tonight, of course." Jordaan paused for a moment. "My quarters are there too. You'll see them later. As a new member, you'll be spending tonight with me."

Blimey, that's rather bold, I thought. She must have been the best part of sixty years old, though still quite attractive. I liked that smooth olive skin and those soft, silvering dreadlocks. It looked like I had an interesting evening ahead.

"I see. Well, jolly good," I replied, with what I hoped was the correct mix of seriousness and enthusiasm.

"That was a joke, Minstrel Hart," said Jordaan. "Not a very professional one, but I was fascinated to see how you would react. Do you think we're some sort of deviant sex cult?"

I blushed so fiercely I was worried the bees would think spring had arrived and start launching themselves merrily into the January darkness.

"Ah, no. I'm glad to hear you're not," I lied.

"Our Minstrel with the greatest appetite, our Invocator called you. He was right there. I trust you'll address that appetite at our dinner tonight."

A clattering of wooden boards from the Top Garden saved me further embarrassment.

"Ah, about time! They're laying the table and I need to supervise. Come on." Jordaan took my hand and led me back up the stairs.

A dozen or so workers were unloading broad wooden planks from wheelbarrows. Each length of timber, heavy enough to need two men to lift, was slotted into place between the trellis's pillars. Jordaan watched the assembly, occasionally directing a pair of workers, until a ring of planks, like a huge circular bench, surrounded the central tree.

Looks a bit uncomfortable, I thought. *I bet House Mercantilist aren't sitting on a park bench in the January cold.* They'll be braying and clinking gold goblets together in front of a dozen roast suckling pigs. And House Archivist will be snug as a bug too, no doubt, deep in their basement lair, sipping ancient vintages as they swap hilarious Latin anecdotes in front of Byzantine treasures. And as for House Hedonist... I imagined Valentina, already stark naked in the Roman baths, drinking Vin Santo from the spout of an obscenely well-endowed ice sculpture.

"You look disappointed, Minstrel Hart," said Jordaan.

"No, not at all. Well, I might have brought my own cushion if I'd known," I said, peering at the rough wooden planking.

"That's the table. Don't worry, cushions are provided. And if rain had been forecast, we'd have deployed canvas covers over the trellis. We're Terroirists, not Spartans."

Sure enough, a workman was making his way around the ring of benches, pushing a wheelbarrow piled with rolls of matting, and placing a thick sausage of fabric every yard or so. Another worker threw sheets of linen over the wooden planks, taking care to avoid trailing the clean cloth on the ground, while another placed paraffin lamps every few yards around the inside of the ring. It was all starting to look quite romantic, with the glowing lanterns hanging from the tree, the vines twisting around the metal latticework and the starry sky above, like a scene from an upmarket wedding brochure.

"Come and see the kitchens," said Jordaan, taking my arm once more.

Steering me through a gap in the trellis, we approached another wall, ivy-covered and dominated by a pair of tall stable doors. Jordaan lifted the catch and, as the door swung open, a warm, delicious aroma washed over us.

"The Mercantilists have their wealth and their fine wine cellars. The Archivists have their museums and their treasures. The Hedonists have their baths and saunas." *And their orgies*, I thought, *don't forget the bloody orgies*. Jordaan pulled the door shut behind us and we descended a broad, shallow slope, the sound of metal implements clashing and shouts of "Chef!" and "Prep!" becoming louder.

"But House Terroirist have the kitchens."

We turned the corner and the passage widened into a scene from a glutton's wet dream. No fewer than a hundred staff, their whites streaked with grease and sauce, bustled around the largest kitchen I'd ever seen. One side was an inferno of flaming gas, dozens of yards long, battled by a platoon of sweating chefs, some jostling angry, spitting woks, others manhandling great bubbling cauldrons of stock. The other side housed a battery of work stations, sous chefs chopping, dicing, thrashing and whipping whatever unfortunate root or flesh found itself before them. Oven doors swung shut with a bang, tongs and spoons clattered into sinks, and above it all, at the tops of their voices, the chefs themselves exchanged orders and curses richer than a regiment of medieval infantry.

Jordaan didn't raise her voice, she just pulled my arm and brought her lips to my ear. I could smell the spiced oil of her perfume again.

"Our kitchens cater for all the restaurants and bars in Minstrels Hall. We keep the best for ourselves, of course."

She guided me through the maelstrom, the chefs holding their pans and plates aside, nodding respectfully as she passed.

We exited the kitchen through a pair of swing doors, into another large room stacked with crates of fruit and vegetables. Staff moved between the piles, some unloading great trays of onions from barrows, others dragging sacks of produce along the flagstones. A sliding door opened as we passed, a blast of cold air making me turn in time to see huge sides of hanging meat, waiting for their turn on the butcher's block. A woman in checked trousers slammed the doors of a goods lift, large enough to carry a mounted horse in comfort. She punched a button and the machine hummed, sending its load deep into the bowels of Minstrels Hall.

"Through here."

After two further sets of swing doors, we entered a cool, quiet room, alone again. Legs of cured ham hung from lengths of rope, scribbled chalkboards describing their origin: Salamanca *jamón ibérico*, Bayonne, *Schwarzwälder*. Through a long window, great rounds of cheese matured on wooden shelves.

"A little more peaceful here." Several hams sat on a counter top, each secured in a vice. Jordaan walked over to one and carved a thin slice.

"What do you know of the philosophy of House Terroirist, Minstrel Hart? Our purpose?" She offered the slice of meat, which I nearly snatched from her hand in delight. I hadn't eaten for hours. "*Jamón de Guijuelo*. Nice, isn't it?"

"Yes, thank you," I mumbled, through the fabulous, salty, melting mouthful. It was useful to have a few seconds to think about the Provost's question. I've always been suspicious of questions of philosophy. Mention a cave, a dream and a golden mean and, with a little practice, you can prove that black is white and if only my auntie had bollocks she'd be my uncle.

"You're supposed to keep the Minstrels honest, I think."

"That's not a bad answer. Wrong, but not bad." Jordaan popped a slice of ham into her mouth.

"Are you going to tell me?"

"No. You'll have to work it out for yourself. Let me show you the cellar."

We passed through yet more doors and down a flight of stairs. We were in a long, curved corridor, dark, cool and moist. As my eyes adjusted, I realised the entire wall of the corridor was a wine rack, from floor to ceiling, the top rows several feet higher than I could reach.

"This is House Terroirist's private cellar. We also share a cellar with House Hedonist. And do you know the purpose of House Hedonist, Minstrel Hart?"

"I thought it was to have fun."

"No. Completely wrong." Jordaan ducked under a tall pair of stepladders. In the dim light, I could see the ladder had wheels, resting on rails that ran the length of the corridor. "You do know their purpose. You've just confused the Hedonists with us."

"The Hedonists' purpose is to keep the Minstrels honest?"

"Yes. House Hedonist practices the precepts for a happy and virtuous life." Jordaan walked on, the dim bulbs making her silver hair glitter like frost.

"By being naked and cavorting in Jacuzzis?"

Jordaan snorted. "I think you'll find there's a lot less cavorting in House Hedonist than everyone claims."

My spirits rose a little. Maybe I wasn't missing out too much after all. Jordaan ducked under another set of stepladders and the corridor widened.

"Here's the barrel room. A place for our winemakers to experiment."

Sure enough, several dozen barrels lined the wall. Next to them, rather more bizarrely, stood a series of upright stone eggs, around six feet tall, supported on metal tripods.

"What are those for? Hatching baby dinosaurs?"

"A little experiment by some of our French members. The theory is that the wine ages more uniformly than in a conventional tank. We use them for our special wines. The results are very promising." A row of wine glasses dangled from pegs embedded in the wall and Jordaan slid one free. She held it under a tap protruding from one of the egg-shaped vessels and turned a valve. A liquid hissed into the glass, milky with sediment.

"It's unfiltered but ready. Try it."

I took a sip, half-expecting the flavour of banana milkshake. But it was sharp, a little fruity, just like wine, in fact. I took a larger sip. A hint of coffee, a leafy pepperiness. Now, a more confident mouthful. A thick breadiness with savoury notes, like fresh tomato, changing to salty, hard cheese on the finish. Very strange. I noticed Jordaan didn't try any. Was she trying to make me drunk? Ridiculous, I'd been drunk for hours. I finished the wine. It was very moreish. It lay on my palate like a hungry paint, begging to be washed away with more of the same. I stepped forward to the egg and held the glass under the nozzle, gently turning the valve. The wine sang into the glass. I'd finished the wine before it occurred to me I should have asked permission. My hand moved to the valve once more but Jordaan's moved faster and grasped my fingers.

"That's enough for three men, even with your appetite. There's plenty more to drink upstairs."

We wound between several large clay amphorae, stoppered with wax bungs. Another little experiment, perhaps? I half-expected a toga-wearing Greek to leap from behind one of them, demanding I try his latest Peloponnese Pinot Grigio. We passed a line of small, steel tanks, like the ones old Hawkins had installed underneath the Flag and Parrot, and we were back in the corridor.

"We can take this staircase. It leads straight to the Top Garden. Mind your step."

I'm not sure I needed Provost Jordaan to hold my hand all the way up, but she did so anyway. Maybe she thought I'd dash back down the steps and fix myself another glass of that strange, moreish wine. I wanted to.

We emerged into the Top Garden, which was now alive with Minstrels. Most stood in groups, chatting merrily, as staff dispensed glasses from wooden trays. Some had already taken their seats, lolling casually on their mats, wine in hand. Candles and oil lamps hung from the trellis, bathing the garden in a warm glow.

"Provost in the Top Garden!" called a voice, and the knots of gossiping Minstrels dissolved and drifted to their places. Provost

Jordaan passed through the ring of seated Minstrels and led me to the tree. I felt like a bit of a lemon, to be honest, with a couple of hundred Minstrels sitting cross-legged in a great circle, all gawping at me. I hoped I wasn't delaying dinner. I felt warmer than I had earlier. Whether that was the paraffin lamps or the wine I'd drunk, I have no idea.

"We are gathered on the twelfth of Dionysus, the Day of Theemeter, as we have for a millennium," said Provost Jordaan. "Tonight, we welcome a new Minstrel to House Terroirist, who has come to us of his free will, in search of our purpose."

Well, that's a load of bollocks for a start, I thought, but I kept my mouth shut.

"As Botwulf of Thanet departed the shores of Cent, so our traveller departs the realm of ignorance."

Now, I'd heard of old Botwulf. I knew he was the founder of House Terroirist, and I even knew the date he departed the fair shores of Cent, better known these days, to the fish-scented citizens of Ramsgate, as Kent. He'd packed his bags in 1067, the year after the Battle of Hastings, during which he found himself on the losing side, a fact which probably hadn't endeared him to the invading Normans.

"And as Botwulf travelled through the Kingdoms of Germany, Arles, Provence and Italy, let our new member absorb, with humility, new knowledge and technique."

From my admittedly brief study of the history of the Minstrels, I knew that Botwulf and his companions, as merry as you might expect a bunch of defeated, dispossessed Saxons to be, had set out on a trek through Europe in search of a new home.

"And when a new master offers him reward, grant him the wisdom of Botwulf, to distinguish good charity from mercenary servitude."

Botwulf had found himself in a spot of bother in Turkey, as far as I can recall. I wasn't sure on the details, but I think he found himself grasping the turd-coated end of the stick after a botched war between the Byzantine emperor and the Turkish

Sultan. He had something of a talent for picking the wrong side, old Botwulf.

"House Terroirist, help him spurn the false gods of mercantilism and celebrate originality, quality and truth!"

"Originality! Quality! Truth!" declared the ring of Minstrels in unison, raising their glasses and making me jump.

I hoped dinner would be served soon. I was feeling distinctly light-headed.

"Our new member will now be subject to *La Vendange Impossible*," said Jordaan. A House member approached me and placed a clay cup, similar to the one I had supped back in the Invocator's loge, upon a small table.

"*La Vendange Impossible*," I repeated. "The impossible harvest? That sounds rather difficult."

"It is supposed to be difficult," said Jordaan. "Drink the wine, all of it, and identify it."

I did as I was told. The spritzy, almond-scented wine slipped down easily enough. But I hadn't a clue what it was; it tasted like nothing I'd drunk before.

"What is your answer?" The circle of Minstrels watched me. I could swear a couple were smirking.

"I've no idea. Sicilian Catarratto?"

"Wrong!" called Jordaan. "Please remove your jacket and shirt."

I'd removed my dinner jacket and unbuttoned both shirt cuffs before it struck me that this was a rather irregular request.

"Why do I have to remove my shirt?"

"Because you misidentified the wine. These are wines free of artifice and pretension. Your clothes are symbols of the same. Everybody else is doing so too."

To my astonishment, she was right. The men were wriggling out of their jackets and shirts and most of the women were down to their bras already.

"Next wine. Quickly please, it's mid-winter." Another cup was placed before me, by a bare-chested man. I drank the liquid down. It was vibrantly fruity, bursting with quince and kumquat, though the finish was tannic and a little bitter.

"This is bloody impossible. Georgian Mtsvane?" I turned to Provost Jordaan and was surprised to see she too had cast off her cloak and shirt, her pert breasts pointing back at me. *She looks bloody good for sixty*, I thought. *No problem at all if that invitation to her sleeping quarters is still open.* I started to feel a rush of heat to the lower portions.

"Clever guess, but wrong. Please remove your trousers."

I kicked off my shoes and hopped out of one leg, then the other, Provost Jordaan slipping a supporting arm around my waist, which gave me a renewed flush down below, and the good members of House Terroirist helped each other wriggle free of their dresses and trousers. I should probably have been a little more embarrassed, but I'm a natural exhibitionist and, with the rest of the House down to their underwear, sporting a stonking boner under my boxer shorts didn't seem quite such an issue.

"Final wine. Let this be the potion that lays deception bare!"

A woman, down to her underwear, placed a third cup before me. This wine was course and medicinal, laced with bramble fruit and nutmeg spice. I swallowed the contents, trying to recall anything similar.

"Bastardo Noir, Dão," I said, wildly.

"Wrong continent completely," declared Jordaan, and stepped out of her knickers.

It says something for my state of mind that this all seemed reasonably normal. Nor did it seem inappropriate when I felt several hands tugging at my boxers, relieving me of my final thread of modesty. As my undergarment was whisked down, my spout sprung free, waving like a branch liberated from the weight of a large bird.

"As Botwulf found his vocation, let us reclothe our new member."

I felt a warm, wet sensation on my chest. I looked down to see Provost Jordaan smearing a reddish mud over my skin. A naked Minstrel with plump breasts stood before me, holding a bowl of wet clay as a queue of her colleagues took turns to scoop a handful and apply it liberally to my chest, neck and back. Soon my torso was covered, the mud forming a warm coat against the brittle air. More hands smoothed the clay over my thighs and down to my feet, others coated my buttocks. A Minstrel placed a gentle, muddy hand over my eyes and others applied the slurry to my cheeks, nose and chin. I could feel the colder spots where the mud was yet to be applied, and one by one they were covered: the tops of my feet, behind my ears, under my chin. There must have been a dozen hands upon me at the same time, smoothing and sculpting the earth over my body.

There was one area yet to be covered, a not insubstantial area, though I say so myself. I could feel the cool air still playing around it. I hoped they hadn't miscalculated and run out of mud. It would require more than a handful, possibly three, I mused. I felt more hands on my face, one on each cheek and one still covering my eyes. The mud smelled earthy but also perfumed, familiar, like a dry vermouth. Fingers caressed my chest and behind, perhaps more than seemed necessary to do the job. Then, tentatively at first, I felt the clay being added to my final bare spot. First one hand, then another, then a third, until I was entirely covered. But the hands didn't stop. I wondered who they belonged to, but I was held quite still by my fellow Minstrels, a layer of clay and hands obscuring my eyes. All I could hear was the wet sound of the clay being rubbed over my ears, while my nose was filled by the spicy aroma of the earth.

My sense of touch felt heightened, as though sensitised by a thousand miniature masseurs. I felt a warm flush spreading from my neck, across my chest, stomach and down still further. A pleasant, very familiar sensation began to build, though in my heightened state I couldn't quite place it. It was only when the sensation burst into life, like the uncoiling of a great snake, the pounding of a huge bass drum, the opening of the sluices in some mighty dam, that I remembered myself.

The hands slid away from my eyes and ears.

"Welcome to House Terroirist, Minstrel Hart," whispered Provost Jordaan. Her perfume and the clay smelt alike.

A Minstrel took me by each hand and led me from the garden. The clay was still caked over my eyes, but I could feel the ground change underfoot, from the bare soil around the tree to the sisal matting beneath the trellis, then the cold paving flags beyond the ring of vines. I felt us move indoors, a just-perceptible brightening through my closed eyes and the screen of drying mud.

"Careful, there are steps here," said a woman's voice, one I didn't recognise.

A first, then a second stone step, then I felt my foot dip into warm water.

"It's a bath. You need to clean up before dinner," said another woman.

"He's not the only one."

Someone gave a little giggle and pressed a cloth into my hand. I soaked it in the water and wiped the earth from my eyes. I was standing thigh-deep in a large tiled bath, large enough to fit a rugby team. I had three companions, all women, standing barefooted around the bath, each holding their purple gowns closed at the neck.

"Are you going to watch?" I asked.

One of the women knelt and washed her clay-soiled hands in the water.

"I'm afraid so," she said. "You've had a lot to drink and the clay can have a soporific effect. We don't want you fainting and drowning on your first night in House Terroirist."

"Fine by me," I said, sitting in the water. I rubbed at the clay with the cloth. It washed off easily enough, leaving my skin cool and light, as though I had bathed in menthol.

"Don't forget your face," said one of the other women. "Dunk yourself underwater."

I held my breath and leant backwards, immersing myself completely, wiping at my face and ears and feeling the cake of mud dissolving. As I rubbed the cloth around my neck, I was surprised to feel a pair of hands under each arm, pulling me to the surface. Did they think I was drowning?

I wiped my eyes to find two of my companions either side of me, cloaks soaked to the waist, wearing very serious expressions. The other woman stood by the door, which I saw had a sliding lock.

"Don't worry, ladies. I haven't fainted yet."

"Shut up," said the woman on my left, bringing a large knife to my throat. That was a surprise, though I still felt strangely calm.

"Have I done something wrong?" I asked, incredibly reasonably.

"Be quiet! We'll ask the questions." She pressed the knife against my skin. It tickled slightly, like a barber beginning a wet shave.

"Fire away," I said.

"He's absorbed too much," said the other woman, peering into my eyes.

"I've had quite a few," I replied.

"Yes, I know you have," said the first woman. "Now pay attention. What is your relationship to Paris-Blois International?"

I thought of Sandra, the diamonds cascading down her chest. "Unconsummated," I said.

The woman frowned. "What do you mean?"

I tried to imagine unhooking that breastplate of glittering gems, untwisting the hundred fiddly pieces of fastening wire. "Difficult, disappointing," I said. I felt warm again, my skin blushing under the water.

"He's babbling," said the woman by the door.

"What do you *do* for Paris-Blois?" said the first woman, shaking my arm.

"I help them with problems."

"Do they pay you?"

"No. Not a bloody penny."

"So why do you work for them?"

"They threaten me. Sex."

The women looked at one another and the one with the knife shook her head. I saw her robe had fallen open slightly, exposing part of a perfect, round breast. My body flushed warmer.

"They threaten you with sex?"

She had beautiful, dark, curly hair. I couldn't help wondering what she looked like under the robe. I felt the tip of my chap breach the water's surface, like a submarine scouting for port.

"That seems very unlikely," said the other woman, spotting my periscope.

"Hurry up, Teasel," called the woman at the door. "They're serving dinner."

"Teasel's a pretty name," I said. "Isn't that a kind of flower?"

"A wildflower, yes," said the knife-wielding woman. "Some might even call it a weed."

"I'm very hungry."

"We're all hungry. What do Paris-Blois want you to do at the Judgement of Basildon?"

"To help their wine win, of course."

"And are you going to do that?"

"Yes. Otherwise they'll kill me."

They seemed surprised at this. "Who's going to kill you?"

"An old woman in the mountains of Calabria," I replied, "and her army of psychopathic knife-wielding thugs." I tried to focus on the knife being held at my throat, but it was too close and the effort made me feel dizzy. I rested my head on the knife-wielding woman's shoulder. "People threaten me with knives all the time these days," I said.

There was a brisk knock and a voice called from outside. "Dinner is served. Is our newest member all right?"

"All fine," said the woman at the door. "He's just cleaning up. Start without us."

"I'm not sure we'll get any sense out of him in this state," said the knife woman. "You two go on. I'll make sure he's ok." The others slipped out and my remaining companion slid the lock home once more.

"Why all the questions?" I asked.

"Shush. I'm the one asking," she said, stepping into the bath, this time without her robe. "We are *Les Malherbes*. Will you help us?"

"Yes, definitely," I replied.

"Good. I could tell you were one of us. Do you find me attractive?"

"Yes."

We were late for dinner.

Chapter Thirteen

Wild Card

I'd agreed to meet Lily in the Olde Cittie of Yorke, an ancient pub with a row of secluded booths down one side of the saloon. It was a lawyers' pub, where legal functionaries from the nearby chambers met to discuss fine and confidential points of the law – a perfect venue for our assignation.

I'd arrived early and installed myself in one of the cubbyholes. Lily arrived soon afterwards and, spotting me, stepped inside and pulled the curtain shut. She removed the pint from my hand, sat in my lap and made it clear she was pleased to see me.

"You're incredible. I didn't know you played the flute so well," I said, once she'd come up for air.

"We all have our talents," she replied. "So, my fellow Minstrel, how are things going with your handler at Paris-Blois? Sandra, isn't it? Managed to get any action yet?"

"I don't think there's a good answer to that question."

"Yes, there is. The good answer is no." Lily popped a couple of buttons open on my shirt.

"How are things going with the tasting preparation?" I asked, mainly to divert my thoughts from Lily's fingers, which were trespassing like a particularly cocksure poacher.

"Fine. Lord Flashman is close to deciding which non-French wines to include in the lineup. We've been ploughing through Pinot tastings every day."

"Sounds like dreadful work."

"It's been quite difficult, actually. The idea is to trick the tasters into thinking they're drinking French. Quite a few of the judges will be very pro-Burgundy, so they'll mark down any wines that don't taste typical, even if they're good."

"So, nothing too super-fruity or extracted?"

"Exactly. Nothing from too warm a climate. I've tasted loads of great Australian and Californian Pinot but most just doesn't taste like Burgundy."

"So, what's made the shortlist? Willing to give me any clues?"

"There'll definitely be a German Spätburgunder. Climate's pretty close to Burgundy. I doubt I could distinguish between a good Burgundy and some of the better German Pinots myself."

"Makes sense. Something from New Zealand too?"

"Yes, for sure. We're deciding between the final three from Central Otago."

"Anything from the States?"

"Probably not. Amazing wines but the style isn't right. And South America has the same problem; they're just too juicy and fruity." Lily unbuckled my belt with her free hand.

"Sounds like you're halfway there then."

"Yes. Lord Flashman really wanted six non-French Pinots from six different countries but we'll probably end up with two Kiwi ones, maybe two Germans."

"I've brought you a little surprise."

"I'd have been very disappointed if you hadn't," Lily replied, and began gnawing on my fingers. With my ungnawed hand, I reached down and lifted the flap of my bag, extracting one of the Little Chalfont wines. Lily released my fingers and looked at the unlabelled bottle.

"What's that? Some kind of tank sample?"

"Try it. It's not Burgundy." I unscrewed the top and poured two half-glasses. Lily leaned back and lifted one, holding my belt for balance, and brought it to her lips.

"That's very impressive," she said. I could tell she meant it; her eyes had opened wide. "Where's it from? No, don't tell me." She took a sniff and another small mouthful. "I assume it's not Burgundy. So... a top end red Sancerre? Is it Vacheron?"

"Not French," I said, smugly.

"Really? It tastes French. Is it a Spätburgunder?"

"Not German either. What will you give me if you can't guess?"

"A good seeing to. But then, I'm going to give you that in the next two minutes anyway, whether I guess or not. So, it's not European…"

She was an assertive one, that's for sure. I liked her attitude, though there was something about Lily's utter unwillingness to compromise that made me slightly nervous.

"I didn't say it wasn't European."

"Austrian then? Really?" She sniffed again. "Actually, I was going to say New Zealand, or perhaps California, reminds me a little of Au Bon Climat…"

I smiled and shook my head.

"Well, bloody tell me then!" She finished the glass and pinched my nose.

"It's English."

"Bollocks. Tell me what it is or I'll punch you."

"I'm serious. It's from my garden in Little Chalfont. Tom Hawkins pressed the grapes and aged it for me. It's had two years in a tiny, old oak barrel. He's just bottled it – there were only forty-two bottles, but he's polished off three and that's another one down."

"You're full of crap. You can't ripen Pinot like that in England." She took my glass and drank some more. "You're kidding me? It's incredible."

"I know. You should put it in your tasting."

Lily stood up, leaned back against the table and raised her hand to the curtain. I thought I'd blown it, that she was about to draw it back and walk out on me. Instead, she tugged the fabric closed where there'd been a small gap at the top and, to my delight, undid the buttons on her trousers.

"I'll talk to Lord Flashman," she said, retaking her position on my lap.

My spirits rose. Courtesy may not have been her strong point but she was a woman of her word.

***

A few days later, my phone gave a little shudder. A text from Lily.

Meet me at 5:30pm. Hyde Park, Dell Bridge.

It was nearly five. I caught the tube to Hyde Park Corner and, as I emerged into the open, the soupy air of the Underground vanished in February's chill. Within a minute I was through the gate and on to the sandy bridleway that rings the ancient park, checking my step as a pair of mounted policemen crossed my path, reins jangling and vapour puffing from the horses' mouths. Beneath a winter-bare tree, a patch of hardy crocuses had pushed through the soil, their petals gasping at the final minutes of cold, bright sun.

As I rounded the bronze statue of Diana atop her fountain, I caught sight of Lily at the centre of the little bridge. But she'd seen me first and as I drew closer she smiled, turned and walked away, disappearing into a knot of trees beside the lake.

I hurried after her then slowed as I reached the quiet of the copse, creeping silently from tree to tree, expecting her to jump out at me at any second. But she was just leaning against a large oak, right at the centre, waiting for me to find her, smirking as she played with her ponytail. She took hold of me and greeted me vigorously.

"Success!" she declared, a few minutes later. I agreed and she giggled, smoothing her skirt flat.

"No, I mean Lord Flashman loves the idea of using your wine. He thinks it's an incredible expression of Pinot. 'Reminiscent of a rich vintage in Ahr,' he said."

"That's great," I replied. I thought of the vine, limbs still bare and outstretched, waiting for the sun to warm her sap and bring her back to life. How amusing to imagine the eminent judges humming and hawing, pontificating as to whether the soil was sandy Burgundy or slatey Rhein, whether the vineyards had been cooled by the frigid Southern Ocean or the rolling Pacific mists.

Then, like a silly sod, I remembered my conspiracy. The winning wine *had* to be Domaine Henri-Leroy, not my wine and not any other either, otherwise I would soon be the subject of a particularly nasty game of 'Garrotte the Felix'. I looked at Lily and felt a strange, tender sensation, something unfamiliar. Was it guilt? Seemed unlikely. It was dinner time, so I decided it was probably hunger.

"Why did we have to meet in Hyde Park? Couldn't we have gone to a restaurant?"

Stupid thing to say, I knew full well why.

"Don't be a muppet. We can't be seen together. The Judgement of Basildon takes place next week. Your Paris-Blois friends are probably keeping tabs on you anyway."

As if I didn't have enough to be paranoid about.

"Ok," she said, "let's run through the plan. Firstly, I need to get my hands on four bottles of your wine. Two will be decanted and two held as reference samples. And the wine will need to be associated with a reputable producer or distributor."

"No problem," I said. "You can pick the bottles up from the Flag and Parrot and declare Hawkins's wine company as the official distributor. I told him the wine might be going into a prestigious competition, which got him giddy with excitement. He guessed it was The Judgement of Basildon straight away, of course. He's probably told half of London he has a wine in the competition, but I swore him to secrecy about the origin of the grapes."

"Good. So, what's the wine called? It has to have a name, Château something?"

"I've thought about this," I said. "Chalfont means chalk spring in Old English. In French, that translates as *La Source Craie*. So, we should call it *La Petite Source Craie*. Little Chalfont. Clever, eh?" Oh, how very clever I was, and no mistake.

"I like it!" said Lily. "God, it would be so good if this beats Domaine Henri-Leroy. Imagine what the press will make of it!"

"I imagine they'll think all their Christmases have come at once." But I couldn't let it beat Domaine Henri-Leroy, of course, much as I wanted to. Not if I valued my own neck, which I did very much.

"Ok," said Lily, "I'll pick up your Little Chalfont bottles from Hawkins and label them. Each of the six wines Lord Flashman and I have selected are to be delivered by our retired Detective Inspector to Sir Francis Walsham and the idiot Percy Woods at Le Grain d'Or on the morning of the tasting. You're more familiar with the next bit, thanks to your dodgy friends at Paris-Blois."

"Indeed," I replied. "Walsham and Percy will have selected their own six wines for the competition, all Burgundies of course. They'll open your six non-French wines, then all twelve will be decanted. Each decanter bears a number. The secret of which wine corresponds to which number remains locked in a safe in the bowels of Le Grain d'Or. But idiot Percy, as you call him, will be communicating the number corresponding to Domaine Henri-Leroy to a Paris-Blois agent, who in turn will pass it on to me."

"How will they do that?"

I shrugged. "For some reason, Paris-Blois won't tell me. I've just been told to stand in a certain place and wait. I don't know how Percy communicates the number to the Paris-Blois operative and I don't know how they communicate it to me. Our Inspector has ensured both decanting sessions take place in deep cellars, so there's no opportunity to use a mobile. Apparently he sweeps the cellar at Le Grain d'Or for electrical devices before the decanting begins, in case there's a telephone or radio transmitter hidden in a magnum of Champagne."

"He intends to do the same at our end," said Lily. "So, however they communicate Domaine Henri-Leroy's decanter number to you, we'll have to assume you're in possession of it by the time you enter Basildon House. In the meantime, I'm stuck in the cellar, three floors beneath you, waiting for the locked chest of decanters to arrive."

"Once Flashman has received the chest from Walsham and taken it downstairs to you, my Paris-Blois friends are in the dark. They weren't able to hack Flashman's emails."

"Ok, this is what happens," said Lily. "Once the chest is opened in front of Lord Flashman and the Inspector, I have two jobs. Firstly, to decant the numbered wines into the *second* decanters, each of which are marked with a sign of the zodiac. Secondly, to record which number corresponds with which star sign. Obviously, that's the only way anyone can track the judges' scores back to the initial bottles. I'll have no idea which wine is which. I'm not even allowed to taste them."

"Signs of the zodiac!" I rolled my eyes. "Right, so I need to communicate the Henri-Leroy decanter number to you, so you can note the star sign on its second decanter and tell me which it is. Then I'll wait for it to be poured and give the wine a properly lousy score."

Hart, you lying swine. I felt like the worst kind of bounder. But what else could I do? I had far more to lose than Lily did. But if I saved myself, would I lose Lily?

"Impossible, Felix. You're going to be sitting around the table in the Grand Dining Room, pretty much under armed guard, twiddling your thumbs while I do the decanting down in the cellar. How are you going to tell me the number?"

"I've no idea. Can you say you need the toilet and pop upstairs, then I'll hold up the correct number of fingers?"

"No, you idiot, I can't."

"Ok," I said. "How about you slip me a note showing the relationship between all the numbers and star signs on the first and second sets of decanters? How are you recording them?"

"I just write it down on a clipboard. It gets placed in a safe for the duration of the tasting then removed when it's time to reveal which wine is which."

"Let me guess; the key to the safe is retained by a certain retired Detective Inspector."

"Yup." Lily gave a grim smile.

"Christ. How are we going to do it then?"

"I don't know. I can't actually see a way."

Despite the February chill, I broke into a sweat.

"There must be a way. We need to make this work. You just need to write the numbers and star signs down on a separate piece of paper and smuggle it to me."

"With the Inspector watching my every move? How am I going to do that?"

"Use copy paper," I said. "Carbon paper. You can make a duplicate as you write."

"Ok… that might work," said Lily uncertainly, "and then how do I get it to you?"

"You're not locked in the cellar for the tasting itself, are you?"

"No. I'm supervising the whole thing."

"Good. Our retired Detective Inspector must trust you."

"He doesn't. He wanted me locked away after the second decanting, for the duration of the tasting, but Lord Flashman insisted I supervise the pouring of the wines."

"Thank God for that. So, you just need to slip me the codes."

Lily shook her head. "That's not going to be easy. The staff aren't allowed to speak to any of the attendees. And there's no clutter allowed on the table, just a white tablecloth, the glasses, a single score sheet and a pencil."

"I'll think of something." I had to. God knows what, though. How difficult could it be to pass a piece of paper to someone under the gaze of a Lord of the Realm, a sharp-eyed ex-detective and my fellow judges – some of whom weren't even corrupt? Thoughts of hidden ink pads, miniature earpieces and lasers projected onto walls filled my mind. I needed a diversion. Maybe I could set off a firework or poison one of the judges? Arrange an artillery barrage from Green Park? Hire a streaker to padlock her tit-rings to the chandelier and sweep across the room in great arcs, screaming *La Marseillaise*?

I had six days left to put the finishing touches to what, in the cold light of day, was a double-crossing, half-baked, witless shambles of a plan. And the penalty for failure was death.

Chapter Fourteen

Amazons and Swallows

Monday 14th February. Valentine's Day. But there was no rosy glow in the breast of yours truly that frigid morning as I and my fellow tasters assembled outside the gates of Basildon House.

We had already surrendered our mobiles, been patted down for hidden earpieces, pagers or other electronic wizardry, and instructed, in no uncertain terms, that we were not permitted to mix with the press, public or anyone else outside our little group. The retired Detective Inspector, a tall man with a bristling moustache, hovered nearby, his beady eyes flitting from one judge to the next. The sod had even confiscated our overcoats.

"You wouldn't believe what I've seen concealed in the lining of a Chesterfield," he'd drawled a few minutes earlier. *Let me guess*, I thought. *A Soviet communication satellite? A loft full of homing pigeons?* But I kept quiet, shooting him no dirtier a look than did the rest of the judges as our coats were whisked away to a locked cupboard somewhere in Basildon House.

I buttoned my suit jacket and rubbed my hands. There was now a fair-sized crowd on the road, half of them press and international TV crews, the other half curious bystanders. Flashman and Walsham had spent the past week cranking up their PR machines and the Judgement of Basildon had even made the BBC news.

"It's Lord Flashman!" someone shouted.

It was indeed. There was a buzz from the crowd as Flashman, a large, almost perfectly round man, in bow tie and waistcoat, bowled from the front door of his mansion. He propelled himself down the drive to the gate, waving his short arms.

"Ladies, gentlemen!" he boomed, small puffs of steam escaping from the more excited parts of his face.

"Has French wine had its day, Lord Flashman?" shouted an oikish member of the press.

"That is what we are here to find out, dear boy!" he replied.

"Who's gonna win then?" shouted another journalist.

"That will be determined by our hugely experienced judges," said Flashman, flinging a hand towards our little crowd. The press turned towards us and a few of them raised their cameras, recording the twenty of us arranged like a punnet of prize prunes, quarantined behind our velvet rope.

"Give us a smile, winos!" shouted one and the rest laughed.

My fellow judges, it was fair to say, were not overjoyed at being called a bunch of winos in front of a large crowd on a chilly Monday in February and it was a sour score of faces that were captured for posterity by the world's press that morning. We were a mixed bunch, from very different backgrounds, united only by our service to the world of wine. Some were journalists, others wine critics, a couple were professional merchants and the rest, me included, were associated with one of the wines due to be tasted. I wondered who else had been nobbled by Paris-Blois.

"Attention please," called Flashman, just about managing to clasp the tips of his fingers together before his vast stomach. "I have been informed that the wines are now in transit!"

Another buzz rose from the crowd and they craned their necks for a view down St James's Place towards Le Grain d'Or. I suddenly remembered my instructions from Sandra.

"Sorry, I'm probably blocking your view," I said to a woman behind me, and eased my way to the rear of our group. I stood, as instructed, with my back to Green Park, scanning the crowd before me.

I still had no idea how the Paris-Blois agent intended to deliver the code. Sandra had steadfastly refused to tell me. She had phoned the evening before, as she had every day of the previous week, demanding a progress update. And, on every call, I'd fibbed like a career burglar at the Old Bailey, assuring her everything was under control, that Lily had fallen deeply in love with me and was in the palm of my hand, and that we had a foolproof plan by which I would identify Domaine Henri-Leroy.

At the end of the street, I could see some kind of commotion. Two white horses were making their way slowly towards us, heads tossing. As they drew closer, I saw they were pulling an open-topped carriage, on which sat a man in a dark suit and top hat. Members of the press and public kept darting into the road to take photos, before being waved back by the marshals.

"Here they come!" called Flashman.

I could see the man on the carriage more clearly now. It was Sir Francis Walsham. Tall, even without his hat, he was perched absurdly high, atop a large wooden box to which he clung, rather desperately, with both hands. His face had clearly been instructed to convey solemnity but was betrayed every few seconds by a flash of panic as the badly behaved horses jerked their load along the street, flinging him forward and backward, as though his hips had been replaced by an over-generous hinge.

"Woah, there!" shouted Flashman, at the top of his voice, as though he were flagging down a pair of galloping stallions. The coach ground to a halt and the horses stared at Flashman, perhaps believing him to be an exotic farmyard animal. Walsham dismounted, grey-faced, and dropped a key into Flashman's outstretched hand.

"Convey this chest to the cellars, men!" called Flashman. A group of footmen surrounded the carriage and passed two wooden posts through the leather loops riveted to opposite sides of the chest. They carefully lifted it over the back of the carriage and proceeded through the gates. The Inspector nodded to another footman, who unhooked the velvet rope holding us in place. Lord Flashman beckoned to us. The front of our little group shuffled forward and through the gate. So, the wines were on their way into Basildon House with us in hot pursuit. But where the hell was my bloody emissary with the code?

"Christ!" I shouted, slapping my hand over my left buttock.

The rest of the group turned to look at me, as did the Inspector. His eyes narrowed.

"Thank Christ for that," I continued. "I was getting cold!"

"Well, we're going inside now. So there's no need for further blasphemy." The Inspector gestured towards the house and continued watching me.

It wasn't the cold. I'd been stung by something. I could feel an object beneath my fingers; a short cylinder, like a tiny pencil stub, hanging from my trousers. I glanced behind me. There was a row of dense rhododendron bushes between our assembly point and Green Park. For a second, I swore I saw the end of a hollow bamboo cane withdrawing into the foliage. The sods had darted me! It was probably tipped with poison, curare no doubt. How long did I have left? A minute, maybe two?

I waited until my body was shielded from the Inspector's gaze by the group in front of me, then I pulled at the dart. The barb popped out of my skin and I winced.

"Arseholes!"

"It's really not *that* cold," said one of my fellow judges, a short, rather serious-looking man.

"Oh, I just remembered I forgot to feed the cat this morning, what with all the excitement," I muttered.

"Well, I hope you don't have any cat hairs on your suit; I am *extremely* allergic to animals," he replied, glaring at me.

"My house is an animal rescue sanctuary," I said. "I share it with a dozen cats, four dogs and a circus donkey with mange."

The man moved away, rapidly. I looked down at the object. It was a tiny black dart, the same colour as my suit, with a barbed tip, a short shaft and black flight feathers. The dart's body was hollow and a tight roll of paper had been tucked into the back end. I glanced behind me again, expecting to see a naked pygmy sprinting through the flowerbeds, but any pint-sized Amazonians had long since vanished.

Our whole group was now on the move. I realised this might be my only chance to extract the decanter number; I'd be far more exposed once we were seated inside. I kept close to my fellow judges as we passed through the gate, our feet crunching on the gravel, trying to keep a person or two between me and the Inspector. His beady eyes flicked from face to face, and every so often his tongue would dart out, like an officious cobra, tasting the air for corruption. I stared dead ahead, hoping to heaven I'd blocked his view of my hands, as I tried to tease out the paper with my fingernails. What the hell had they done? Superglued it in? *Come on, you sod*, I prayed, *for the love of God!* But it wasn't budging and I didn't dare look down.

We'd arrived at the front door and our group filed inside. I stepped over the threshold, bringing up the rear, and we bunched up and stopped. The Inspector shut the door and, with a final scowl at me, moved through our group into the hall. Balancing on tiptoes, I saw the footmen had placed the chest on the floor and were sliding the wooden poles from their loops.

"Careful lads!" said Flashman. "That's the way, good job!"

Four footmen lifted the chest once more and manhandled it towards a doorway, presumably leading to a stairway down to the cellar. While the Inspector and the rest of the group were distracted, I glanced down at the dart. It took just a second to tweezer the paper between fingernail and thumbnail and, finally, it pulled free of the shaft.

"Cheat!" boomed a voice. My buttocks clenched like a vice and I looked up wildly, blood pumping.

There was a round of polite laughter and there was Flashman, a pair of joke cardboard glasses on his face with the words 'X-ray specs' printed across each lens. He peered down at the floor and clapped his hand over his mouth in a mock expression of surprise.

"Cheat!" repeated the voice, jovially. It was one of the judges.

"Are these permitted, Inspector?" guffawed Flashman.

Whether the Inspector was in on Lord Flashman's little jape was unclear. He merely held out his hand, like a headmaster confiscating a schoolboy's fake dog turd, until Flashman surrendered the spectacles. The Inspector folded the cardboard into a small square, his face neutral, and placed it in his jacket pocket.

"Ahem, anyway," said Flashman, "please carry on through to the dining room, my friends. I shall join you shortly."

Our group shuffled forward. I didn't fancy catching that horrible little barb on my skin again, so, with a flick of the wrist, I threw it down on to the thick doormat and stepped on it. It sank, satisfyingly deep, into the bristles.

We proceeded into the grand dining room, a high, wood-panelled space lined with gold-framed pictures of earlier generations of Flashmans, none of whom appeared a stranger to the pie shop. The dining tables had been arranged to create three sides of a square, with a separate table for two replacing the fourth side. A footman, consulting a plan, nodded to me and gestured towards a chair. Next to it lay a neat little place card: *Felix Hart (MinWin)*.

One by one, the judges took their seats, the conversation low. Clearly, everyone was rather overawed by the surroundings, which was probably the intention. Walsham, now looking a touch less grey, placed his ridiculous top hat on the table and sat down.

I took my seat. Twelve empty wine glasses lay before me, forming a gentle crescent. A single sheet of paper and a pencil sat enclosed by the curve of glasses, the page blank except for the numbers one to twelve and a small box next to each digit. A chunky crystal water glass, also empty, completed the place setting.

The Inspector cleared his voice. "Ladies and gentlemen, please allow me to remind you of the rules of this competition." He looked each of us in the eye, tongue darting in and out, before continuing. "You are asked not to place any objects upon the table, except those that are already before you. It is strictly forbidden to refer to any materials that might be on your person. Anyone contravening these rules will be asked to leave the table and their scores will be discounted from the competition."

There was a whisper of excitement at this point. What a strict man our Inspector was! What must he have been like before he retired? The criminal fraternity of London must have been quaking in their boots!

"Please avoid any unnecessary conversation. We ask that you do not speak to one another, though you may address the two chairmen at the front." The Inspector nodded to Walsham and the empty chair awaiting Lord Flashman's rear.

"No-one will be permitted to leave their seat until the tasting is finished. So anyone requiring refreshment," at this the Inspector cleared his throat and his moustache gave a little twitch of distaste, "should avail themselves of the facilities forthwith."

A couple of judges rose to their feet and were directed, blushing, to a side door. The rest of us remained silent as a cacophony of antique plumbing made heavy weather of transporting the weak-bladdered judges' sprinklings through the bowels of Basildon House and into the sewers of St James's.

As the final judge retook his seat, the main door flew open and Flashman rolled into the room.

"Ladies! Gentlemen! The wines have been decanted and are on their way to the dining room!" The room broke into applause. Flashman took his seat next to Walsham and slapped his hands on the table with excitement. He then began a speech on the epoch-defining majesty of the occasion and how history was about to be forged before our very noses.

I tuned out and slowly slipped my hand into a trouser pocket, feeling for the scrap of paper. I hadn't had time to unfold it and had stuffed it away as we entered the dining room. It was now a crumpled little knot, carousing with the fluff and loose threads in my pocket's farthest depths. I located it, teased it into my palm and withdrew my hand, resting my fist on the table, as though inspecting my fingernails. With agonising slowness, I tried to smooth the tiny scrunch of paper flat with the tip of my finger, feeling its growing dampness as it squirmed around the centre of my sweaty palm. *Flatten out, damn you!* I prayed the ink wouldn't run...

146

"Felix Hart!" said Lord Flashman, loudly. I looked up with a start, tightening my fist, my blood running cold. The entire room was looking at me. Why had he said my name? Had he spotted my suspicious, idiotic finger movements? Everyone appeared to be waiting for a response.

"Yes!" I declared, emphatically. It's always best to be confident in such situations.

There was some tittering from my fellow judges and Flashman beamed. "Excellent, sir! It's good to see a man aware of his own importance!" He looked at another judge further along our table. "And our final Minstrel of Wine is Percival Howard, an honour to have *you* here too!"

"The pleasure's all mine," fawned a tall, red-nosed man, as he peered back down the table at me.

My heart slowed a little. I'd not been busted. I rolled my finger tip over the piece of paper and, at last, felt it flatten against my palm.

"And here are the wines, not a moment too soon!" declared Walsham.

Lily strode into the room, dressed in her dinner jacket and black tie. It reminded me of the moment I'd first met her, in Vougeot, though there was no smirking now, she was in full professional mode. Her long hair was tied back, off-centre, the ponytail curling over her shoulder. The room followed her, taking in her fine features and slender limbs, and Flashman beamed and wiggled his sausage fingers. She moved to the back of the room, followed by a line of footmen, each of whom carried two crystal decanters. The footmen placed the decanters on a sideboard and lined up before it.

"Excellent! Thank you, Lily. Thank you, gentlemen!" Flashman leaned forward. "The Judgement of Basildon will begin shortly. Let me take you through the order of play. This is a blind tasting, of course. Of the twelve wines you will taste, six are fine Burgundies, provided by my good friend Sir Francis Walsham, who declares red Burgundy to be the finest expression of Pinot Noir in the world." Walsham nodded solemnly. "The other six wines have been chosen by myself. They are also one hundred percent Pinot Noir but have been selected from countries outside France, from regions I believe give Burgundy a run for its money!"

Flashman addressed the back of the room. "Yes, yes, of course." I turned to see Lily directing two footmen, each of whom held a carafe of water.

"Water from my estate in the Highlands. I hope you don't mind drinking non-French water, Sir Francis?"

"If we must compromise, we may as well start as we mean to go on," drawled Walsham, as Flashman guffawed at his own joke.

The footmen moved around the table, pouring Flashman's finest spring water into the crystal beakers. I heard Lily tut behind me as my glass was filled.

"Those two are dirty!" she hissed to the footman. She leaned over and plucked my neighbour's and my own water glass from the table, removing them to the back of the room. She returned with fresh glasses and the footman refilled them. "The judges must remain hydrated!" she whispered. I felt her elbow knock against the back of my head. Not hard, just a slight, glancing blow. She didn't apologise. The Inspector, now sitting in a high chair in the corner of the room, watched us. I remained motionless.

"I'm sure I checked the glasses," protested the footman, in a whisper.

"Never mind. Just carry on," she whispered back.

"You may notice that each decanter has been marked with a sign of the zodiac," continued Flashman. "This is its identification mark. It allows us to trace each wine back to its first decanter, then the original bottle from which Sir Francis poured it this morning." Flashman looked at Walsham, who cleared his throat.

"Yes, indeed. After the tasting, while you are all enjoying Basildon House's wonderful hospitality, the two of us, along with our friend here from Scotland Yard, will collate your scores. We will match them to the codes secured under lock and key beneath us, then match them to those locked in the cellars of Le Grain d'Or."

Flashman smiled and the Inspector allowed his moustache to twitch in agreement.

"And when you've finished your pudding," said Flashman, "we will reveal the results to the world!"

Chapter Fifteen

Double Blind

Lord Flashman and Sir Francis Walsham shook hands.

"Let the best Pinot win!" declared Flashman.

The room erupted in applause and I saw my chance. I tapped the fingers of my right hand against my left in delicate applause, half-opening my fist to reveal the scrap of paper. My eyes flicked down and I stole a glance. My blood froze. The fragment, now rather grubby, was blank. Oh, sweet Jesus! Had I erased the ink as the paper smeared around inside my sweaty palm?

"First wine, please!" called Flashman. Lily marched to the centre of the room, followed by a footman with a decanter. I glanced down at my palm and turned the scrap of paper over with a finger, revealing a neat number six, written in pencil. I closed my eyes in relief. Thank God! Number six. Or was it number nine? Hell! Six or nine? I opened my eyes to check on the Inspector. He was observing the progress of the wine around the table, the footman pouring an inch into each glass under Lily's watchful eye. I looked at the judges either side of me. There was an aristocratic-looking French woman to my left and a bald, smartly dressed Indian man on my right. We were all seated well apart, presumably to foil any attempt to read each other's scores. The whole room was watching the decanter's procession.

I risked another look at my palm. It was a number six, it had to be. The line was curly, not straight. But did blowpipe-toting pygmies know how to write their number sixes versus their number nines? Especially when they were crouched in a rhododendron bush on a chilly Monday morning in Central London, while attempting to aim a dart up the arsehole of a pillar of the international wine trade? *Oh God*, I thought, *just make a decision. It's only life or death.* Right, number six it is.

The pourer and Lily were now attending to my neighbour. She had introduced herself as the proprietor of a Burgundian wine estate as we took our seats, so presumably she was rooting for Team France.

"*Merci,*" she said quietly, as a stream of red flowed from the decanter's spout to her glass.

As my wine was poured, I stole a look at Lily. But she was watching the footman and didn't return my glance. I stared at the decanter. It was a large, teardrop-shaped vessel, with a tapered neck and a slightly fluted spout, sliced at an angle to leave a sharp, asymmetric top. The neck was engraved with a small symbol, a pair of parallel wavy lines, suggesting water. Aquarius, the water carrier, perhaps? I wasn't sure; I wasn't big on horoscopes. Christ! How was I supposed to know what my number six corresponded to? I looked frantically back to Lily, at her face, her hands, waiting for a sign. But there was nothing.

The pourer moved on to the man on my right. I'd overheard him talking to a fellow judge as we assembled outside, he was Chairman of the Mumbai Wine Society. "Wonderful, thank you," he said softly, as his wine was poured. *There's nothing wonderful about it*, I thought miserably. I was up Diarrhoea Creek with a canoe holed below the waterline. My mouth was dry. I reached for the water glass. Lily had definitely nudged me, deliberately, with her elbow. That had to be a sign, but what? An elbow in the back of the head. Did that mean Domaine Henri-Leroy was wine number one? No. She was hardly going to elbow me eleven times in the head if the bloody wine was the penultimate one, was she?

What had she said when she nudged me? 'The judges must remain hydrated?' Was that a code? Just sounded like common sense, especially when you're sweating like a burglar in church, facing what was probably the final tasting of your poor, blameless life. I took a sip of water and stared into the glass, hoping for inspiration.

There was something in the bottom of the tumbler. At first I thought it was the logo of the manufacturer printed on the base. I took another sip, going cross-eyed as I tried to focus on the squiggles. A disc of transparent plastic had been stuck to the inside of the beaker's base, quite invisible to a casual observer, and upon it someone had drawn a diagram in thin, black pen. The disc was divided into twelve slices, like a neatly sliced cake, and inside each slice, around the edge, like the numerals of a clock, was a symbol. The symbols were the signs of the zodiac. Good God, this was it!

"Judges, you are welcome to observe the wines," said Walsham, peering at his first glass, "but please do not smell or taste until all have been poured, out of courtesy to your fellow judges."

I scanned the room. Everyone was watching the footman and Lily make their second circuit of the table, delivering wine number two. I brought the rim to my lips and peered at the runic clock face once more. How did the code work? I spotted the letters N, E, S, W around the edge of the disk, outside the circle itself. I could work that one out. I twisted the glass very slowly through ninety degrees, allowing the rim to slide between my lips, until the N for North was at the top and the symbols were upright. I spotted the two parallel wiggly lines at seven o'clock. That was Aquarius, the first wine we'd been poured. The symbols' position on the clock-face corresponded to the number on the first decanter! Lily must have written each one down as she conducted the decanting earlier. Very clever. I wondered how she'd managed that in front of Flashman and the Inspector.

Concentrate, Felix! I was glad I wasn't drunk yet. If the wiggly Aquarius symbol was at seven o'clock on my little cheat sheet, that meant the wine I'd just been served had been poured into decanter number seven this morning, back at Le Grain d'Or, before Lily and Flashman had re-decanted it. The number on my painfully delivered scrap of paper said six. So, I needed the symbol at six o'clock. I squinted again. There was a six and a nine on their side, one lying rather obscenely on top of the other. Sixes, nines, it all felt a little confusing. But that had to be the one.

I looked up and my heart missed a beat. The Inspector was staring straight at me. Had he been watching as I peered like a village idiot into the glass, rotating it between my lips? My stomach churned but I kept my nerve, letting my eyes slide, as calmly as I could manage, towards the front table where Flashman and Walsham whispered to one another. I jumped as something gurgled next to my ear. It was a footman with the next wine, directing a thin stream of red into my second glass.

"Wonderful, thank you!" I said, slightly too loudly, jutting my head forward to spot the symbol etched on the decanter's neck. It was a crossed arrow, pointing north-east. Sagittarius. Didn't matter, it wasn't the wine I wanted. The pourer moved on to my Mumbai friend. I glanced back at the Inspector and was relieved to see his eyes had also moved on.

The footmen now speeded up their service. Every few seconds, Lily gestured to the back of the room and a new decanter began its journey round the table. The third, then the fourth, then the fifth wines were deposited in each judge's glass and I made sure to note the symbol etched on each vessel as it passed. A V-shape with little horns, then a circle with a squiggle on top. The fifth decanter was marked with a pair of back-to-back brackets joined by a line. The sixth and the seventh passed by, depositing their ruby load, each sporting the wrong symbols. Then, suddenly, there it was! A six and a nine, each head nestling into the other's tail. Gemini, the Twins, though they looked like a pretty damn kinky pair of twins to me. So, Domaine Henri-Leroy was the eighth wine along! I made a little mark on my tasting sheet next to number eight. At last, I could relax.

I watched Lily work the room, checking each footman was pouring at the correct rate, whispering words of encouragement, waving the next wine forward when the time was right. She was very impressive; no wonder Flashman had insisted she supervise the tasting. I suddenly realised that I was going to betray her. Our intimate little conspiracy-within-a-conspiracy would soon be a fiction, trodden underfoot by my own selfish needs, even if it was in aid of my own dear life. There'd be no more mischievous smiles or gentle assaults in the corners of pubs. For a few minutes, I felt miserable. Was I making the right decision? I had to be. It was a simple matter of self-preservation. Surely there's no nobler calling than that?

I observed my fellow judges. Which were the bribed and the blackmailed? Was it the curmudgeonly wine correspondent of a major Sunday paper, preparing to nose his way through the glasses like a pig on a truffle hunt? Or the intense lady winemaker from Sonoma, beside him? Perhaps it was the celebrated négociant from Dijon, perspiring under his tweed three-piece suit. Or the all-powerful, purple-nosed wine critic of *American Goblet*? How had Paris-Blois bent them to its will? By intercepting emails between a man and his mistress, perhaps? Tempting someone into a breach of their employer's code of ethics, like the hapless Percy Woods at Le Grain d'Or? Perhaps it was straightforward bribery; a discreetly lubricated bank account in Zurich, or part-ownership of a tasty racehorse. It didn't matter. All I had to do was deliver my line, the one I'd been practicing all day under my breath. It might lose me Lily, but I'd remain in Sandra's good books. And that, in turn, meant a dramatically lower probability of a lunatic Mafioso leaping out of a tree and slitting my throat when I least expected it.

"Ladies and gentlemen, my most esteemed judges," called Flashman, rising to his feet. "The Judgement of Basildon has begun!"

"The scoring regime is the Le Grain d'Or system," said Walsham, also rising. "So please mark each wine out of one hundred. And do try to write legible notes please; we would like to publish them after the results are made public."

"And," grinned Flashman, clambering his way up to an amusing punchline, "try to avoid any obscene adjectives. I'm aware the wines are exquisite, but we *are* hoping to keep the archive a family-friendly affair!"

The room tittered at Flashman's witty banter and he wiggled his fingers in delight.

And so began The Judgement of Basildon. Each taster grasped their first glass and buried their nose in the aroma. I gave the wine a little swirl, inhaled the bouquet and took a generous sip. The wine was fabulous, a symphony of ethereal, perfumed fruit and satin chewiness. I reckoned on this one being a real Burgundy, though Flashman's final selection of non-French Pinots had been chosen with immense cunning, so I might well have been wrong.

The judges were now tasting in earnest, some sucking air through their mouths, a couple of the faster tasters already expelling thin streams of second-hand wine into the silver hourglass spittoons beside each chair. I wouldn't be spitting, I decided, partly out of deference to Dionysus, but also because I felt I deserved it after a morning of oppression at the hands of deranged frog-poison merchants, humourless ex-detective inspectors and the extreme-toffee-nosed wing of the international wine trade.

A couple of the judges were smirking at each other and nodding; I suspected the first wine would be receiving good marks. I wrote a suitably lyrical tasting note and gave it ninety-six out of a hundred, a pretty damn good score. All I had to do was meander my way to the eighth wine, raise my glass and say my magic phrase. It might earn me a tutting from the chairmen but, as Sandra had suggested, I was sure I'd get away with it. I focussed for a second and practiced the phrase under my breath, ready for my delivery. 'The wines are quite open; they have clearly been aerated.' Then I lifted my second glass, took a deep sniff and a vast mouthful. Good Lord, this wine was more magnificent still!

"Ze wines are quite open; zey have clearly been aerated," said a French-accented voice somewhere to my left.

I choked, violently, and barked like a hippopotamus. The wine exploded from my mouth, projecting a cone of red spray across the table, covering my tasting sheet, several glasses and a large acreage of white tablecloth. Smaller jets of wine erupted from my nose, squirting down my shirt front and into my lap.

"Whaaaa?" I squealed, between coughs, trying to identify the owner of the French accent. That was my line! My bloody line! I became aware of a humming of disapproval from around the room. The Inspector had leapt from his seat and was staring at my wine-decorated tablecloth, his moustache quivering with dismay at the proceedings' sudden decline in decorum.

A clean piece of linen appeared before me, held by a neutral-faced footman. He fixed his eyes a foot or so above my head, as though the blank wall was more interesting than a man with Burgundy-laced snot dangling from his chin.

"Dank-du," I said, wiping the sheen of Pinot Noir from my face.

"Is everything… quite all right?" said Walsham, slowly, his tone making clear that things were not in the slightest all right.

"Er, ah, yes," I stammered, still in a fair degree of shock. "I… I don't think the wines *are* that well aerated actually…" I tailed off. The other tasters stared at me.

"I disagree," sniffed Walsham. "The wines are very open. Well done Lord Flashman." Flashman smiled briefly and nodded in acknowledgement.

I felt like an idiot. I looked like one too. As I dabbed at my shirt, I looked again to see who had spoken. It was a young man, about my age. He had introduced himself earlier as a Burgundian winemaker from somewhere in Morey-Saint-Denis. I'd forgotten his name, Jean-Pierre something. But more importantly, he had just uttered my code phrase, word for word. Which wine was he holding? The second one! The wrong wine! He nosed the glass, without a care in the world. Could he have said it by accident? No, impossible. He'd been briefed. Had Paris-Blois hired someone else to take part in the plot, in case I flaked out? But that was the wrong wine! A footman glided to my table with a length of absorbent paper and began pressing it against the tablecloth. I looked around for Lily, but she was nowhere to be seen. She must have left with the serving staff once the wines had been poured. Lily. Oh no... the bleeding obvious slowly dawned on me. She'd set me up.

Given that I had a dozen of the finest wines known to humanity before me and absolutely nothing to do but drink them, an unworldly spectator might imagine the rest of my morning taken up by a pleasant canter into a Pinot-infused daze. But there was nothing pleasant to look forward to. There was a wider conspiracy afoot and yours truly wasn't on the inside track. My precious code phrase had been blurted out by some Gallic fifth column and Paris-Blois's bribed judges would now be merrily marking the wrong wine as Domaine Henri-Leroy, writing gushing tasting notes and scoring it ninety-nine out of one hundred.

Sandra and that arsehole Boulle would explode when the tasting results were unveiled, their precious, super-premium wine exposed as a pathetic runner-up, to the glee of the media and every Pinot merchant from Limari to Queenstown. Then they would make a call to an unsmiling man with a very thick neck, residing in a small mountain village in the toe of Italy. The man with the thick neck would call his friend in London, an even less smiley man with an even thicker neck. And that man would make it his business to leap through my bedroom window in the middle of the night and snap my significantly less thick neck like a twig. I drained the remainder of the second wine, which even in my misery I could see was damn impressive, and tried to think of a plan. I would have to flee the country straight after the tasting and lie low. Perhaps I could find work as a cellar-hand somewhere in Argentina. Or Kazakhstan.

I trundled my way through the rest of the wines, ensuring I didn't waste any further drops. When I reached the eighth, I spotted the little mark on my tasting sheet indicating it was the real Domaine Henri-Leroy. *I'd better fulfil my side of the bargain*, I thought.

"Erm, yes, the wines are quite open; they have clearly been aerated," I murmured, feeling even more of an idiot.

"Oh, you agree now do you, Mr Hart?" smirked Walsham. A couple of the judges tittered. I tasted the wine, miserably. It wasn't bad, quite intense and brooding, though far from the best of the lineup.

By the end of the tasting, I'd cheered up slightly, partly because I remembered we were due an excellent lunch, and mostly because I was well on the way to being rather drunk.

"Dear judges," called Flashman, now slurring slightly; he clearly hadn't been spitting either. "Please check, one final time, that you have legibly scored each wine out of one hundred. I can quite understand some of you may have lost the ability to write, given the liquid genius before you!"

Our notes were collected by a flunky, who danced around the room whisking each paper from the table with a flourish. When he reached my liberally wine-stained effort, he paused, wrinkled his nose and lifted it slowly between thumb and finger. The sheets were placed in front of the two chairmen, who nodded to one another, Flashman grinning and rubbing the tips of his fingers, Walsham pursing his lips. Then the Inspector, dismounting once more from his corner chair, placed the papers into a box file and, with an officious twitch of his moustache, snapped it shut.

"Luncheon will now be served, ladies and gentlemen. Do enjoy it and think of us as we're toiling away, deducing the results," said Flashman. He and Walsham stood and walked to the door, followed by the Inspector.

The room gave the departing men a round of applause, whereupon a line of footmen, bearing silver serving dishes, filed into the room. In a seamless and near-silent dance, our glasses were removed and replaced by cutlery, plates and fresh linen. Even my splattered tablecloth was replaced, leaving the scene of my crime spotless once more. The food was excellent, creamy Bresse chicken and morel mushrooms, and the wine was more excellent still; a Puligny-Montrachet and a Sonoma Chardonnay served side by side, a white salute to our earlier Pinots. I ate and drank quickly, making no complaint as my plate and glasses were replenished over and over again.

As I tucked into the crème brûlée, I wondered whether Flashman and Walsham had decoded the results. They would have carried out the morning's procedure in reverse, descending into the cellars beneath us, collating the scores, then comparing the zodiacal codes to the numbers locked in the safe by the Inspector. Then they would have trooped down the road to Le Grain d'Or, descended to the cellar, and Walsham would have unlocked his own safe, finally de-anonymising the wines, revealing which numbers corresponded to the empty bottles.

I prayed that Domaine Henri-Leroy had done well on its own merits. Hopefully, I'd be able to lie and tell Sandra the evening had progressed perfectly according to plan. Even with six corrupt judges, it was mathematically possible for another wine, maybe even two, to beat the Paris-Blois Burgundy. I would commiserate with the blackmailing sods, declare *c'est la vie!* and advise them to employ a new winemaker. Then I remembered that all the scores were due to be published, together with the identity of the judges. It would be clear as day that a different wine had been given top points.

Oh Lordy, I was screwed.

Chapter Sixteen

Pinotgeddon

"Ladies and gentlemen, the results of the Judgement of Basildon will be announced shortly! Please follow me to Le Grain d'Or where Lord Flashman and Sir Francis will reveal the results to the world." The flunky who had collected our tasting sheets gestured to the door.

My stomach churned as we filed out of the dining room. We were helped into our coats then wove our way towards St James's Street. The other judges were talking excitedly but I remained silent, at the back of the group, my utterly desperate predicament now clear. A large crowd had assembled, far bigger than the one that had watched this morning's procession. St James's Street had been closed to traffic and the crowd stretched all the way from James Fox's cigar merchants down to Pall Mall.

"Excuse us, please!" shouted the flunky, carving a passage through the spectators. "The judges are here to witness the result." The crowd parted and we joined a small crowd of VIPs on a temporary stage constructed next to Le Grain d'Or. Lord Flashman and Walsham stood at the front, alongside the Mayor of London, who was already a couple of bottles down judging by the colour of his nose and his attempts to incite the crowd into a chorus of The Drinking Song from *La Traviata*. A tall, well-dressed man with a cane was introduced as the French commercial attaché, presumably there to cheer on his country's wines, and a small scrum of senior Minstrels of Wine were present too, resplendent in their purple and gold hooded gowns.

"Good afternoon!" boomed Lord Flashman, little clouds of condensation puffing from his mouth into the frozen air. "On behalf of myself and Sir Francis, thank you for joining us today, to hear the results of the most definitive tasting in the history of wine. The Judgement of Basildon!"

The audience clapped.

"For centuries, millennia even, Burgundy has been synonymous with the finest expression of Pinot Noir. But times change! And, as we enter the twenty-first century, we find the rest of the world snapping at Burgundy's heels!"

"Bullsheet!" declared the French commercial attaché, loyally.

"So today, we have tested that assumption by the most rigorous method possible. Six Burgundies and six non-French Pinots have been blind-tasted, in a random order, and marked out of one hundred by the finest palates in the world. To ensure balance, ten of the tasters were French, while ten hail from other countries."

"Wish he'd bloody get on with it," muttered a chilly-looking member of the press.

"So! Did Burgundy retain its crown as the world's pre-eminent Pinot Noir?"

I inspected Walsham's face for clues, but it wore its default expression, somewhere between a depressed beagle and an under-tipped toilet attendant. Flashman continued to burble on, milking the occasion, as my mind wandered back to my own plight. What would I tell Sandra? Or, worse still, that horrible fellow Boulle? It suddenly struck me, much to my surprise, that I was probably best served by telling the truth. It had to be Lily who'd betrayed me. Was it my fault that she'd had her own, despicable agenda? I had no choice but to grass her up and throw her to the wolves. And yet, I found I didn't really want to. I shook my head in disbelief. "Man up, Hart," I muttered to myself. "This is no time to be a gentleman."

Walsham now took the microphone from Flashman. "I can tell you that most of the Burgundies were indeed placed in the upper half of the league table, a definitive endorsement of the superiority of the region!" He gave a grim smile.

"*Vive La France*!" shouted the French commercial attaché, waving his cane and leaping up and down.

"And so, the results, in reverse order," continued Walsham, in a solemn drawl. He slid a large piece of card from a gold envelope. "With an average score of eighty-six, it's Moa Creek Pinot Noir. A very respectable score from down under."

Thank God for that. The lowest placed wine wasn't Domaine Henri-Leroy. That was something at least.

"Second last, with an average eighty-six and a half points…"

Anything but Domaine Henri-Leroy, please God. Work with me, oh Lord.

"Domaine Henri-Leroy!"

A few of the wine-savvy members of the crowd let out an "oooh!" at this point and my bowels let out a little oooh of their own. I was shafted, truly and utterly shafted. I wondered if that blowpipe-wielding Amazonian was this very second raising his weapon, this time loaded with the deadliest of poison-tipped darts. I glanced round to check for shrubs large enough to conceal a murderous pygmy but there was no nearby vegetation, just Le Grain d'Or's sturdy old shop front.

"A shock result for one of Burgundy's most prestigious estates, eh Sir Francis?" said Flashman mischievously. "Dear, oh dear! And now, in eighth place…" There followed a long, drawn-out roll call of Pinots, the Burgundies on average doing slightly better than their non-French competitors. The hum of the crowd grew in volume as each wine was revealed, the journalists scribbling notes and tapping at their phones.

"And now, the medallists!" boomed Flashman. "The bronze medal for the Judgement of Basildon goes to…"

The third place was won by a German wine. I tried to recall which wines remained. We'd had four Burgundies, meaning the top two spots were the final Burgundy and a non-French wine. We'd had the Kiwi, the Aussie, the South African, the German, so...

And then, to my astonishment, I realised that in my obsession with Domaine Henri-Leroy, my outrage at the cruel harpooning of my delicate derrière, my sweaty fumbling to extract the dart's magic number, the furtive squinting at the code in the bottom of my water glass, the collapse of my conspiracy into a double-crossing fiasco, and the expulsion of a perfectly good mouthful of wine across the table and down my shirt, that I'd clean forgotten about *my* Pinot Noir. My very own Little Chalfont wine, the grapes plucked by my own fair hands, that Lily had induced Lord Flashman to include in the competition. I flushed with shock, my cheeks burning. An image of the vine filled my head, naked and gnarled in the February sun, that black trunk emerging from the earth, its branches crawling inexorably towards me…

"The silver medal…"

I already knew. The silver medal, of course, was won by the final Burgundy. Ninety-seven points out of one hundred, a famous estate wine from Vosne-Romanée. And therefore, the gold medal went to my own creation, the vineyard next to a municipal car park, dominated by that single vine, heavy with rich, dark, late-summer fruit.

"And the gold…"

Flashman milked the silence for all it was worth, looking up and down at his sheet, a wide smile painted across his face. "It looks like a French wine!"

"*Naturellement!*" declared the French commercial attaché.

"The estate's name is *Clos de la Petite Source Craie,*" Flashman giggled. Walsham remained po-faced.

I didn't hear much of the rest of the announcement, just little snippets of Flashman's voice: "a micro-pressing by Tom Hawkins"; "greatest upset in the history of wine!"; "England, this England!" I could hear a rushing sound, as though my body was trying to surface in an angry sea. I realised the crowd were cheering and laughing.

"*In England's green and pleas-ant land,*" sang the mayor, attempting once again to conduct the audience.

The French commercial attaché was waving his cane. "*Merde!*" he screeched, "It is not true wine; it is against the EU regulations!"

"A fart to your regulations, *monsieur*, any reasonable person would consider this a wine," replied Flashman. "It is a micro-pressing of organically produced grapes, from a single vine in a secret walled vineyard in the Buckinghamshire countryside, known only to Tom Hawkins. It was fermented at Hawkins's urban winery in the cellar of the Flag and Parrot, not one hundred yards from this very spot!"

"*A firkeeng feex!*" hollered the furious commercial attaché. "*Feeex!*"

"It is no fix, *monsieur*! This is the most intelligently devised and rigorously policed tasting in the history of wine. It is quite impossible for anyone to have compromised our methodology."

I counted the number of people involved in the conspiracy. There was me, Sandra, Boulle, the blackmailed Percy and the six bribed tasters, of course. There was the Paris-Blois team who'd set up the sting on the hapless Percy and communicated the decanter number to me, including the psychotic pygmy who'd propelled that dart into my posterior. Then there was Lily, of course, and her partner in crime, the Frenchman, who had wrecked my carefully crafted plot for his own nefarious reasons. And God knows who else was in on it, probably the Lord Mayor, the Tiller Girls and the Grand Panjandrum himself. All in all, I doubted there had been a tasting with less integrity since the Spartans pissed in an amphora and sold it to the Athenians as the latest trend in biodynamic wine.

By now, the journalists were shouting into or frantically tapping their phones. An English wine beats the massed ranks of Burgundy! It's Agincourt! Waterloo! Where did he say the wine was from? The Flag and Parrot! No, the grapes, where are they grown? Buckinghamshire? Where though, where's the vineyard? Anyone got old Tom Hawkins's number? He's been banging on about that superstar wine of his for weeks. Let's get down the Flag and Parrot!

The sick realisation dawned on me that Tom Hawkins was the least discreet human being on the planet. He loved a bit of publicity and wouldn't be at all shy about dropping ripe, juicy hints to the next journalist who clapped him on the back and tickled his beard. It only needed someone with a passing familiarity with schoolboy French to translate *Clos de la Petite Source Craie*. Christ, why hadn't I called it something less obvious, like Château Kurdistan?

It was quite one thing to have utterly, catastrophically failed in the task Paris-Blois had set me. But quite another to have been responsible for growing, fermenting and inspiring the competition's winning wine, and therefore to have single-handedly humiliated the Burgundian wine trade in general, and Paris-Blois's most profitable brand in particular. My vicious corporate friends would come to the only sensible conclusion, that I had been responsible for a particularly odious little double-cross, expressly designed to smear their faces with rich, pungent manure. I could see Pierre Boulle making a grim little phone call right now to a cruel-looking receptionist in 'Ndràngheta head office. I wondered how long it would take the Calabrian mafia to do a whip-round, hire the world's most depraved assassin and dispatch him to London for a little light murdering.

I had to get to Hawkins first and force him to keep quiet, though God knows how I'd manage that. I'd probably have to commit to buying half the Chilean Merlot harvest from him, at double the market price.

I hadn't a second to lose. I could see a couple of the journalists were already pushing back through the assembled spectators, no doubt on their way to the Flag and Parrot. How the hell was I going to overtake them? I was surrounded on all sides. I'd just have to barge my way through. I was preparing to leap off the stage and hurl myself into the crowd when I remembered that Le Grain d'Or had a garden terrace they used for summer suppers. It backed on to an alleyway, just a low wall separating the terrace from the passage below. I'd rested my Port on that wall many a late summer's evening, while enjoying one of Le Grain d'Or's game pies and a cigar from Fox's.

The Mayor was talking now, singing the praises of English wine while the French commercial attaché heckled him from the other end of the stage. I jumped off the back of the platform and made a run for the front door of Le Grain d'Or. An absurdly dressed doorman, looking like a cross between a Grenadier Guard and a Zimbabwean customs official, held up his hand.

"The wine shop and restaurant are closed for…"

His sentence finished prematurely, with a theatrical *ooof* as my shoulder made contact with his chest and propelled the two of us through the door and into the shop. The doorbell pealed with joy as the footman sprawled on the floor, the tassels of his gold epaulets leaping like a gypsy's skirt. I hurdled his body and charged through the store, my feet thundering against the wooden boards. I narrowly avoided colliding with the antique weighing scales hanging at the rear, leapt up a short staircase and into the empty restaurant. I slowed slightly to slalom around the tables, then barged open the patio door, thanking the gods of health and safety who'd seen fit to install a quick-opening fire exit.

Half a dozen bounds later, I was across the terrace and vaulting the back wall. But in my haste, I had forgotten the adjacent alleyway was some way below the level of the terrace. In a pair of running shoes and with a foam mat beneath, the leap wouldn't have been a problem. But, as I vaulted the wall in my smart leather brogues and spotted the piss-streaked flagstones gleaming ten feet below, I realised I'd misjudged. In a panic, I twisted and attempted to grasp the top of the wall but I only half-succeeded, my hands slipping on the moss-covered bricks and my shoes scraping uselessly against the masonry. I fell backwards, feet first, and flexed my knees for a hard impact. Through far more luck than judgement, my feet made simultaneous contact with the ground, and I winced as the shock rocketed up my shins. But I was hopelessly off-balance and I toppled backwards, hunching my shoulders and screwing my eyes shut, waiting for the inevitable crack of my head against the pavement.

I landed hard and with a shout of distress. But, as I came to a stop, I realised the shout had not been my own.

"Arrghh! Bloody hell!" wailed a muffled voice beneath me. A man, well-padded in a damp sleeping bag and winter clothing, had broken my fall, his soft body absorbing the impact of my back and head.

"I'm terribly sorry!" I said, pushing myself to my feet, astonished that apart from a pair of smarting ankles, I was completely unharmed. A more generous man, and one who was not engaged in a race to preserve his mortal body, might have donated a few coins at this point, but I lacked the luxury of time. So, making a mental note to return and reward my saviour later, I broke into a tender canter, praying my legs wouldn't give up beneath me.

I emerged on to King Street and picked up speed, leaving the busy afternoon pavement and running along the road. I careened around the corner, ignoring the single-syllable Cockney roar from a swerving taxi driver, and raced past the clubs and art galleries of Duke Street. There it was, the Flag and Parrot! I reached the door, panting, and glanced back down the street. To my horror, I spotted the two journalists turn the corner at a half-trot, their pale trench coats marking them out from the darker-suited pedestrians of St James's. They were moving more slowly than me, making heavy weather of the gentle slope, but they'd be at the pub within a minute or two. I ducked through the door and burst into the bar.

"Is Tom in?"

"Hiya Felix!" smiled Jenny, loading a tray with pints of ale. "He's down below, checking on the barrels."

I tore through the back of the pub and down the stairs.

"Hey, what's the rush? Where's my kiss?" she called, but I'd already reached the bottom of the steps and was hurrying along the passageway, into the dark.

I slowed down. Where was the light switch?

"Tom?"

The place was silent. I felt my way forward, trailing a hand against the cold, cobwebbed wall, the glow from the pub upstairs nowhere near sufficient to pierce the gloom. I knew there were more stairs ahead and took short steps, feeling ahead with each foot. I could hear a faint glug-glugging sound from somewhere ahead of me. What the hell was Hawkins doing working in the dark?

There was a scrubbing of feet against the stairs behind me. The journalists had caught me up.

"Where is he? I can't see a bloody thing in here!" said one, breathlessly. I heard the zip of a cheap lighter and the two men made their way down the passage, the first one jumping slightly as the dim halo from the flame illuminated me.

"Christ! Oh, it's you. Felix Hart. You're one of the judges! What are you doing here?"

"I'm as curious as you two, clearly."

The man with the lighter stepped further into the room.

"Ah, there's the light switch."

He flicked it on and the bare bulbs strung across the cellar hummed to life.

"Jesus bloody Christ!"

There was Hawkins, lying motionless on his back on the floor of his cellar. His eyes and mouth were open, frozen in a mask of pain. The cause of his contorted face and general stillness was obvious, namely the large barrel of wine lying across his chest. The bunghole was open and the contents of the barrel were still gurgling out onto his neck in little bursts, creating a wide pool of red across the floor.

"Quick, get it off him!"

With much grunting, we rolled the great oak barrique off his body, but he was completely lifeless. I looked at the wall where the barrels were stacked, three rows high. There was an obvious gap in the top row where the dislodged barrel had lived. A ladder lay on the floor nearby. Hawkins must have been clambering over the casks, presumably checking the fill, and somehow pulled one of them down on top of him. A full barrique of wine weighs half a ton, there was no way anyone could survive an accident like that.

"Suppose an interview's out of the question then," muttered one of the journalists. "Better call the Old Bill."

"That's the rest of the afternoon buggered then," said the other.

Out of the corner of my eye, I saw a movement, in the darkest recess of the room. I turned and, to my horror, saw a short, squat man running at us, completely silently. I had no time to move before he was upon us, colliding hard with one of the journalists, sending him spinning into the wall of barrels. The man ran on, heading for the stairs.

"Stop 'im! He's a murderer!" shouted the other journalist.

I don't know what subconscious reflex kicked in, possibly the same one that obliges a spiteful schoolchild to extend a leg in front of a passing fellow student, sending the victim headlong on the floor to general hilarity, but out shot my leg, tangling itself between the ankles of our mysterious friend and sending him sprawling to his knees.

The squat man rose to his feet and growled. In the half-light, I saw I had made a terrible mistake. Though short, he looked like a barrel himself, shoulders broad and arms curled, a shaven head sitting atop his torso like an unfriendly artillery shell.

"Oops, sorry," I blurted.

The half-barrel-half-man ran at me, noiselessly. I barely had time to wonder what type of plimsoll he was wearing before he barged me, his arms clamping around my sides and his head burying itself into my chest. It was like being hit by a locomotive. I was lifted off my feet and driven hard against the cellar wall, his shoulder winding me as my back slammed into the brickwork.

"Help!" I whispered to my companions, but they just stood, open-mouthed, utterly failing to come to my aid.

I knew I was in trouble. I thumped my fists down onto the sides of his neck as hard as I could, but I may as well have given him a back rub and lighted a scented candle; he didn't even flinch. Then I felt one of his arms draw back and I knew what that meant. My plums have had a fair few arguments with the fists of rugby players, bar room brawlers and insensitively trained police officers over the years and they rarely benefit from the interaction. I twisted myself violently to the right just in time, his clenched fist driving into my hip. I squealed with pain, certain he'd broken my pelvis. I flung my arm out across the wall in a desperate attempt to find some finger hold, anything to try and pull myself free of the monster.

There was a dull clank of metal on brick and my palm struck something cold. The brawler was still driving me against the wall, only the back of his shaven head visible, and my winded lungs were burning from the lack of air. I sensed his arm withdraw for another punch and I knew he'd take care to be on target this time. I winced, waiting for the impact, and looked at the object against my hand. It was Hawkins's Champagne sabre, hanging from a hook like a gift from the gods. I ripped it from the wall and plunged the end into the side of the brute's head. Through excellent judgement, mixed with blind panic, I managed to drive the point a good couple of inches into his ear. He felt that one all right, screaming like a burgled baboon, and he dropped me, clutching the side of his head with both hands.

I pushed myself free and hobbled to the stairs, one leg semi-paralysed and my hip burning from its encounter with the thug's fist.

Another roar, more emotional than the first, suggested my friend was down but far from out. I turned and jumped out of my skin. The freak was already three-quarters of the way across the room on his creepy rubber-soled shoes, one hand holding the sabre high above his head, the other clasping his ear, which judging by the generous flow of blood running between his fingers, was causing him a spot of grief.

I raised my hand, clenching my teeth for the horrible, inevitable slicing of sword into forearm, but instead of metal meeting flesh, there was a gentle tinkling sound. The brute stopped and looked up, puzzled. He'd entangled his sabre in the lighting cables and the bulbs were swinging wildly on their wires, sending shadows see-sawing across the walls. With an angry grunt, he tried to pull the blade free, removing his hand from his oozing ear and grabbing the handle of a nearby wine tank to steady himself.

There was a low hum and the lights dimmed. The thug froze and shivered, eyes bulging, as though taking part in a psychotic version of musical statues. An unpleasant crackling, like angry bacon, joined the tinkle of the light bulbs, as the mains electricity supply liberated itself from its wiry confinement and passed joyfully through sword, human and stainless steel tank, to freedom in the earth below.

I'm not one to look a gift horse in the mouth. I seized the nearest non-conducting heavy object, an enormous book lying atop a nearby barrel, and brought it, with the most violent downward force I could muster, upon the monster's head. The man took a step back and his head rolled sideways in a horribly loose manner. Then he toppled over backwards, leaving the sabre entangled in the wires above.

The journalists peered down at the gently smoking man. "I'll tell you what," said one, "this is a far more interesting afternoon than I'd expected."

Chapter Seventeen

Pain in the Butt

The police were dismayed at the scene in the cellar and it was a full twenty-four hours before I was released on bail. Luckily, my journalist friends proved themselves valuable witnesses; it would have been a far trickier job explaining the presence of two heavily traumatised corpses without their help. The authorities accepted I had been defending my life from extreme peril and it was with great relief that I received the news, two days later, that they were dropping all charges.

Hawkins's death was treated as murder, motive unknown. The terrifying little muscleman, who had damn-near extinguished my own tender life, took the blame for that. The murderer's cause of death was given as orthopaedic trauma, caused by the impact of Jancis Robinson's *The Oxford Companion to Wine*[*], second edition, with his cranium. The coroner declared he had not seen a corpse in such a distressed state since the 1978 British tour of the Volgograd State Circus, when Kirill the Clown miscalibrated the explosive charge on his cannon, overshot his safety net, and collided with the company's star silverback gorilla, Gregor the Angry.

The media made a song and dance about the whole thing, of course. Some speculated the thug had been a Burgundian assassin, sent to take revenge on the creator of England's fairest wine, and to knock off one of the judges into the bargain. Others hinted at a conspiracy between the late Tom Hawkins and the

---

[*] *The Oxford Companion to Wine is an exceptional piece of work, bursting with meticulously researched detail. I thoroughly recommend it to all prospective Minstrels of Wine.*

organisers of the tasting, though all sensible folk dismissed such talk as fanciful in the extreme, not least the retired Detective Inspector who had his reputation to protect. I found myself, not for the first time in my largely unblemished life, the subject of intense media interest. There's nothing the papers like more than a good-looking, have-a-go hero, defending the weak and giving the guilty a good thrashing. I took the opportunity of a foreign trip to escape the brouhaha and the attentions of Paris-Blois with whom, I suspected, my relationship had soured.

As luck would have it, this was the perfect time for a getaway masquerading as a business trip. The tiptoeing arrival of spring heralds the start of the wine fair season, where the great and good of the international beverage trade assemble to argue prices and to taste the first mewling gasps from the recently delivered vintage.

The first fixture of the season is the *Salon des Vins de Loire*, an exhibition of wines conjured from the slopes that border France's longest river, from the zesty Sauvignons of Sancerre all the way to the bone-dry Muscadets of the Atlantic coast. The fair takes place in the city of Angers, a pretty, history-soaked kind of place, dotted with castles and fine gardens. My plan was to attend all three days of the fair then, at a leisurely pace, wend my way back up the Loire to Orléans, dropping into châteaux here and there for a little research, before taking the train to Paris to recover. I allotted two weeks for the trip, partly to burnish my knowledge of the region's wines, partly in the hope that by then the British press would have moved on to a more wholesome story – a pensioner mauled by a rabid fox, perhaps, or a bishop evangelising over-enthusiastically in the taverns of Old Compton Street.

And so, the morning after my release from police custody, I fled the country. That evening, nursing a carafe of fine Anjou Blanc in a wine bar in Anger's old town, I separated my wine trade acquaintances into two groups: those I could trust and those who were actively, or passively, supporting my imminent murder. The first group was distressingly small, the second far too large for comfort. Paris-Blois was my main concern, of course. When

Sandra or Boulle finally caught up with me, my only hope was to plead loyalty and claim to be a victim of the same nefarious plot to which they had fallen prey.

The most important thing was to prevent anyone connecting me with the Little Chalfont wine. That would spell my death sentence, for sure. With the demise of Tom Hawkins, the only people who knew anything of the origin of the winning Pinot were Hawkins's winemaker and my two flatmates, fellow guardians of the vine. The winemaker had returned to Australia over a year ago and, though he'd met me briefly, was unlikely to remember my name, while Wodin and Fistule were far enough removed from the world of wine not to be a problem.

That just left Lily. I hadn't seen or heard from her since the Judgement of Basildon. That was probably for the best, though I had missed her. During my police interrogation, I'd avoided mentioning our relationship, not to mention my involvement with the Little Chalfont wine. If there's one thing the police like, it's an open and shut case; there was no need to introduce a vast conspiracy into an already complicated situation.

I pondered Lily's motives. One thing was clear, she hadn't played a supporting role for yours truly – she'd stitched me up like a Brunswick kipper. And she certainly hated Paris-Blois, that much was obvious. Did she have any more plans for me? Strangely, and very much against my better judgement, I hoped so.

The second day of the wine fair was busy. I was officially on Gatesave business, so I thought I'd better do a little work. I visited a couple of dozen stands, concentrating on finding a tasty, well-priced Touraine Sauvignon that I could profitably flog on a half-price deal later in the summer. After an afternoon of slurping and precision spitting, I'd narrowed my search to a couple of promising wineries. Better still, a rather glamorous sales executive, spotting my Gatesave name badge and, no doubt, my raffishly unbuttoned shirt, invited me to a promotional tasting and dinner at Château Trélazé, just out of town. Just the thing to round off a day of Sauvignon gargling.

If I ever win the lottery, rob a bank, or fluke my way to the top of the corporate ladder, I'll be sure to invest some of my loot in a Loire Valley castle. They really are a smarter class of château, particularly compared to the tumbledown versions one finds further south. This castle was on the smaller side but was beautifully appointed, as was the magnificent dinner the winery had laid on for the two-dozen guests.

I'd had a long day, the dinner was very well lubricated, and it was after the fourth course, with another half-dozen to go, that I felt myself starting to flag. I never leave home without a sachet of *Madame Joubert's* blessed pick-me-up, so I excused myself and nipped off to the gents for a quick sharpener. I added a dose of the invigorating powder to a glass of water, waited for the fizz to settle, and swallowed the gentle, chalky liquid down. The day's belly-load of acidic Sauvignon and heavy game pâté soon softened, my limbs began to tingle and I felt my vim return.

It was gone midnight when, with a gut full of Sancerre, pork rillette and Crottin de Chavignol, I meandered my way down the moonlit drive towards the waiting taxis. Halfway down the slope, as I passed through the shadow cast by an overhanging oak, the hairs on the back of my neck prickled. I'm usually alert to robbers and other ill-willed folk creeping up behind me, though that night, I confess, my senses were somewhat dulled from over-consumption. But I still had my edge, thanks to *Madame Joubert*, and my wits told me to duck.

Something solid whisked over me, skimming the top of my head. I skipped forward and tried to turn, but I was too slow. A dull thump in the small of the back, from what felt like a bag full of lead shot, and I stumbled, arms spinning. Before I could regain my balance, there was a sack over my head and an unsporting fist in my stomach.

"Stop struggling or you'll get another," said a familiar, French-accented voice. It was Boulle, of course. With a sinking feeling, I realised the invitation had been a trick. *Nice of Paris-Blois to wheel out their best cheese trolley before my execution*, I thought, miserably. A strong accomplice grasped my arm and the back of my neck, and I was marched off the driveway and up a path at an uncomfortably fast pace, stumbling every few seconds on the rough paving.

"Mind the step," muttered Boulle, as a heavy farm door scraped against the flagstones. I was pushed inside, tripped and fell headlong on the ground. Someone heavy sat on my back and tied my hands behind me, then my ankles.

"Welcome to Château Trélazé," said Boulle, unpleasantly. "One of our minor Loire properties, but you weren't to know that."

"It wasn't my fault!" I gibbered, from inside the sack.

"Shut up. You'll have plenty of opportunity to talk."

"I did exactly what I was told, I promise!"

"I said shut up."

The sack was pulled from my head. I was in an untidy winery, with barrels and lengths of hose lying all around. The light was low but, from my nose-in-the-dirt position, I could see Boulle's smart, polished shoes. The man sitting on my back climbed to his feet and there was an uncomfortable silence.

"Someone else used my code phrase!" I said, pathetically.

Then, another set of footsteps. A pair of low-heeled, black ladies' shoes stopped a foot from my face.

"You're an idiot," said Sandra.

"Yes, sorry," I said, "but it wasn't my fault."

"Do you like Loire Gamay, Hart?" asked Boulle.

That seemed an odd question. Mind you, they'd just fed me some excellent cheese and wine so perhaps it wasn't so odd that an interrogation might be accompanied by more of the same. The French are, after all, a highly civilised nation. I relaxed slightly.

"Actually, I find it a little light. Do you have any Cabernet Franc?" I replied.

Boulle drove one of his posh shoes into my kidney, which hurt.

"I dislike you very much, Hart. I'm glad you don't like Gamay."

Peering over my shoulder, I saw the thug had looped a hook through the rope around my ankles, which led to a winch suspended from the roof. A long cord hung from the winch, at the end of which dangled a control panel. Boulle took hold of it and pressed a button. A clatter filled the air, the sound of a chain running over metal. Gradually, my ankles rose until they, then my knees, were free of the ground. My face began to press into the grubby concrete so, with a lunge, I twisted myself on to my back. My head came to rest on one of Sandra's shoes and I realised I was looking straight up her skirt. I should have shut my eyes, of course, but the perilous situation meant I'd quite forgotten my manners. I glimpsed the briefest flash of white thigh and, with a rush of excitement, realised she was wearing stockings. It occurred to me she probably wasn't wearing them for my benefit.

"Excuse me," I mumbled, letting out a little cheese-infused burp. Sandra stepped back, letting my head bump against the floor. She had her eyes closed and didn't look pleased.

By now, my feet were pointing at the ceiling, with only my shoulder blades and the back of my head in contact with the floor. I realised I was probably in a lot of trouble.

"Let me down!" I ordered.

As the pulley took my full weight, the top of my head dragged along the concrete for a second and suddenly I was swinging free. Boulle kept his hand on the control panel and I span slowly as I rose, my eyes at the level of Sandra's knees, then her waist, finally her chest.

I was pretty frightened by this time and would have been squealing and gibbering if it weren't for my general dizziness and the earlier cheese course, which was repeating on me in an increasingly assertive manner.

"What are you doing?" I wailed, accompanied by a Crottin-flavoured gurgle.

"The Common Agricultural Policy pays farmers to grow grapes for which there is no market," said Boulle. "Our only option is to distil the unwanted wine or pour it away."

"How can I help?" I said, hoping a conciliatory tone might soften my treatment.

The thug grabbed my shirt and swung me over a nearby barrel. Glancing down, I saw the cask was open and full of dark liquid.

"You can drink it!" shouted Boulle.

The chain screamed through the pulley and, before I could take a breath, I plunged in. Everything went dark and quiet. The wine was cold and burned my eyes. My surprise turned to terror and I flipped and wriggled inside the barrel, my head banging dully against the staves. The wine trickled into my nostrils and I could feel it creeping like acid up the back of my throat. I spluttered, took an involuntary gulp and the wine roared into my mouth, forcing its way down my throat. My lungs screamed, my head span and, as a high-pitched noise filled my ears, I realised these were my final seconds on earth.

I don't know if I passed out. If I did, the fist driven into my stomach certainly woke me. I wheezed like a pensioner in a brothel and heard Boulle's mocking voice close to my ear.

"Did you enjoy your *digestif*, Hart?"

I couldn't reply, what with my burning throat and the uncontrollable spluttering, but my angry stomach answered for me. Through a combination of gravity and fist-induced peristalsis, the cheese course charged up my throat and I experienced a most unsettling sensation, as if my own innards were squirting out of my face.

"Argh!" shouted Boulle, in a tone of distress.

I was in no position to worry about my tormentor. I was far too busy coughing fragments of that evening's cheese course from my poor, abused windpipe, and my eyes were streaming.

"Oh God, that's disgusting!" said Sandra.

I blinked the wine and tears from my eyes to find I was hanging at my initial, pre-dunking height once more. Sandra and the thug were observing me with distaste, while Boulle furiously wiped a revolting-looking paste of cheese and wine from his shirt.

"My suit!" complained Boulle. "Why couldn't we use water?"

"Death by over-indulgence," said Sandra. "When they find his body, his lungs need to be full of wine."

And that, I must say, put the willies up me far worse than a thousand punching, kicking thugs ever could. Huge, hot tears of fear washed away the remnants of the wine and I gibbered uncontrollably.

"I did my best, I promise! Why are you doing this? It's not my fault!"

"Why did you sabotage the Judgement of Basildon, Felix?"

"I didn't! It was someone else, I swear! Someone else said my code phrase. A French man."

"You're lying!" shouted Boulle. "Drown him again!"

The thug positioned me over the barrel, grimacing as his hands pressed against my slimy, wine-soaked shirt.

"It was Lily! It was Lily, Lord Flashman's cellar master! I told her the code phrase and she must have told someone else!"

"Why did you tell her?" said Sandra.

"I had to; it was part of our plan! I was pretending to help her make Henri-Leroy lose, but I always intended to make it win!"

"What rubbish is that?" spat Boulle. "Domaine Henri-Leroy *did* lose. You made it lose! And now we're a laughing stock. Sales have dropped by eighty percent!"

"I didn't, I promise! I told Lily to give me the codes, I worked out Henri-Leroy was the eighth wine, I was going to say the code phrase but the other man sabotaged it. Ask any of your bribed judges! It was a Frenchman, some guy from Burgundy, who said it!"

I stopped, conscious I'd sold Lily out to save my own skin. Whatever her role in this foul conspiracy, that seemed ungentlemanly. Perhaps I wasn't a gentleman after all. Sandra gestured to the thug and he released me, leaving me swinging back and forth in a rather sickening manner.

"That's quite easy to check," said Sandra, "but why didn't you report back to us after the tasting instead of running off to France?"

"I thought you would have me killed."

"You thought right, *imbécile!*" said Boulle. "You have made a mistake with this boy, Sandra. I knew he was untrustworthy. It wouldn't surprise me if he had cooked it up with that arsehole

Tom Hawkins. What were you doing in the cellar at the time of his death?"

At that, my blood froze. Did they know about the Little Chalfont wine?

"Did you kill Tom Hawkins?" I blurted.

"People with loose tongues deserve what they get!" replied Boulle.

Maybe it was hanging upside down, maybe the residual effect of my *Madame Joubert's*, but the improved blood-flow to my head and the involuntary expulsion of my gutful of wine had sent my mind racing. Loose tongues... Hawkins had been bragging he had a wine featuring in the Judgement of Basildon. He wasn't known for his discretion. But I was confident Boulle and Sandra didn't know the wine's true origin, or they'd have mentioned it already.

"Answer Pierre's question, Felix," said Sandra. "Why were you with Hawkins in the Flag and Parrot after the tasting?"

"I was curious," I said. "Everyone knew Tom Hawkins had a wine in the tasting."

"Go on."

"Hawkins and Lily knew each other. He sells wine to her, for Lord Flashman's cellar. That's why he offered her one of his wines for the Judgement of Basildon." *Keep your nerve, Felix old boy*, I thought. I had to make this work otherwise I'd be inhaling my personal quota of the EU wine lake before the next minute was up. My soaked shirt clung to me in the chilly air and I shivered.

"What are you implying?" said Sandra.

"I think Hawkins decided to fix the tasting. He stood to become famous for entering the winning wine."

"Yes. That's what we think too. The day of the tasting, word reached us of Hawkins boasting he had a wine in the lineup. He also claimed he had an inside track on the process and was sure to win."

My heart sank a little. I was his inside track, of course. No doubt he'd exaggerated the story for effect, as he did most things. Unfortunately, his exaggeration had been a little too close to the truth. And Paris-Blois, already paranoid about the risk to their precious overpriced wine, must have dispatched one of their interrogators to clarify Hawkins's unexpected role in the conspiracy.

"So why are you blaming me?"

"Because your behaviour doesn't match that of an innocent party," said Sandra. "Why were you in the cellar with Hawkins at the time of his accident?"

"I told you. I was curious about the origin of the wine."

"Sounds fishy to me. Let me tell you a more likely story. Hawkins was at the centre of a conspiracy to hijack the Judgement of Basildon and ensure his own wine won. He recruited your friend Lily then they persuaded you to take part too. When our operative confronted Hawkins, he managed to send word to you, and you intercepted our man before he could report back."

"It was an accident! He attacked me and I hit him with the *Oxford Companion to Wine*."

"You killed one of our toughest operators with a wine book. You're cooler than you look, Felix, I'll give you that. All that drunken bumbling around, accidentally ending up in the right place at the wrong time. It's quite an act!"

"I'm innocent! Ask the other judges!"

"It's too late."

And then I realised, to my horror, that I knew too much. That all the clever stories in the world couldn't save me and this would be my final few minutes on earth. I crumbled and my eyes moistened with self-pity. I'd always intended my final drink to be vintage Krug, sipped from a sliver goblet on my deathbed at an ancient age, surrounded by loved ones dabbing tears from their eyes. Instead, my last taste would be cheese-flavoured vomit blended with taxpayer-funded surplus plonk, too miserable-tasting to even give away to a passing peasant. How the gods laugh at us.

"Why did you score Domaine Henri-Leroy so badly?" said Boulle.

"What... what do you mean?"

"The scores were all made public," said Sandra. "If you knew which wine was Henri-Leroy, why did you give it the worst mark out of all the wines you tasted?"

I thought back to the tasting. After the Frenchman had ruined everything, it hadn't even occurred to me to go through the motions of scoring the Paris-Blois wine highly. I'd given it the score it deserved. But I hadn't scored it the *lowest*, I was sure of that. Unless I'd confused the numbers... what the hell did it matter, anyway?

"Well... I just didn't think the wine was that good," I said.

From Boulle's face, I could see this was the wrong answer. He turned redder than the vomit patch on his shirt and prepared to hurl himself at me.

"Kill him!" he screamed to the thug.

The man directed my dangling body over the barrel and Boulle stabbed at the control panel. Panicking, I jack-knifed, taking my handler by surprise and breaking his grip. The chain whirred and I plunged downwards, but I was off-centre and, instead of dropping neatly into the barrel, my shoulder struck the rim. The chain rattled through the pulley and my body draped itself across the barrel's open mouth.

"Get him in! Get rid of him!" shouted Boulle.

The thug pushed my head into the barrel, but my face remained several inches above the surface; the level was lower following my earlier dunking. As the last few feet of the chain rattled through the pulley, my legs descended over the outside of the barrel until my toes touched the floor. To my distress, the thug leapt on top of me and grasped my neck, trying to drive my head further into the cask, but he only succeeded in splashing my forehead against the wine. I was safe from drowning, but with that brute on my back the metal hoop around the rim was digging painfully into my stomach. I felt his thick fingers move over my mouth and I sunk my teeth into them, bringing forth a splendid roar of pain, but it was no use. My only options appeared death by suffocation or being sliced in half. For the second time in five minutes, I realised I was done for. Barely able to gasp, I emitted a long, low moan, a death-rattle, my final breath.

But just as I felt my life slipping away I sensed the barrel tip forward, unbalanced by the weight of the thug above me. With a final ounce of effort, I pushed my toes against the ground, willing myself forward. The cask tipped further, balanced on its rim for a sickening second, then toppled over. The brute's head hit the concrete, rather hard, and I somersaulted, his body breaking my fall. The cask's contents washed over us and I ended up lying on top of the motionless thug, observing the ceiling, while the barrel rolled lazily into the corner.

I felt my creative escape deserved a round of applause but Boulle was not in an appreciative mood. Even as I gasped for breath, he ran at me, face contorted, clearly intending to aim a kick at my innocent head. Fortunately, his shoes slipped on the wine-soaked floor and he landed hard on his backside, his arse bouncing a couple of times through the puddle of dirty wine and his legs becoming entangled in my own. He screamed several French curses and, now on hands and knees, began to rain blows upon my face, most unsportingly given that my arms and legs were still bound. I tucked my knees up to my chest and thrust my feet at him, my shoes making satisfying contact with his head and sending him sprawling backwards.

"Pierre! Stop!" shouted Sandra. "It can't look like he was in a fight."

I didn't like the sound of that at all. Time to improvise, damn fast.

"They're going to kill your CEO!" I shouted.

Boulle had climbed to his feet and was advancing on me, murderously, but he paused.

"What?"

"The people disrupting your events around the world are going to assassinate your CEO. I know who they are."

"You're a liar."

"Sandra asked me to join House Terroirist in the Minstrels of Wine to discover who's attacking your business," I gabbled. "She knows what I'm talking about."

"Sounds like more rubbish!"

But Sandra held up her hand. "Wait. What have you heard? Tell us, Felix, very quickly."

"Untie me!"

"Not until you answer the question. Why would they tell you something like that?"

"Because I'm the assassin, for Christ's sake!"

Well, I've told a few porkies in my time, but that got their attention.

Chapter Eighteen

Les Malherbes

"*Les Malherbes*!" I declared.

The unconscious thug's head was digging, rather painfully, into my back. I wriggled off him and into a more comfortable position, using his stomach as a pillow.

"What new crap is this?" spat Boulle.

"Pierre, please," said Sandra. "Go on, Felix."

"They're the organisation targeting you. They despise Paris-Blois and everything you stand for. Their leaders are members of House Terroirist and their headquarters are inside the Minstrels of Wine. Their mission was to humiliate you, to embarrass you. But, since Hawkins's death, they've changed tactics. Now, they intend to fight fire with fire. An eye for an eye."

"You said you were an assassin." Sandra peered down at the comatose thug beneath me. "You're pretty handy but you don't strike me as a fanatic. Why would you want to kill our CEO? Are they paying you?"

"Blackmail. And it's all your fault."

Sandra narrowed her eyes. "What do you mean?"

"You sent me to Burgundy to meet Lily Tremaine. I did meet her, as you know. We… developed a relationship. I told her everything. About my part in The Judgement of Basildon, of course. And… about the death of the Mafiosi."

Sandra closed her eyes. "You idiot."

"I thought we were in love!"

"You feather-brained idiot!"

"Lily was shocked and told me she didn't want any more to do with me. She told a friend, who turned out to be a member of

Les Malherbes. They got involved in the Judgement of Basildon. And now…"

"And now," interrupted Sandra, "they're blackmailing you. They're obliging you to work against us. Not just to ruin The Judgement of Basildon but to commit murder."

"Yes," I said, miserably.

Despite being tied up, soaked in wine and lying next to a man who had just attempted to strangle me, I was feeling quite pleased with my little story. You see where I got the idea, of course. And if I'm going to be subject to blackmail by one bunch of arseholes, why not invent another bunch and use the same excuse to explain away my ineptitude?

"Tell us the names of the *Malherbes*," said Boulle.

"I'd be delighted to tell you. But I think I'd like to be untied now. We can reconvene in London."

***

"You do know I wouldn't have hurt you, Felix?" said Sandra. "I'm sorry for the unpleasantness but it was vital to find out what you knew. To protect us all." She smiled and gave my arm a squeeze. A waiter placed a tiny saucer of olives between us.

It was one week later. We were back in London, perched at the bar of an upmarket tapas restaurant, at a launch party for the new vintage of Finca Tormenta, Paris-Blois's super-premium Rioja brand. To a casual observer we might have been two lovers, about to share a piquant dish of *pimientos de Padrón*. A glass or two of chilled Albariño, perhaps, and back to hers for coffee. Then, whispered conversation, intimate laughter, before the lights were dimmed and she slipped out of that dress. I wondered if she was wearing stockings. Perhaps she only wore stockings when she was drowning people.

"Forgive me for not believing you in the slightest," I said. Rather abrupt, perhaps, but it's not nice to discover an object of your affection has your very worst interests at heart. Being used is one thing, but I do resent being murdered.

"I apologise for Pierre's behaviour. You shouldn't have wound him up."

I was glad I had. Boulle and his thuggish friend had got what they deserved. And I knew Sandra had been secretly impressed that, despite being tied up, I'd been able to give the pair of them a good kicking. More impressive still, I felt, had been my spinning of a seamless tissue of lies, knitting together the lightest threads of truth into a fabrication as opaque as a vintage Port.

"How were you intending to assassinate our CEO, Felix?"

"Your CEO is generously hosting my boss, the Director of Commerce, at Paris Fashion Week," I said. "He's been boasting about it all month. I know which Michelin-starred restaurant they're dining at the night before – he's been boasting about that too. I was going to hide in the toilet and bash your CEO's brains out with a brick."

"I must say, Felix, you're coming across less convincingly than you did when you were tied up and soaked in wine at Château Trélazé."

But now I'm eating fancy olives in Portland Place, I thought, *not tied up and suspended over a barrel of plonk in one of your chateaux.*

"Tell us who's blackmailing you and working against Paris-Blois," said Sandra. "We'll solve the problem and your little secret's safe again."

"*You're* the one blackmailing me. When I've helped you solve this problem, you'll just oblige me to do something else. Then again and again."

"Just remember who started this, Felix." Her tone was sharper now. "You killed a senior mafioso and his accomplice. A man by the name of Signor Rizzo, remember? That's not the action of an innocent man. You also cocked up the Judgement of Basildon, very badly. You owe us."

She paused then put her hand on my arm. "Maybe I will make you do something else. When this is over, we should visit Maison Flavigny again. Not on business, either. A thank you, from me."

"Aren't you worried I might kill you?" I stared into her beautiful blue eyes. Christ, she was attractive.

"I remember what you wrote in the guest book. I trust you. Maybe you should tie *me* up this time."

A fabulous offer and, of course, utterly insincere. I looked across the crowded restaurant to the central table, where Boulle and the winemakers from Finca Tormenta were pouring samples and holding court before the drinks media. Boulle glanced up and held my eye. It wasn't a friendly look.

"What do you want me to do?"

"I've told you. We want the names of the conspirators who are blackmailing you and trying to destroy our business. We've tried to track down Lily Tremaine and find out what she knows, but she's vanished. Taken a sabbatical, according to her colleagues."

I was pleased to hear it. I hoped she'd hidden herself somewhere safe.

"Lily Tremaine isn't one of them. I don't know their real names. They're all named after weeds. It's a House Terroirist tradition."

"Weeds?" Sandra sighed. "Just find out their bloody names, Felix. Better still, take photos. You've got until Friday."

"That's only a week!"

Sandra didn't reply, just placed an olive in her mouth and stared at me. My phone, wedged in my trouser pocket, gave a little buzz. A message. Grateful for the chance to break her gaze, I fished it out and looked at the screen. It was Lily.

Miss me?

I felt a rush of excitement then looked up, guiltily.

"Message from another girlfriend, is it?"

"Well... kind of," I said.

"I'll leave you to it then. We're releasing a new expression of our prestige Cognac next week; there's a launch party at the Brixton Grand. I'll send you a ticket. Be there and bring the information."

She kissed me and stalked over to join Boulle. I tapped out a reply.

Been busy. Fancy a drink?

I held the phone for a minute, then five, waiting for another affectionate little vibration. But the phone remained still, its screen dark. Perhaps a ruder message might have been appropriate. Lily *had* deliberately ruined my plan at the Judgement of Basildon, leaving me in horrible jeopardy. In fact, I'd barely escaped with my life. Did she care? Was I only attracted to women who wanted to kill me? That seemed a worrying character fault. I consoled myself with the thought that a successful man probably can't help attracting his fair share of murderous enemies, some of whom, in this age of equality, are bound to be female.

None of this idle speculation was going to resolve my current crisis, I mused, as I wandered up Park Lane. I'd escaped death at the hands of Boulle and his stock of European-taxpayer-funded surplus wine, but I'd only bought myself a few days. I now had to invent the names of my phantom accomplices in an entirely fictional conspiracy to assassinate the CEO of Paris-Blois.

I could always name a couple of people I wasn't keen on, I thought, perhaps some of Gatesave's senior management. The Dick was top of my list. He'd torn a strip off me after my Loire adventure, claiming I spent far too much time in wineries and not enough time in front of spreadsheets. Then, in a very low blow, he'd publicly halved my travel budget, suggesting it might focus my attention on delivering shareholder value.

Tempting as it was to arrange The Dick's execution, it was unlikely to succeed. For a start, Sandra had already met him, when she and Boulle had buttered up the credulous toad at Maison Flavigny, as part of her company's pre-millennium trick to bankrupt the rest of the Champagne industry. And Paris-Blois was expecting me to grass up alleged members of an eco-cult – they'd need to look like fanatical anti-capitalists or sabotage-inclined environmentalists, not clean-shaven supermarket board members.

A little buzz from my phone. Lily again!

Drink sounds great! I'm at the Balladeer. You free now?

This was turning out to be a much better weekend than the last.

The Brompton Balladeer was no normal pub. It was owned by House Terroirist, functioning as an informal venue for meetings between House members and non-Minstrels. It was open to the general public too, though its eccentric drinks list, dominated by orange biodynamic wines, and its refusal to sell any beer other than naturally fermented Belgian gueuze, meant its patrons were mainly cutting-edge young foodies with waxed beards.

"Minstrel Hart," said the barman, as I entered.

"Have you seen…?"

"Minstrel Tremaine is in the back, waiting for you."

I passed through to the private dining room and there sat Lily, casual as you like, in frayed denim shorts, her legs and bare feet propped on the seat opposite. But she wasn't alone. Two men sat at the table, side-by-side, unsmiling. One was large, with yellow, waxy features, the other small and beady-eyed.

"Hey, Feel, good to see you. Sit down. Have some wine."

Lily moved her feet from the chair and poured me a glass. As I sat, she replaced her legs over mine, playfully digging her toes into my thigh. I took a sip. The wine was a cool, vivid red, a Beaujolais from a tiny biodynamic producer, refreshing after Paris-Blois's rather turgid Rioja.

"Thanks, nice to see you too. Wondered where you'd got to," I said.

"Yes. I got your warning message, thank you. I couldn't reply, of course. I wasn't sure whether they had you under duress. You did sound a little stressed."

I'd phoned Lily from France, as soon as I was clear of Boulle's and Sandra's clutches, gabbling that an assassin was probably attempting to track her down and that she should flee for the hills, preferably the Andes. The call went straight to voicemail, of course, as had every attempt to contact her since the Judgement of Basildon, but I'd felt a sense of responsibility. God knows why, after the way she'd derailed my innocent life. Just my innate chivalry, I suppose. But I was glad the message had got through.

"There was a touch of duress, I must admit. I'll tell you about it later." I glanced at the two men. The small, beady-eyed man made a little jerking movement with his head and I smiled and nodded in return. He jerked again and I realised it was a nervous twitch.

"I'm staying here, at the Balladeer, for now," said Lily. "We've not caught up since the Judgement of Basildon, have we? Great job there, by the way."

That was a rash thing to say. Startled, I looked at our companions. Who the hell were they? Whose conspiracy were they part of?

"I don't believe we've met," I said, extending my hand to the waxy-faced man. He shook it, briefly and clammily, without giving his name.

"Don't worry, Minstrel Hart, we know everything," he said. "We're members of House Terroirist too. You met a couple of our colleagues on the night of your induction. In the bath, I believe."

"Oh, I see," I said, slightly embarrassed. I suspected I'd walked into another trap. "That was a rather intimidating introduction."

"The knives were blunt, Minstrel Hart," he said. "A little prop to focus your mind. We had to check whether you were trustworthy or not. Good to have you working with us." He didn't seem that pleased, I thought, but then neither was I.

"I don't recall offering to work with you," I said, refilling my glass. "And who are you, anyway?" I knew, of course.

"We are *Les Malherbes*," said the waxy-faced man, smugly.

Well, it's nice to have official confirmation, I thought. *But, more importantly, are they friend or foe?* Let's stay optimistic, I decided. It seemed unlikely that *every* conspiracy on God's earth involved jeopardising my life and liberty.

"This is Cranesbill," said Lily, gesturing at the beady-eyed man. Cranesbill nodded twice, like a fierce chicken pecking corn. Lily waved towards the waxy-skinned man. "And next to him is Sow-Thistle."

I nearly spurted my Beaujolais across the table but, just in time, clapped a palm over my mouth. Sow-Thistle's expression hardened.

"Cranesbill? Sow-Thistle? You guys really *are* named after weeds, aren't you?" I smirked. "What's your weed name then?"

"Bittercress," said Lily, "and don't mock us."

I raised my hands. "No offence meant. What do you want with me?"

"We want information on Paris-Blois," said Cranesbill, fixing me with a bird-like eye. "Details of their events and product launches, help with our little interventions."

"Like the Judgement of Basildon?" I said.

"Yes, like that. And the Champagne auction at Louis Beaufort."

"You were responsible for all the Champagne being corked?"

"One of the serving staff was *Malherbes*," said Sow-Thistle. "It's amazing what you can do with a small bottle of TCA solution and an eye-dropper. It's a shame you were so effective at rescuing the situation for Paris-Blois. If you'd kept quiet, the auction would have been a disaster and retailers like you might not have ended up overstocked with millions of bottles of their Champagne."

And perhaps I wouldn't have been sent to Vougeot and met Lily, I thought, her feet cool against my thigh.

"Who was that Frenchman who stole my line at the Judgement of Basildon then? I was about to say my magic phrase and I was gazumped."

"Ah, Jean-Pierre," said Lily. "Well, we weren't sure we could trust you. Sorry we doubted you, but I was going to–"

"Yes, it would have been idiotic to trust you," interrupted Sow-Thistle. "It was clear we had to plant one of our own into the party of judges. One of the more inspired parts of my plan, in fact. The original judge was one Monsieur Fabius, the Director-General of the Burgundian Export Authority. Unfortunately, a couple of weeks before the tasting, he was informed of a video showing him *in flagrante* with an attractive young Australian woman." He smiled. "The woman in question was a *Malherbes* operative, of course, not that Monsieur Fabius knew that."

"That hardly seems a solid foundation for blackmail," I replied, pouring myself a refill. "In my experience, the French regard evidence of an older man getting his end away as a laudable sign of vigour, not a source of shame."

"Indeed. But the video also showed the two lovers consuming a bottle of Coonawarra Cabernet Sauvignon, a wine which Monsieur Fabius is heard comparing favourably against the produce of his own, native region."

"I see how that could be awkward."

"Yes. We only had to play the recording to him once. The point where he stated, 'If we lazy Burgundian bastards could produce wine like this, instead of our normal *vin de merde*, we could conquer the world' was probably the clincher. He soon agreed to step down and nominate our own candidate in his place." Sow-Thistle leaned back, looking extraordinarily pleased with himself.

"So, you had your own judge on the panel. But how did he know when to say my phrase?"

"He didn't!" said Lily, laughing. "Jean-Pierre just had to say your catchphrase at random – or at least before you did. All we wanted was for Paris-Blois's wine to lose and, of course, it was a 90%-plus probability that he'd pick the wrong wine. And we couldn't take the chance you might still be working for Paris-Blois, you might have come up with an alternative method of identifying Domaine Henri-Leroy. The code sheet I placed in the bottom of your glass was completely made up, by the way. I wrote it the day before the tasting!"

"I see. Why did you even bother?"

"Well, I thought it might help when you were explaining the cock-up to your Paris-Blois friends."

I can't deny I wasn't a little peeved. No-one likes to find that they're the monkey when they thought they were grinding the organ. But I was pleased Lily appeared to believe I'd been on her side in the end, rather than Paris-Blois's.

"Come on, Feel. It's pretty funny that Domaine Henri-Leroy scored second last, even without your help. And it's hilarious that Jean-Pierre ended up nominating the Little Chalfont wine, isn't it?"

At that, my stomach gave a sick little lurch. Surely she hadn't told her fellow *Malherbes* about my Little Chalfont connection?

"Yes. Absolutely side-splitting," I said. "I don't see why you need me. Looks like you're doing fine without my help."

"But Paris-Blois must still trust you," said Lily. "After all, it wasn't *you* who ruined the Judgement of Basildon for them, was it?"

"No, it wasn't."

"Why are you so grumpy? I thought you'd be pleased that their wine did so badly. That night in Burgundy, you told me Paris-Blois would end up blackmailing you if you helped them win, just like they did Percy. They're no friends of yours."

You don't know the half of it, I thought.

"And our understanding is that you promised you'd help us," said Cranesbill, "that night in the bath with Teasel and her friends. Isn't that correct?"

I recalled being heavily drugged and a knife being held to my throat, which I'm pretty sure counts as duress. *Les Malherbes*, however, appeared to have mistaken my tactical agreement for enthusiasm.

"I'm not exactly in Paris-Blois's good books right now. I expect they're arranging my assassination as we speak."

Luckily, my companions took my rather reckless comment as jest. I leaned forward to pour more wine, but the bottle was empty.

"Let's get another," said Lily. "Cranesbill, give the guy a shout, will you?" The man rose, put his head round the door and called for another bottle of Chénas.

Lily leaned forward and brought her lips to my ear. "I missed you," she whispered.

Sow-Thistle watched us, a smirk on his waxy features. The new bottle arrived and Cranesbill poured us each a glass.

"Good. You're with us then," said Lily, after we'd savoured the new wine. "We're stepping up our activities. There's a Paris-Blois Cognac launch event next week. All the drinks media will be there. We know you've been invited."

"What are you going to do? Roll a burning barrel of brandy into the nightclub?"

"Mass murder isn't really our style," said Lily.

"Paris-Blois's new Cognac is a bland spirit with minimal ageing; its high price justified solely by its ridiculous packaging," sneered Sow-Thistle. "Paris-Blois are serving it in cocktails to disguise its mediocrity. We're going to add a mystery ingredient."

"I see. I'll stick to beer that night then."

"Oh, I wouldn't do that," giggled Lily. "We're planning a rather potent inhibition-loosener. Right up your street, I reckon. It could be quite fun."

"What do you expect me to do?"

"We need you to ensure Paris-Blois's management get their medicine. You know what these senior executives are like, they barely drink at all, especially at their own events. Too afraid of losing control."

"Which executives?" I asked. I already knew the answer, of course.

"The European sales director, Pierre Boulle. And the UK director, your *friend* Sandra."

"That's not a good idea."

"Why not? You told me you were hoping to get some action. This could be your chance. Unless you've managed to get some already?" Lily smiled at me, but her eyes flashed dangerously.

"That's not the kind of question a gentleman answers."

"But you're not a gentleman, are you?" said Cranesbill, more coldly than I cared for.

"I am, actually."

"Come on, Feel," said Lily. "Cranesbill's only joking. You have to help us. It'll be exciting!" Lily paddled her feet against my thigh. "Do it! Or you're not staying with me tonight."

My time as a high-powered executive has trained me to weigh up complex situations and competing interests, and I recognised this argument as a game-changer. Despite my misgivings, I signalled my consent.

***

"I have a meeting," whispered Lily the next morning. "We've got some logistics to take care of."

"Remind me why you're mixed up with the *Malherbes* again? I don't see the attraction. Especially those two humourless bores."

"Because I believe in it. You should try believing in something, Felix."

"Just be careful."

"You are funny, Feel. What are you so worried about?"

"Paris-Blois know about the *Malherbes*. They know you're conspiring against them."

"And how do they know that?" She pulled back the curtain of the Balladeer's guestroom, revealing a clear dawn sky, before turning back to me. She was no longer smiling. "Because you told them?"

"No. They have spies within the Minstrels of Wine. They worked it out for themselves." *I'm pretty sure that counts as a white lie*, I thought to myself.

"There's something you're not telling me. You wouldn't have left that message warning me about Paris-Blois otherwise. What is it?"

"They killed Tom Hawkins. He was boasting he had the inside track on The Judgement of Basildon. They think he was a member of the *Malherbes* and part of a conspiracy to embarrass them."

"That's… insane. They killed Hawkins? We need to tell the police."

"Please don't. There's no evidence, anyway. Just be careful. Stay away from work and home for a while. Don't repeat what I've said to your friends. And I wish you hadn't mentioned the

Little Chalfont wine in front of those two yesterday. I hope you haven't told them about it?"

Lily's eyes dropped and she slipped out without answering. *That's a yes then*, I thought. Were they trustworthy? They certainly fancied themselves as master conspirators. I hoped they knew how to keep a secret.

I rose, gazing down into the pub's beer garden as I stretched. Beyond the railings lay the forty acres of Brompton Cemetery, its monuments and chapel yet to catch the morning sun. A clattering of pans told me the Balladeer's kitchen had opened, so I headed downstairs and, arming myself with a half-pint of coffee and a hot bacon butty, set out on the two-mile walk back to Minstrels Hall. I still had work to do. And as I strolled through Hyde Park's morning mist, my body fortified with buttery bap and strong cabbie's coffee, an idea sprang into my head.

I speed-marched the final half-mile and, stopping only for a quick shower in my Minstrel lodgings, grabbed my camera. My destination was Speakers' Corner, that venerable area of Hyde Park where crowds of wing-nuts, God-botherers and political imbeciles gather to screech their half-baked jibber-jabber for the amusement of the promenading public. I identified a handful of suitably tousle-haired individuals, who all claimed, at high volume, they were under the protection of some deity or other. I took a few surreptitious shots, making sure to avoid any landmarks that might betray the location, then dropped into Heywood Hill Books, heading straight to the science and nature section. A quick perusal of *The Young Scholar's Guide to Common British Flora* later, I had christened each lunatic with an appropriately weed-themed name: Herb Robert, Wood Spurge, Chickweed.

An afternoon of printing and red marker-penning later, my dodgy dossier was in tip-top shape, a job worthy of the *Securitate* themselves. I dropped into a Mayfair wine bar for a congratulatory glass of Romanian Pinot Noir.

The phone twitched against my thigh.

Balladeer. 8pm. x

Lily must have finished her day of scheming with the *Malherbes*. I killed a couple of hours by strolling back to Brompton, popping into a pub or two on the way. I arrived at the Balladeer a few minutes early and ordered a glass of biodynamic Beaujolais before heading to the back room.

"Glad to see you're keeping organic, Minstrel," said Lily, winking. She was accompanied by Cranesbill and Sow-Thistle.

"We have further instructions for your Brixton job next Friday," said Cranesbill, giving a little involuntary nod.

"Have you now?" I replied.

Cranesbill grimaced, awkwardly. "Yes, so please listen. Sow-Thistle will explain."

"A *Malherbes* operative has infiltrated the serving staff at the event," said Sow-Thistle. "You must await his approach and follow his instructions. He will inform you of the target…"

To be honest, I'd had quite enough of drinks-based conspiracies for a lifetime. No doubt the next stage would involve me standing on a podium in the centre of the room, while a Zulu hurled a barbed spear into my nether regions, to which would be taped a set of instructions obliging me to shove a Roman candle up my arse and dive into a piranha-infested tank of brandy and soda. Well, I had my own plan, and this one would be putting Felix Hart and his tender, innocent body first for a change.

"I'm sorry Sod-Thistle, but I've had second thoughts about the whole thing."

"It's *Sow-Thistle*," he said, hatefully.

"Well, whatever thistle you are, you can forget your love-drug cocktail conspiracy. I'm not doing it."

I felt the dodgy dossier in my jacket pocket. I'd be delivering that to Sandra, then as far as I was concerned my job was done. Of course, Paris-Blois would soon be back in touch, after their operatives failed to match the photos to any members of House Terroirist, but I'd have made up some other cock-and-bull story by then, along the lines of the conspirators having fled the country and expired in a freak grape harvesting accident.

Lily raised her eyebrows and the other two *Malherbes* glowered at me. Then waxy-faced Sow-Thistle spoke again.

"That Little Chalfont wine you created with Hawkins. The World's Greatest Pinot, as the idiotic media have christened it. How do you think it will look when the news gets out it's your wine? The winning wine of The Judgement of Basildon, at which *you* were a judge."

My buttocks clenched, involuntarily. So, Lily *had* blabbed the story. I looked at her but she just smiled, defiantly. "Why would you do that?" I said, holding her eye. "Lily's up to her neck in this too." But the shameless hussy just glared back, without the slightest hint of remorse.

"Worse still," continued Sow-Thistle, "straight after the results, the wine supplier, poor Tom Hawkins, was murdered. A murder witnessed by *you*. How peculiar."

"I bet you didn't tell the police about your connection with Hawkins and the Little Chalfont wine, did you?" said Cranesbill, nodding like an excited fowl.

I drained my Beaujolais, which, despite being rather splendid, failed to improve my spirits.

"I didn't think so," smirked Sow-Thistle. "Would have made the whole situation a little complicated, wouldn't it?"

"I don't understand," I said, my dismay turning to mild panic. "You do all realise Lily here is heavily involved? And that she was hardly an unwilling participant. She'll be in trouble with Lord Flashman, possibly worse."

"You forced me into it, Felix, don't pretend you didn't," said Lily, giving me a big wink. "Who are they going to believe, a defenceless girl like me, or a horrible supermarket buyer like you?"

What a cow. Disgraceful, pitiless trollop that she was, though, I had to admire the way she'd played this one. Lily was a class act and no mistake.

"The thing is," she continued, "I'm committed to our cause and willing to make sacrifices, unlike you, you cowardly mercenary. So maybe you should rethink your attitude. Help *Les Malherbes*, Felix, and help me. We're the good guys here, remember?"

"Of course you are," I said, miserably.

"Good," said Cranesbill. "We'll be in touch. You can go now."

I left the Balladeer a far less happy man than when I'd arrived. That cowardly mercenary jibe had hurt. I wandered up the darkened street, wondering why the innocent and trusting always drew the short straw, while the real villains got away with murder.

"Cheer up," said a low voice.

I turned to see a pair of goths, all in black save their unsettlingly white faces, standing arm-in-arm before the gates of Brompton Cemetery.

"Take our picture?" said the female goth, twirling her black parasol, presumably deployed for protection against the bright moon. She extended a lace-gloved hand, in which she held a camera.

For a second I thought it was a trick, that she'd pickpocketed me and was handing back my own camera. I patted my pocket but there it was, alongside the envelope containing my dodgy dossier. And then, in a flash, I realised what I had to do. I couldn't believe I hadn't thought of it earlier. Clearly, my brain had become fogged by the past two days' barrage of blackmail and double-crossing.

"No problem," I said. "Smile!" They didn't, of course. I clicked and returned the camera, and the two of them peered at the screen. Whether they liked my photograph or not, I have no idea, for I was already striding back up the street towards the Balladeer.

I crossed the road and ducked into a restaurant just opposite the pub. It was perfect, barely a quarter full, with plenty of free tables at the front, overlooking the street. I installed myself, then placed my camera on the windowsill, zooming in and out on the

Balladeer's doorway a couple of times. I was all set. I ordered a bottle of Malbec, a rare steak and an extra side of chips.

Two hours later, the steak was a distant memory and there was no sign of Lily and the double-crossing *Malherbes*. I wondered if I'd missed them. Perhaps they'd left straight after me, or used the rear exit through the beer garden. I'd finished the wine and a second plate of chips and was considering phoning the Balladeer to ask if they were still in the back. But then the pub door opened and there, framed in the doorway, was Lily. I powered up the camera, zoomed in and took half a dozen shots, the camera nice and steady on the windowsill. She stepped on to the street and Sow-Thistle and Cranesbill emerged right behind her. I kept clicking as they hailed a taxi, not stopping until the vehicle had nosed its way into the evening traffic and disappeared up the street.

Threaten Felix Hart, would you, my weedy friends? It was time for a new dossier.

Chapter Nineteen

Revelations

Friday arrived and I headed to the Brixton Grand for Paris-Blois's Cognac launch party, the real *Malherbes* dossier tucked in my jacket pocket. I passed my invitation under the nose of the gigantic doorman and was waved past the velvet rope, running a gauntlet of young women proffering trays of Sazeracs. After a couple of sharpeners, I drifted around the dancefloor, mixing seamlessly with the beautiful people and keeping an eye out for Sandra.

I patted the dossier once more. What had Lily said? That she was committed to her cause and willing to make sacrifices, unlike me? Well, we'll see who's willing to make sacrifices. With a bit of luck, Paris-Blois would quickly track down my *Malherbes* and put the frighteners on them, then I'd be free of at least one set of blackmailing lunatics and back on a more even keel with Sandra. Maybe Boulle would have them drowned in a butt of Malmsey.

My phone buzzed. It was Lily.

Be careful tonight. X

How nice of her. I tapped out a reply.

Don't worry. Taking care of business.

The hip-hop quietened and the DJ piped up.

"Ladies and gentlemen, boys and girls!"

The crowd whooped and waved their cocktails.

"A few words from our host and brand ambassador for Bâtisse Cognac, the very lovely Lady Redoutable!"

Lady Redoutable strutted on to the stage, firm of thigh, her gigantic hooped earrings bouncing, and whipped the crowd into a frenzy of gratitude for the generosity of Paris-Blois.

"Check out the all new French Connection, you fine, fine people!" she called, as an army of servers marched through the crowd, distributing more cocktails.

"You have something for me?" said Sandra, slipping her arm around my waist. She was accompanied by a brooding male model, who nodded to the music and avoided meeting my eye. Clearly, my position as favoured escort had expired in the wake of my incompetence at the Judgement of Basildon.

"Here," I said, removing the envelope from my jacket. I cast my eyes over Sandra's figure-hugging dress and wondered where she intended to tuck the dossier.

"Just give it to James," she said. The model took the envelope without looking at me.

"Now, y'all gonna drink sensibly, yo?" called Lady Redoutable. The happy crowd made clear they wouldn't be. "That's why I love you, Brixton!" she sang back.

"Come and join us in the VIP area." I followed Sandra and her partner into a moodily lit lounge. Low tables and deep leather armchairs surrounded a small dancefloor.

"I'm glad we're working together properly again, Felix. Let's keep it that way, shall we?" Sandra ran her hand over my chest and winked, which had me flushing all over like a giant squid.

"Now, please excuse me, I need to join Pierre and take care of our media friends. Feel free to enjoy yourself. Within reason, of course." She sashayed across the dancefloor to a curved banquette, where Boulle was courting members of the drinks press.

"Sazerac, sir?" A waiter proffered a tray of tumblers, each holding a potent-looking measure of spirit garnished with lemon peel.

"Thanks," I said.

"Maybe you'd like a couple more, for your friends," said the waiter. He raised his eyebrows.

"Oh. Right," I said, my mood souring as I remembered my mission. I wondered whether I'd already drunk some of the

Malherbes' adulterated cocktails. A potent inhibition-loosener, Lily had said. What kind of loosener? I lifted two more glasses. The waiter melted into the background and I crept towards the media table, heading for Sandra.

"Felix! Are you joining us? Come and sit here!"

It was Justin Carter, news editor of *Drinks Digest*, the glossy trade magazine. Carter waved me over.

"I was just bringing Sandra a drink," I explained, lamely.

"I bet you were! Never mind that, I'll have it. I'm sure the UK sales director of Paris-Blois can manage to procure her own drinks tonight!"

The rest of the table watched us – Sandra neutrally, Boulle hatefully – as I joined Carter at the far end of the table.

"Lovely, thank you!" said Carter, grabbing one of my glasses and downing it in one. My phone buzzed. A message from Lily.

You're being set up. Stay near exit.

"Naughty!" declared Carter. I jumped, thinking he meant me, but he was wagging his finger at Boulle, who smiled, thinly. "Too much absinthe for a school night, I think!"

My heart quickened. What did Lily mean? And why was she helping me? Was someone watching? I wondered if they'd seen me pass the envelope to Sandra's assistant.

"These youngsters, always looking at their phones!" said Carter. "Felix, it's good to see you. I trust you've recovered from your awful episode in the cellar of the Flag and Parrot?"

"Yes, thank you. It was quite traumatic."

"I bet. But how serendipitous that we meet today!"

"Is it?" I said, not liking the sound of that at all. Boulle glared at me. I gave a little shrug and sniffed my cocktail. I wondered how the hell I was going to persuade him to drink one.

"Of course it is! You were a taster at the legendary Judgement of Basildon. And here we are, in the company of Paris-Blois, owner of Domaine Henri-Leroy." Carter leaned forward, mock-conspiratorially, and lowered his voice. "Which, as we all know, came a bit of a cropper that day!"

Shut up, for God's sake, I thought. I glanced around, just in case I really did need an escape route. I spotted a fire exit behind the bar.

Boulle stood and held up his hand. "I'm sorry, Justin. We've invited you tonight to enjoy the new expression of Bâtisse Cognac, not to discuss Burgundy. Mr Hart, thank you but we don't require you here."

"Fine by me," I said, turning on my heel.

"No, but I *insist*," said Carter, grabbing my sleeve. "What did you think of the winning wine, Felix? The World's Greatest Pinot! I believe you're quite familiar with the *terroir*?"

A chill stabbed through my chest, like an iced dagger.

"I… am I?" I mumbled.

"Can we talk about the Cognac, please?" said Boulle, louder now.

"I believe you are, Felix, yes," continued Carter. "The winning wine, an *English* wine of all things, was made from Buckinghamshire grapes, was it not?"

"Yes, so they say," I said.

Sandra now rose to her feet. "Justin, can we talk about this later, please? It's a little bit rude in front of our Cognac friends. And I don't think your colleagues are terribly interested in last month's news."

"Actually, I'm quite interested," called one of the other journalists. "Carry on, Justin."

"I believe the vineyard is located in Little Chalfont. Did you know that, Felix?" said Carter.

"I… didn't really, no."

"It's very simple when you think about it. The wine's name is *Clos de la Petite Source Craie*. Anyone speak French here?"

"*La Petite Source Craie*… little chalk spring?" said another journalist.

"Exactly! And Chalfont means 'chalk spring' in Old English. Little Chalfont! Clever, eh?"

A murmur of agreement hummed around the table. Carter turned back to me.

"You live near Little Chalfont, don't you?"

My sweat turned to frost.

"No. Well, yes. Not much though, these days."

The whole table was watching me now. I glanced at Sandra, whose eyes had narrowed.

"Yes, I thought so. They've identified the location of the vineyard. It's a tiny little communal garden, surrounded by flats, next to a council car park, of all things! I visited there yesterday, had a chat to the neighbours. Funny little place, quite remarkable. Who'd have thought a site like that could produce such exquisite fruit?"

"Ah... argh," I replied.

"Little Chalfont's a *very* small place. You must know where I mean. It's round the back of a branch of Charlie's Cellar."

Boulle was glaring at me, his fists balled, knuckles white. I kept my face in my tumbler of cocktail, not daring to look at Sandra.

"Good Lord!" said another of the journalists. "That's a hell of a scoop you've got there, Justin. We've been trying to find the source of the World's Greatest Pinot ever since the Judgement of Basildon. We thought the secret was buried with poor old Tom Hawkins."

"I have my sources," said Carter, smugly. "I had a bit of luck, actually. I was in Wagga Wagga last week, researching a piece on the Australian vintage. And guess who I bumped into at a winery there? Only Hawkins's old winemaker! He'd heard about the Judgement of Basildon, of course, and knew a wine supplied by Hawkins had won, but hadn't made the connection with a micro-fermentation he'd done a couple of years previously at the Flag and Parrot. You can read all the details in tomorrow's online edition of *Drinks Digest*."

Two of the journalists were already on their phones. I felt my presence was no longer strictly necessary and began to take slow steps backwards.

"Stay there, Felix. We need to talk," ordered Sandra, pointing at me.

That was my cue to flee. I suspected Paris-Blois would be more rigorous next time they tried to kill me. They'd probably tie Lily and me together and drown us in the same barrel. The photographs! I looked frantically for Sandra's manservant. There he was, next to the bar. I strode over.

"I'm going to need that envelope back, I'm afraid." Where was it? Had to be inside his jacket.

The man looked at me, a sneer on his buffed, moisturised face. "I'm sorry, who the hell *are* you?"

"I'm a Minstrel in peril!" I shouted, and thrust my hand into the man's jacket. I felt the envelope against my fingers, but before I could withdraw it he grabbed my wrist.

"What are you doing, you *freak*?"

"Hold him!" shouted Boulle. The man tightened his grip and two large bouncers, who'd been guarding the entrance to the lounge, trotted across the dance floor towards us.

I judged I had about five seconds before they reached me. I looked around, wildly, for a weapon but there were no bottles within reach, just an ice-filled Champagne bucket. With my free hand, I lifted it and hurled the contents across the dance floor, towards the approaching doormen. Then I drove the upturned bucket down hard on my opponent's head, giving it an extra thump with my fist. He released my wrist and clutched his silver helmet with both hands, screaming blue murder. I tore the envelope free and vaulted the bar, just as the bouncers, arms wheeling, came sliding towards me.

I landed awkwardly, grabbing the edge of the bar so as not to lose my balance. I was in a half-crouch, my eyes just above the counter top, facing back towards my hosts. Boulle was on his feet, staring at me, face like thunder. He held my gaze and raised his hand, palm down, then made a cutting movement across his throat. I turned, barged open the fire exit and ran for my life.

I considered catching a cab to Heathrow and taking the first flight to Tashkent. But I kept thinking of Lily and that she might be in more danger than she knew. It suddenly struck me that if there was any fleeing to be done, I wanted to be doing it with Lily or not at all. And it was in this moment of astonishing selflessness that my mind cleared and I chose my destiny.

I flagged down a taxi and dived inside. "Brompton Balladeer, fast as you can please." As the driver pulled away, I called Little Chalfont.

"Wodin! Has anyone been sniffing around, asking questions about the vine?"

"Yeah, how did you know? A wine journalist dropped by a couple of days ago. Really nice guy. He knew all about the wine we made with that old guy who got murdered."

"Oh God! What did you say?"

"He just asked where you were and how we went about making the wine. Fistule told him about the harvest and driving the grapes into London. He thought it was a great story. He took some photos too. That's not a problem, is it?"

"Yes, probably. Why didn't you tell me?"

"I was going to, but you've been hanging out with your new girlfriend. I wanted to give you some space."

"Did he ask about Tom Hawkins?"

"Not really. We just all agreed it was bad he got murdered."

"Look, if anyone else turns up asking questions, say I've moved away. Say I've gone abroad or that I'm dead or something."

"Ok, man."

The taxi pulled up outside the Balladeer and I rushed through to the back room. As I burst in, Cranesbill and Sow-Thistle leapt to their feet. Lily remained seated, glass in hand, but her eyes widened.

"What the hell are you doing here?" shouted Cranesbill, nodding angrily.

"Frankly, *Malherbes*, I feel there's a trust deficit in this relationship," I said. "I was executing your plan, exactly as instructed, only to find you've double-crossed me, quite horribly."

"Yes... well," said Sow-Thistle, "the spiked cocktail story was a little work of fiction, as you probably realise. We just needed to get you next to those Paris-Blois executives in time for the big reveal."

"Blowing open the Judgement of Basildon conspiracy is too good an opportunity to miss," said Cranesbill.

"It's unfortunate that you're at the centre of it, but it's far more important to land a blow on Paris-Blois," said Sow-Thistle. "Our friend Carter will publish his story tomorrow, linking Hawkins's winning wine with Little Chalfont. Then we'll inform him of your own relationship with the vine and point out how strange it is that the grapes that produced the winning wine were grown in the garden of a house inhabited by one of the judges."

"I'm sorry you've been dragged in, Felix," said Lily, "but Cranesbill is right. We won't get another chance like this."

I looked at her. Did the others know about her texts? That she'd warned me? Her face was neutral, giving nothing away.

"Obviously, the story's going to look very fishy," continued Sow-Thistle. "But the fact that Hawkins was murdered straight after the Judgement of Basildon, and the fact that you were present at the time of the murder, takes it into another league of suspiciousness."

I was feeling rather dry-mouthed. I wished there was some decent wine on hand.

"I suspect the police will want another chat with you," said Sow-Thistle. "They'll probably want to understand how you, as a supposedly neutral judge representing Paris-Blois, are in fact the co-creator of the winning wine. And they'll probably be interested in your thoughts on why the only person connecting you with the wine, namely Tom Hawkins, was murdered, with you present at the scene of the crime."

Sow-Thistle smirked. *What a self-satisfied prig*, I thought.

"My advice is to confess to the entire Paris-Blois conspiracy. The blackmailing of Percy Woods. The bribing of the judges. And, of course, your attempt to force Lily into your nasty little scheme."

"If you don't confess, we'll be tipping off the police ourselves," said Cranesbill.

In the olden days, I reflected, this would be the moment to draw one's sword and deal bloody murder to one's tormentors.

But it wasn't the olden days and I was out of swords. It was clear, however, that I needed to flee the country and give myself as many days head start as possible.

"Is it too much to ask Carter to hold off on exposing me, just for a week? I need to put my affairs in order before I'm arrested."

"What sort of affairs?" said Sow-Thistle, oily lips curling.

"Payments to my sick infant son," I said, with exquisite inspiration. Lily rolled her eyes, but discreetly.

"Oh," said Sow-Thistle, "I didn't know."

"Not many people do," I said, quietly. "His mother, my ex-girlfriend, looks after him, but they rely on my money for the treatment. I need a few days to get some funds together. When I lose my job, the income will dry up, then…" I tailed off.

"Our operative in the Brixton Grand did say he tried to deliver the cocktail to Paris-Blois's management," said Lily, "so I suppose he's shown a *degree* of loyalty." I could tell she didn't believe me in the slightest.

"All right," said Sow-Thistle, "we'll delay revealing your connection with Little Chalfont for a week. The discovery of the vine's location is enough of a scoop for now."

"I appreciate your kindness." *And I'll have an Oscar for best actor in a bloody fiasco while you're at it*, I thought. "I'll be staying in a Balladeer guestroom tonight. I'd like to remain out of sight of any Paris-Blois employees for the foreseeable future. Goodnight." I lifted the tasty-looking bottle of Burgundy from the table and headed upstairs.

I was lying on the bed, watching the television in my shirt and boxers, the bottle three glasses down, when my phone buzzed. A text from Lily.

Hope the door's unlocked?

I didn't want to appear too keen, so I left the message unanswered, though I muted the television and quietly unbolted the door. I also moved a sturdy chair next to my bed, ready for protection against any knife-wielding *Malherbes* who might fancy a little late-night filleting. I emptied the rest of the wine into my glass and sat on top of the bedcovers, keeping the bottle handy in case a rapid counter-attack was required.

There was a barely perceptible tap and the door opened. Lily slipped inside and bolted it behind her.

"Not bringing your friends?" I said.

"They don't know I'm here. And I don't want them to know."

"So, how can I help?"

She didn't reply at first, just leaned against the locked door and stared at me.

"What was in the envelope?"

"I don't know what–"

"The waiter at the Brixton Grand was working for us. He told me you gave an envelope to a Paris-Blois employee. Later, you assaulted him and snatched it back."

"Take a look yourself." I nodded to the chair. "It's in my jacket."

Lily withdrew the envelope and tore it open. She looked through the photos of her, Cranesbill and Sow-Thistle emerging from the pub, then placed them on the desk.

"I suppose, if you hadn't retrieved them, we'd be going the same way as Tom Hawkins?"

"Quite possibly. Which would be a shame."

Lily was silent for a while. When she next spoke it was a near-whisper. "Cranesbill and Sow-Thistle think this is a big game, all these dodgy wine tastings and public relations battles. But I'm not sure it's a game at all. I think you're in a lot of trouble with Paris Blois. Aren't you?"

"Is that why you sent those text messages tonight, warning me?"

"Are you in danger?"

"Quite possibly. Last time I encountered a female *Malherbe* in a locked room, she pulled a knife on me."

Lily didn't break eye contact. She unbuttoned her shirt and shrugged it off, then peeled off her trousers, then her underwear. "Unarmed," she declared, hands on hips. "Now, your turn."

I complied. She pushed me aside and slipped under the bedclothes.

An hour or so later, she leant across me and lifted my glass from the bedside table.

"I'm sorry about the trouble we've caused you," she said. "What are you going to do? Leave the country?"

"I'm working on it," I said. "And I can't see Lord Flashman continuing to employ you when this story gets out, even if you claim I forced you into it. So, if we're playing the blame game, it's my fault for dragging you into it in the first place, back in Vougeot."

"No, it's not," said Lily. "I knew about Paris-Blois's efforts to hijack The Judgement of Basildon before you did. When silly Percy at Le Grain d'Or realised he was being blackmailed by Paris-Blois, he told his boyfriend. Their relationship's a secret, hardly anyone knows. But his boyfriend's a Minstrel of Wine. A member of House Terroirist."

"Why didn't you tell me?"

"Because that wasn't the plan." Lily took a mouthful of wine.

"The plan?" Yet again, I was starting to feel like I'd not been invited to the after-show party.

"Yes, Percy's boyfriend informed *Les Malherbes* and they approached *me* to help derail Paris-Blois's conspiracy."

"You knew everything? I don't believe you. How did Percy communicate the decanter number to the Paris-Blois operative then? You know they attached the number to a dart and shot it into my buttock?"

Lily nearly spat her wine across the bed.

"Oh, my poor darling!" she said, once she'd swallowed. She slipped her hand under the small of my back. "Where's the scar?"

"It's healed now, just about. Tell me how they passed on the decanter number."

"I don't know the details. Percy told us that one evening, a few days before the Judgement of Basildon, he was ordered to allow a Paris-Blois operative into the cellar of Le Grain d'Or. The man rewired one of the light switches. Percy was instructed to use it like a Morse code button on the day of the tasting, once he was alone in the cellar, to transmit the Henri-Leroy decanter number."

"Cunning," I said. "A rewired light switch wouldn't have shown up when the Inspector scanned the room for radio transmitters. The wire must have run up to ground level, where another Paris-Blois operative was waiting for a bulb to flash, or a buzzer to sound."

"Yes, I'm sure you're right."

"And then, as the chest of decanters trundled down the road on the back of Walsham's carriage, he would have called my blowpipe-wielding friend hiding in the undergrowth and told him the number."

"If they'd spent as much time on their wine quality as they did corrupting the Judgement of Basildon," said Lily, "they could have saved themselves a lot of trouble."

"Indeed." I tugged the glass from Lily's hand and took a mouthful. "So, after Percy's confession reached the *Malherbes,* they approached you. What did they ask you to do?"

"To hook up with you, Felix. At the tasting in Burgundy."

"What? I approached *you*. Paris-Blois ordered *me* to target *you*! They gave me your picture at a briefing in Champagne, last year."

"No Feel, you just think you did. The *Malherbes* weren't sure, initially, how Paris-Blois would approach me. We guessed they had stolen the plans for the Judgement of Basildon and we knew the double-blind process meant they'd have to compromise both ends of the tasting. Apart from Lord Flashman, I was the only person who'd be handling both sets of decanters. So, at some point, someone working for Paris-Blois would have to approach me. I was asked to play along."

"I'm surprised they didn't try the same trick Percy fell for," I said.

"They did, actually. I started getting invitations from Paris-Blois for all sorts of glamorous trips. A weekend tasting First Growth Bordeaux in Monte Carlo. Then a study trip to the Napa Valley, another to Tuscany. I turned them all down."

"You accepted the trip to Burgundy."

"Yes. I couldn't resist that one. It was an official event, at least, not a complete jolly. The *Malherbes* agreed I should go. We wanted to see how Paris-Blois would approach me. I assumed some salesman would creep up and try to bribe me in exchange for some orders. When I arrived at the Vougeot château, I checked the guest list and saw your name."

"And you already knew the names of the participants in the Judgement of Basildon."

"Yes, too much of a coincidence." Lily smiled. "So, there we both were. Under orders to meet. Romantic, isn't it?"

"Positively idyllic."

"Never mind. I'm flattered they sent a *real* Minstrel of Wine to seduce me, anyway."

"But you *Malherbes* had your own person in the Judgement of Basildon, that Jean-Pierre fellow. Why did you carry on seeing me? Stringing me along with the Little Chalfont wine, pretending to help with the conspiracy."

"Yes, once we had Jean-Pierre on board, Cranesbill and Sow-Thistle told me to drop you. But I was having fun. Just like I am now."

"I'm glad someone is."

Lily punched my arm. "Give me the rest of that wine."

We didn't sleep much. Well before sunrise, the sky still dark-grey, Lily slid out of bed, pulled on her clothes and kissed me.

"I'm sorry Felix. Take care. And good luck."

As I dozed, I dreamt of her voice, first calm, then passionate, like that first night in Vougeot when she condemned Paris-Blois for spraying poison over the vineyards. Then her tone changed, dropping to a cold fury. I woke, completely alert, my sleep vanishing like snow under scalding water. But the only sounds were the creaking of the Balladeer herself and the whisper of the wind around the gravestones of Brompton Cemetery.

Chapter Twenty

The War on Terroir

My escape plan was to volunteer as a deck-hand on a yacht heading to the Caribbean, grow a beard en route, and apply for a groundsman's job at a minor Trinidadian cricket club. As I worked out the details, I hunkered down in Minstrels Hall, judging it far safer than Little Chalfont, which I imagined was already under surveillance by scowling men wearing black leather gloves and comparing neck-breaking techniques. Minstrels Hall's security was pretty tight, with bearded staff-bearers guarding all entrances and patrolling the corridors. And, to the uninitiated, the place was a gigantic maze, making it mightily difficult for mafia assassins to track down someone as hell-bent on concealment as I was.

I phoned the Gatesave office, explaining I'd caught a horrific stomach bug from a plate of poorly cured ham, and booked myself into one of the ninth-floor bedrooms reserved for out-of-town Minstrels, in the farthest extremity of House Terroirist. I spent a sleepless night wondering if every clank of the plumbing was an assassin outside the door, rummaging through his murder-bag of lead piping.

In the morning, I fired up my laptop and loaded the *Drinks Digest* website. Sure enough, there was Carter's exclusive, describing the exact location of my vineyard, complete with pictures of Wodin and Fistule next to the vine, grinning like a pair of half-sharp Languedoc peasants. But the *Malherbes* had kept their word. There was no mention, thank God, of yours truly. Presumably, that would be next week's scoop, followed, if I hadn't made my escape, by my arrest, humiliation and inevitable murder.

I phoned Wodin to warn him of his newfound drinks industry fame.

"Wodin's phone, man."

"Fistule! Where's Wodin?"

"He's out scoring, man. He takes his other phone when he's working."

"Listen, there's a picture of you and Wodin with our Little Chalfont vine on the *Drinks Digest* website. You might receive some enquires."

"Oh wow, that's really cool. The vine's famous, man."

"Yes, but *I* don't want to be famous. If anyone asks, say you've never heard of me, ok?"

"Yeah, Wodin said you were uptight about something." The sound of a bubbling bong warbled down the phone, followed by a long, satisfied exhalation.

"I *am* very uptight about something, Fistule. This is important–"

"There's someone outside!"

"What? Who is it? Don't answer it!"

I heard a noise, very much like a front door opening.

"Helloooo. Who are yoooo?" said Fistule.

"You've never heard of me, Fistule, remember!" I shouted into the phone.

"Good morning. Is Mr Hart here?" said a man's voice.

"Mr Hart..." murmured Fistule.

"Is no longer here!" I screamed.

"Is... no longer... alive," said Fistule, finally.

"Not alive?" said the man.

"Long gone. Long dead. Completely... unknown," said Fistule.

"Oh dear, I am sorry. I'm Doctor Rose from the Chorleywood Wine Society, I live just down the road. Mr Hart did a wine tasting for us last year. I've just been reading about the vine in your garden. Do you mind if I take a look?"

"Oh, yeah. Go ahead, man. It's famous."

"Yes, so it would appear, Mr...?"

"Fistule."

216

"Mr Fistule. Yes, this is *quite* an oddity. Did you know Tom Hawkins?"

"Do I know Tom Hawkins…? Felix?"

I suddenly realised Fistule was addressing me. I hung up.

The Chorleywood Wine Society was a relatively benign organisation. But next time, no doubt, it would be the *Little Chalfont Gazette*, followed by the *Daily Telegraph*, *Le Monde* and the *New York Times*. And then, finally, in all its glory, the story would find itself principal feature in that most august publication, the Weekly Digest of the Holy Brotherhood of Calabrian Throat Slitters.

I pushed my imminent murder to the back of my mind and spent the day working on my escape plan. By the time evening arrived, I was thirsty. I decided to risk a couple of glasses at the Salon de Dijon. The little bar was busy, but I found a gap at the far end, next to the wall, and perched on a stool.

"Burgundy or Jura?" called the barman.

"I'll have the Volnay," I said. The man placed a glass before me and sloshed in a generous measure of Burgundy. I took a sip and relaxed. Cherries and sweet perfume, I mused. Perhaps I could live as a goat herder in the Jura Mountains, dropping into town occasionally, heavily disguised, to restock my shepherd's hovel with fine wine.

"Amazing how excited everybody gets over Pinot," said a voice.

"Indeed," I said, without looking.

"I prefer Sangiovese myself."

It was an Italian voice. I turned, quickly. A short, neat man with a moustache. He leaned against the bar, swirling the last inch of red around his glass, then gave the wine a long sniff.

"Yes, well, everything has its place," I said.

"It does. The place for Pinot is Burgundy. The place for Sangiovese is Tuscany." He took a sip. "And the place for the dead is a cemetery."

I froze and my bowels did a somersault. But the bar was busy. Surely he wouldn't pull out a pistol and shoot me right here?

"Wouldn't you say?" He stared at me.

"Yes…" I whispered.

I wanted to flee, but I was trapped in the corner. Perhaps that was his plan, to panic me and send me rushing out of Minstrels Hall, into the street, where his knife-wielding accomplices would finish the job.

"You agree. Good. Saint or sinner, all deserve a proper burial."

"It was an accident," I said, feeling rather wobbly.

The man shrugged. "I'm not here to judge."

What was he here for then? To commit grisly, bloody murder upon my innocent, defenceless body, from the sound of it.

He took another sip. "I'm here to give advice."

"Oh?" I squeaked.

"London has some wonderful cemeteries. Hampstead. Kensal Green. My favourite is Brompton. It would be wonderful to be buried there, I think."

"I… suppose." My guts were gurgling with horror. I spotted a couple of familiar faces at the bar. Would anyone come to my aid if I screamed murder?

"Yes, Brompton Cemetery. You know it, I think." The man finished his wine and took a step closer. I shrank back, trying to slip off the barstool, but I was already pressed hard against the wall. He moved his hand to his pocket and I whimpered, expecting a blade to flash out and plunge itself into my stomach. Instead, he produced a business card and placed it on the bar.

"See those men receive a proper burial, Minstrel Hart, and redeem yourself. That is my advice. But do it quickly."

He turned and disappeared into the crowd. I looked around, wildly, expecting someone to leap out and embed an axe in my head. But none of the other patrons looked like Mafiosi. My eyes dropped to the business card. *Poletti & Sons, Funeral Directors, Brompton.*

With an unsteady hand, I gulped down my wine. I pocketed the card and scurried back to my room.

***

I slept badly, dreaming of small, neatly moustachioed men with knives between their teeth, creeping through my bedroom window. I spent the next day in my room with a chair against the door, ordering meals from room service and researching jobs at Botswanan game reserves.

The heavy knock, wood against wood, made me jump out of my skin. Peering through the spy-hole, I was relieved to see a staff-wielding guard rather than a garrotte-wielding assassin, but I kept the door bolted.

"I'm just getting changed. Can I help?"

"A message from House Mercantilist. You're invited to dinner at the Salon de Bordeaux. Eight o'clock."

House Mercantilist. The mercenary House, the one that counted Paris-Blois agents among its membership. And at the Salon de Bordeaux too, the only part of the building where Minstrels were permitted to entertain guests. A trap, surely?

"I'm a bit busy, sorry."

But the guard had gone. Did this mean Paris-Blois knew my room number? Probably. They wouldn't dare attack me in Minstrels Hall, would they? That would be very bad form. No, Sandra wanted to send me a message. She was hardly likely to send me a text or email, now that her company was arranging my murder. Well, knowledge is power, I mused, and I was probably better off knowing what they had to say than cowering, silently, in my room. Having said that, silent cowering did have its appeal. But no, I'd head down early, to wrest back the initiative.

At half-past seven, I checked the spy-hole then opened the door a crack, keeping my foot against it and my leg braced, in case a crazed brigand was waiting to charge through and hurl himself upon me. But the corridor was deserted. I crept out and, via a series of back passages, made my way to the Salon de Bordeaux.

"Good evening, Minstrel Hart," said the *maître d'hôtel*. "Your colleague is already here."

So much for initiative, I thought. The *maître d'hôtel* led me across the restaurant to a corner table. A man rose and shook my hand. He was tall and silver-haired, typical House Mercantilist in his immaculate suit and polished shoes.

"Minstrel Hart, I am Minstrel Delacourt. Nice to make your acquaintance and thank you for finding the time to meet me. I trust I haven't disturbed your plans?"

"No problem at all. I had a gap in my schedule."

"Good. I ordered the Château Nenin, 1990. You're a fan of Right Bank claret, I trust?"

"Who isn't?" If there was a silver lining to my predicament, at least I was being hunted down by a better class of assassin.

The man poured me a glass and raised his own. "Sandra sends her regards."

It suddenly occurred to me the wine might be poisoned. I clinked my glass against his and brought it to my mouth slowly, taking care not to let the wine touch my lips. The aroma was superb, voluptuous blackberry fruit and spicy cigar box, and I began to salivate. The man took a mouthful and swallowed. *Oh well,* I thought, *I'll probably be dead soon, one way or another.* I did the same.

"Sandra wishes to convey her disappointment at the direction your mutual relationship has taken," said Delacourt.

"Yes, well, we've had our ups and downs. And we're somewhat at the bottom of the current cycle."

"I fear this may be the end of the cycle, Minstrel Hart. I've been instructed to convey the news that your relationship with Paris-Blois is due to come to an end."

That sounded ominously, chillingly final.

"What does that mean for me?"

"I'm not party to your commercial arrangement with Paris-Blois, I'm afraid. But I understand the termination clause is to be invoked next Monday, on the personal instruction of the European Sales Director. Sandra wanted to be very clear on that."

The European Sales Director. That would be Boulle, the sadistic sod. A termination clause, indeed. I wondered whether my claret-sipping friend had any idea what he was talking about.

Monday, though. Five days from now. Why the warning? Was this part of the plan, to toy with me first?

"Sandra does, however, regret the situation," he said, frowning slightly as I refilled my glass to the brim.

"Well, that's nice to know."

"Sandra expressed her hope you might find a way to dig yourself out of your contractual difficulties."

What was that, some sort of sick joke? I took a long, assertive mouthful of wine.

"I'll leave you to enjoy the rest of the Nenin, Minstrel Hart. Compliments of Paris-Blois." Delacourt rose and offered his hand. I shook it but didn't bother standing.

"I'm afraid the table's only booked until quarter past. You'll have to finish that at the bar." He paused for a second. "Remember, you have until Monday." Delacourt nodded, once, and disappeared. I sighed and finished my glass.

"Can I help, sir?" said a waiter, appearing from nowhere. Before I could karate-chop his hand, he swept the bottle from the table. "There are a few spare seats at the bar, sir. Where would you prefer to sit?"

I considered taking the wine back to my room and finishing it alone, but the thought depressed me and I suspected I was safer in public. The Salon de Bordeaux's bar ran the length of the restaurant and, as the waiter had said, there were several vacant seats. I recognised a pair of wine importers from Gascony at one end, chatting animatedly. Further along, a crowd of elderly merchants chortled together in a cloud of cigar smoke. But I didn't want to sit near anyone I knew or, in my current mood, anyone having too much fun. There were a couple of free seats at the far end, the only nearby patron a small, innocuous-looking chap staring down at some papers.

"Put me over there, please."

The waiter strode off, leaving me to trot after him idiotically with my empty glass. He placed the wine at the end of the bar and wafted away. I pulled up a stool and refortified myself.

"Exquisite taste there, Minstrel Hart," said a voice. My heart sank. The small, innocuous man grinned at me from the next stool down. He pointed at the bottle. "Fabulous stuff."

If I'd been in any normal restaurant I'd have told him to get knotted, but there is a convention at Minstrels Hall that one should never ignore another Minstrel's gentle hint.

"My pleasure," I lied, half-filling his empty glass.

"*Most* generous, thank you!"

It occurred to me that the man knew my name.

"My apologies," said the man. "I'm Minstrel Balic. We haven't met; I only know you by reputation."

"All dreadful, I'm sure." I hoped the man wouldn't keep talking to me.

"Oh, ha ha. No, all good. I lease agricultural machinery to the viticulture and forestry industries, actually." He grinned again. I prayed he was waiting for someone who would arrive extremely soon and lead him away for a vigorous discussion on combine harvesters.

I gave a sympathetic smile and stared at my claret.

"I was wondering if you might introduce me to some of your wine suppliers," he said. "I have a great business opportunity for them."

"Machinery isn't really my area of expertise."

"Oh, I understand."

I desperately hoped he did.

"We've just signed up a fantastic Dutch company, actually. They make the most incredible machines." It was clear he hadn't understood at all. "I have a brochure."

"Please, this really isn't the best time. I'm waiting for someone." *Waiting for the sweet embrace of death*, I thought, miserably.

"Here we go," said the man, pushing a laminated sheet towards me. "It's called a Truck Spade. Brand new. Ever heard of them?"

"I can't say I have." I continued to stare into my wine.

"Quite incredible machines." The man tapped on his laminated sheet several dozen times, until he'd forced me to look. There was a picture of a huge dump truck, the type of thing you'd see removing rubble from a building site. But instead of a hopper it carried an enormous claw, big enough to enclose an elephant.

"They use them in the States, in tree nurseries." He turned over the sheet and pointed. "Look."

I poured another glass and followed his finger. Sure enough, there was the truck, this time deploying its huge claw on the end of a hydraulic arm, next to an unsuspecting tree.

"You see, the claw is hinged and fits around the base of an adult tree, like so. Then, the hydraulic spade sections sink into the earth, a little at a time, around the roots. The peripheral roots are severed, but the main root ball is unharmed. Finally, when the spade sections have met under the tree, they lift the entire thing, root ball and all, from the ground. You can pick up an adult tree, drive it one hundred miles and replant it, unharmed!"

He tapped on another picture, showing the surprised-looking tree, now on its side on the back of the truck, its roots and tons of earth safely clasped within the spade-claw's jaws. Where there had once been a tree, minding its own business, there was now a perfectly smooth, cone-shaped hole, big enough for a family of bears to enjoy a Jacuzzi.

"I also lease machine harvesters to the wine industry. So, when I saw these Truck Spades in action, I thought they might have an application in vineyards. Let's say you have a mature vine but it's in the wrong location, and you want to plant it further up the slope. Impossible to move it conventionally, without doing a lot of damage."

A faint light flickered into life in the back of my mind. I looked more closely at the pictures, showing the pointed segments of the spade-claw slipping into the soil, taking their vast ice-cream scoop out of the earth and lifting the tree free.

"Don't suppose there's any more of that wine going, is there?" The man pushed his glass a couple of inches towards my bottle.

I poured him a full one.

"How big is that spade-claw? How deep does it go?"

"That's the Truck Spade 2000," said the man, proudly. "The largest model. It takes a bite ten feet wide and twelve feet deep. It'll lift a tree with a trunk a foot thick."

"That's very interesting," I said.

"In fact, you wouldn't need one that big for a vine," he continued. "You'd be fine with the Truck Spade 1000."

"No, no," I said. "I want the big one."

"Oh," said the man. "You mean, you already know a vineyard that might need one?"

"Yes. Well, I suspect they might be interested."

"Well, I am glad I bumped into you, Minstrel Hart. Thank you. Here's my card."

"No, thank *you*. I think this calls for another bottle."

***

I woke the next morning and tried to piece things together. The Italian in the Salon de Dijon had scared the willies out of me with his talk of cemeteries, but even in my fevered horror I'd realised he was referring to the corpses buried in my Little Chalfont garden, rather than my own cadaver. Frankly, I thought it was a bit of a cheek expecting me to give them a Christian burial, given that Rizzo and his mafioso friend had been attempting to murder *me* all those years ago. Perhaps they expected me to dig an extra grave and leap into it myself.

And Delacourt, that smooth-talking member of House Mercantilist, who'd shared the bottle of Château Nenin and Sandra's best wishes. He'd suggested my 'termination clause' would be invoked on Monday. Why had Sandra warned me? Unless, of course, they were lulling me into a false sense of security. Maybe they would strike now, when I was least expecting it.

I spent the rest of the day online, researching tour-guide jobs in Oman. By the evening, I'd worked out a plan to join the Bedouin and disappear for a year into the Wahiba Sands. But after hours of staring at dunes and camels, I was feeling thirsty once more and I found myself pining for a glass of something refreshing at the Salon de Dijon.

A couple of quickies will be fine, I thought. I wouldn't let myself be trapped in the corner by any Italians this time. Checking the coast was clear, I darted out of my room and headed to the third floor by way of the kitchens. Five minutes later, I was nursing a generous glass of white Jura.

"Felix!" called a voice from the end of the bar. It was Bertram, a portly wine educator and Burgundy enthusiast. "Haven't seen you for ages!"

"Well, it's been a bit frantic recently, Bertram," I said, relieved to have found a friendly face.

"Bet it has! Oooh, now then, what do you make of this Little Chalfont business?"

I froze.

"What... part of the business?" I said.

"The whole thing!" said Bertram. "The fact that the World's Greatest Pinot has been grown in the garden of a liquor store in a small Buckinghamshire village! The frenzy! The crowds!"

"The crowds?"

"Where have you *been* for the last two days, Felix? These crowds!"

Bertram pushed today's *Times* in front of me. There, at the bottom of the front page, beneath the headline 'Grape Fever', was a photo of my garden, overflowing with visitors wielding cameras and secateurs.

"People are trying to take cuttings. I heard someone even tried to dig it up last night!"

I choked on my wine.

"Luckily, the neighbours heard and chased them off!"

"Thank God for that," I said.

"I was hoping to pay a visit myself but it's bloody carnage, you can't get within a mile of the place during the day. It's virtually a holy site. Apparently, the Napa Valley Pinot Society is planning a pilgrimage next week!"

"That's great," I said, feeling sick. "Excuse me, I just need to make a call."

"Look at them. Animals!" continued Bertram, stabbing at the *Times* with a cocktail stick. They'll end up dismembering the poor thing, trampling it to death."

I hid myself in a corner and phoned Wodin. As he picked up, I could hear the buzz of a crowd in the background.

"There's some outrageous behaviour going on round here, Felix. It's insane!" said Wodin.

"What's happening? I heard someone tried to dig up the vine?"

"Oh yeah, probably some Pinot Noir obsessive, there are lots of them about. Fistule's rigged up CCTV to keep an eye on it during the night."

"Why didn't you tell me the garden was full of sightseers?"

"Didn't want to worry you, man. Fistule said you were stressed out."

"Has anyone been asking questions? Anyone Italian?"

"Everyone's asking questions! They all want to know about the soil type, what we're feeding it, whether there's some crazy rock formation underneath. One guy had a great big soil probe; he wanted to take samples."

"Don't let him!" I shouted.

"Woah, take it easy, man! Don't worry, Fistule won't let anyone hurt the vine. He's out there now with a bamboo cane, whipping anyone who tries to take cuttings. He's very protective."

"Good. Tell him to keep whipping."

"We've got a problem though. The local council aren't happy."

"Why? What's the matter with them?"

"They say it's their land and we're not permitted to grow agricultural crops. They're threatening to spray it with weed killer and dig it up! Fistule's beside himself. There are some hardcore Pinot Noir fans here, though, and they say they'll chain themselves to the vine to stop it happening. It's totally crazy, man!"

"Oh. Oh God," I said. I returned to the bar.

"You look a little pale, Felix," said Bertram.

"Oh… I know someone in Little Chalfont. Apparently, Buckinghamshire Council are threatening to dig up the vine. They say it's unauthorised farming activity on council land."

"What?" said Bertram. "That's outrageous! Felix, we must save that vine. This is a pivotal moment in the history of the English wine trade. I shall go and speak to the Provost of House Archivist immediately. The Institute should dig up the vine themselves. We could replant it here, on one of the balconies."

"No!" I wailed.

"Yes, Felix! This is our vinous patrimony! I must find the Provost now." Bertram jumped off his bar stool and made for the door.

"Oh, hell," I said.

"Another glass, sir?" said the barman.

"Make it a bottle."

Chapter Twenty One

Transplant

"Well, it's very nice to meet you, Mr Spott-Hythe," said Minstrel Balic. He gazed, wide-eyed, at Wodin's sarong, as Wodin grasped his hand and pumped it vigorously.

"Mr Spott-Hythe is my biggest English wine supplier," I said. "He has a vineyard in Kent and is interested in testing your Truck Spade."

Wodin was always up for a little adventure. To help save the vine, he'd agreed to play the part of Mr Spott-Hythe for a meeting with Balic at Gatesave's headquarters. We'd had a bumpy start when it emerged Wodin had interpreted 'business casual' to mean a freshly ironed sarong and tie-dyed shirt, but I'd ushered him through reception into a ground-floor meeting room without challenge from any suspicious senior managers.

"Yes, the estate has been in my family for three generations," said Wodin. "We have a thirty-year-old Pinot Noir vineyard planted near the bottom of a valley. It's a frost risk in spring and suffers from heavy mists in autumn, which gives us rot problems. We want to transplant our vines a hundred yards higher up the slope and your Truck Spade sounds most ingenious."

I had written Wodin a brief script, which he had memorised admirably.

"Well, we'd love to help," beamed Balic. "We can send one of our trucks down to Kent at your convenience. Next week, if you like?"

"How about tomorrow?" said Wodin.

"Oh, goodness. Well, that might be ok. I'll need to check we have a driver available."

"And the test is in Buckinghamshire, not Kent."

"Right. Which vineyard's that then? Hale Valley? I'm trying to remember what other vineyards there are in Buckinghamshire…"

"It's an experimental plot," I explained. "Very small. Near Amersham."

"Yes, very experimental," nodded Wodin.

"Is it? Right. Well, I'm sure that's fine. We usually demonstrate the Truck Spade by creating a hole a few yards away, then lifting a tree – or vine in this case – and dropping it into the new hole."

"Can you take the vine to Kent?" I said.

"What? From Buckinghamshire? Well, in theory, yes, although we don't usually do that for demonstrations."

"Well, if it's a matter of money," I said. "I'm sure Mr Spott-Hythe will pay. There could be a lot of business in this for you, though. We have several English wine suppliers already interested. Apple producers too. I'm sure you're aware that I also look after Gatesave's cider procurement."

"And I would be delighted to provide a testimonial for other vineyards," added Wodin.

"Ooh, well, I'm sure we can forgo the expenses on this occasion," said Balic, rubbing his hands.

"Oh yes, and it needs to be at night," I said. "The local authority won't allow large vehicles through the village during the day."

"At night?" Balic frowned. "That's very peculiar. I don't think we've ever used the Truck Spade in the dark. Where's this vineyard again?"

"Oh, it's a tiny plot, part of an academic study by the Buckinghamshire College of Agriculture. It's not a commercial vineyard."

"I'm not sure we can do it at night, really. The operator probably won't like it."

"Oh well, if you can't help, then that's that," I said, rolling my eyes. I turned to Wodin. "I'm sorry I've wasted your time, Mr Spott-Hythe. Looks like you'll have to dig up your test vine the old-fashioned way."

"Now, that is a shame," said Wodin, shaking his head.

"Ah, oh, well, hang on, let's not be hasty. Look, let me call the driver. We only have two people qualified to operate the vehicles." Balic pulled out his phone and made a call. After a brief conversation, he nodded.

"Much obliged, Mr Balic, much obliged," said Wodin, pumping his hand once more. "Here's my number. I look forward to seeing your driver at 9 p.m. tomorrow. Tell him to call when he's outside the White Lion."

***

The next night, I holed up in the White Lion, in the heart of the Buckinghamshire countryside, waiting for the driver's call. It had been a beautiful, cloudless summer evening, but the sun was long gone and twilight had faded to black. The bell over the pub door chimed and a man walked in, carrying a small dog.

"Have you seen the size of that bugger outside?" he asked the pub.

"Holy Mary!" said another man, pressing his nose to the window.

Sure enough, the Truck Spade had arrived. The vehicle was colossal, the wheels some six feet in diameter, the cab high above the ground. The giant spade-claw itself lay closed on the truck's flatbed, like a great metal teardrop. I abandoned my pint and strode outside.

"Evening!" I called to the driver. "I'm here to direct you to the vineyard."

The man opened the passenger door and I clambered in.

"It's about a mile from here." The driver crawled his way down Little Chalfont's narrow roads, tutting as tree branches swatted against the cab windows. Bemused dog walkers pressed themselves against the hedgerows, gaping at the monster as it passed. We reached the High Street and I pointed to the municipal car park. The cold night had chased away the Pinot groupies, but they'd be back tomorrow, no doubt.

"Just in there."

"I've never seen a vineyard in a bloody car park," said the driver.

"It's experimental. Just turn in here and drive to the end."

"What the hell is this?" said the driver, as he approached the end of the tarmac, his headlights illuminating the boundary fence.

"The vineyard's on the other side of the fence," I said.

"How am I supposed to get in there then?"

As if by magic, a ten-yard length of the fence began to wobble, gently at first, then more and more vigorously. There was a sound of splitting wood and the fence toppled backwards onto the grass behind. Wodin's and Fistule's grinning faces popped round the sides.

"Hey, man," said Fistule. "Cool truck."

"What in God's name is going on?" said the driver.

"That's the vine," I said, pointing. The headlights, shining through the gap in the fence, now illuminated its bare branches, projecting unsettling shadows onto the houses behind.

"This is the most lunatic job I've ever seen," said the driver, shaking his head. "You want me to pick that up and take it to Kent?"

"Actually, we want you to take it to Brompton."

"You what? Into London? You're off your head."

The driver's eyes widened as Fistule, shining in the headlights, lifted his bong and sucked a lungful of smoke into his body.

"I'd like you to get out of my cab, please," said the driver. "I'm leaving."

"You must be doing all right to walk away from a five-grand job," I said.

"I promise you mate, I don't get paid five *hundred* to do this, let alone five thousand."

"Yes, you do," I said, placing a fat, brown envelope in his lap.

The driver considered the package for a few seconds, looked at me, then opened the envelope. He peered inside, extracted a couple of twenties and held them up against the cab light. I'd withdrawn most of my savings and this was my last roll of the dice.

"All right," he sighed, "let's get on with it."

I leapt from the cab and the driver executed a slow three-point turn, backing the truck through the gap. Wodin and Fistule dragged the fallen fence panels aside and, when the vehicle was a few feet from the vine, I held up my hands.

The driver climbed down and inspected the vine. As instructed, Fistule had hard-pruned it, removing the smaller trailing branches. A stepladder, a saw and a pair of telescopic-arm secateurs lay nearby.

"I had to help Fistule," whispered Wodin. "It was tragic. He was crying so much he couldn't see where to prune."

"I don't get it," said the driver. "Why have you insisted on the Truck Spade 2000? You could lift this with a much smaller model."

"The taproot goes very deep," I said, "and we need to preserve the root structure. It's a very important vine."

"What about cables, pipes? We're right next to this block of flats."

"The whole site was excavated before the vine was planted," I lied. "There's no sewerage or mains beneath the site."

"Must be a bloody important vine…" The driver stopped and looked at each of us. "Hang on. We're in Little Chalfont, aren't we? I saw this on the telly! This is the bloody vine that won wine of the year, or something!"

Fistule removed a rolled-up copy of *Drinks Digest* from his back pocket. He opened the magazine at a well-thumbed page and presented it to the driver.

"That is me, man," said Fistule, illuminating the article with his torch. "The nurturer of this very piece of vinous history."

The driver looked at the picture of Fistule embracing the vine, then back at me.

"Are you stealing this vine?"

"We're not stealing it. It belongs to these gentlemen. But the council have ordered it destroyed. We're taking it to a new home in... Brompton Cemetery."

"They sentenced it to death, man," said Fistule, his voice wavering.

"Bloody nutcases," muttered the driver. "Right, this won't take long. Stand back from the truck."

The driver climbed on to the flatbed and manipulated a panel of levers. The hydraulics hummed into life and a huge piston roused the spade-claw from its sleep, pushing it up and back until the great metal teardrop hung over the ground behind the truck, its sharp end pointing to the earth. Then, with a hiss, like some steampunk Pharaoh's coffin, the teardrop split from top to bottom and opened, revealing a clasp at its centre.

"Stay back," warned the driver. He hopped in the cab and, very slowly, backed up the truck until the vine sat in the centre of the open claw. He climbed back on the flatbed and pushed a lever. The spade-claw closed, imprisoning the vine inside.

"Don't worry," called Fistule. "I won't let them hurt you!" He waved at the driver. "Hey man, can I do the next bit? Please?" He inhaled a lungful of smoke and held out the bong.

"I'd like you to step away from the machinery, please," replied the driver.

The truck emitted a loud, pulsing beep and a row of self-important warning lights on the cab's roof began to flash.

"Christ! Can't you turn that off?" I called.

"No, it's a safety thing."

The spade-claw juddered and hummed and the garden flashed bright orange in time with the beeping, throwing terrifying silhouettes of the vine against the surrounding houses.

"I think the neighbours are going to notice," said Wodin.

The shell of the teardrop split into four huge, curved blades, each ending in a wicked-looking point, and the machine began to dig. Almost politely, the blades took turns piercing the ground, a few inches at a time. As the blades gouged deeper, the huge truck heaved and shook, its rear wheels occasionally lifting clear of the ground. Then, after a minute or two, when each blade had buried itself to the hilt, the machine suddenly stopped and the beeping ceased, leaving the garden in silence.

"Are you all right, my love?" called Fistule. Despite the spade-claw's violence, the vine itself looked fine, a lonely gnarled bush sitting inside the ring of sunken blades.

"Right, the claw's engaged underground. Now we raise it. Stand back, please."

"Pagans!" screeched a woman's voice.

Everyone looked up.

"First Muslims, now pagans!"

It was Mrs Hall, our deranged next-door neighbour, screaming from her bedroom window.

"Yes, thank you, Mrs Hall. You can go back to bed. Nothing to worry about," called Wodin.

"I'm sick of it! You've had pagans in the garden all day and now all this noise! I'm calling the police."

"No need for that, we're going now."

"I'm calling the police!" Mrs Hall's head disappeared.

"We can't have her calling the police," I said to Wodin. "Do something!"

"What do you want me to do?"

"I don't know. Gas her with Fistule's bong or something!"

"I could cut the phone lines, man," said Fistule, brandishing his telescopic-arm secateurs.

"Brilliant! Do it!"

Fistule moved his stepladder in front of Mrs Hall's front door and climbed to the top. He extended the secateurs' telescopic arms to their full length, pointed them to the sky and, rather wobbly, caught the phone line between the jaws.

"It's a bit chewy," he said, swaying alarmingly.

"Keep going!" I called.

The driver was watching Fistule, open-mouthed. "Never mind him!" I shouted. "Extract the vine!"

The driver looked at me, then back to Fistule, then down at his controls. He pushed a lever, the beeping and flashing restarted and the machine began to hum, louder and louder. The suspension creaked and the truck's front wheels rose, inch by inch, from the ground. Then, with a shudder, the spade-claw heaved free of the earth and the wheels bumped down on the tarmac. The teardrop, caked in mud and topped by the vine's naked branches, rose into the air, with the roots, a ton of soil and God knows what else imprisoned within its blades.

I rushed over to the pit and peered in, praying I wouldn't see a stray leg, or a skull, grinning back at me. But there was just a perfect, earthy scoop, pitted here and there with stones and the odd severed root.

"Praise the Lord, it worked," I whispered.

My prayers were interrupted by the crash of a toppling stepladder and a cry for help. I spun round to see Fistule dangling ten feet from the ground, still holding the handles of his secateurs, the jaws of which were enmeshed in Mrs Hall's phone line.

"I'm stuck!" he cried, wiggling his legs.

"Help him, Wodin!" I shouted.

There was no need. The junction box, attached to the telegraph pole opposite, decided the combined weight of Fistule, a pair of secateurs and a dozen neighbourhood phone lines was more than any self-respecting junction box should be expected to bear. In a shower of sparks, it parted company with the top of the telegraph pole, leaving Fistule to swing, feet-first, in a lazy arc through Mrs Hall's kitchen window.

"Argh!" screamed Fistule, as the sound of shattering glass mingled with the chimes of tumbling crockery.

Mrs Hall's head shot out of her bedroom window. She stared at the gigantic hole in the garden, then down at Fistule, whose torso now protruded, face up, from her kitchen. Fistule gazed back up at her, still holding his secateurs, his lower half entangled in her kitchen sink.

"Don't worry, Mrs Hall. I'm fine," he called.

"The police are coming!" she screamed.

"We need to leave," I said to the driver.

"Yes, that's very clear," he replied, manipulating the controls and bringing the spade-claw to rest on the flatbed.

"Wodin, please extract Fistule from Mrs Hall's kitchen. It's time to leave!"

Wodin strode up to the splintered window and grasped Fistule's jacket, dragging him from his resting place, accompanied by the tinkle of glass and distressed crockery.

"Let's go! Let's go!" I shouted, climbing into the cab.

With an arm around Wodin's shoulder, Fistule limped to the truck. I pulled him up and Wodin climbed in behind him. The engine roared to life.

"I'm limited to twenty miles per hour when we're fully loaded," said the driver.

"If the police catch us, you can kiss goodbye to that five grand," I said. "I'll tell them it's the proceeds of crime."

The driver gunned the truck through the car park gates and roared out of Little Chalfont.

Chapter Twenty Two

A Fine Mess

The triumphal arch of Brompton Cemetery emerged from the gloom and our driver slowed.

"How do we get in?" he asked.

"Actually, we're dropping the vine off next door. At the pub. We'll move it ourselves when the cemetery opens." I gave an encouraging smile.

"At the pub," said the driver, flatly.

"Yes, the Brompton Balladeer. Just here, on the right."

We turned off the main road and stopped just beyond the entrance to the pub's beer garden. Wodin and I leapt from the cab and ran to the gate. The Balladeer's manager had required some persuasion to lend me the key but my status as a member of House Terroirist and my promise of a fabulous but mysterious present for his beer garden had done the trick.

The padlock clicked open and I yanked back the bolt. Slowly, the great truck reversed and turned until it lay across the road, its rear wheels nudging up the curb and onto the pavement. I retreated into the beer garden and held up my hands. The truck stopped, just inches from the gate posts. The driver descended from the cab and climbed aboard the truck's flatbed once more.

"Stand back, for Christ's sake. There's hardly any room." He fiddled with the levers and the beeping and orange lights began their performance once more.

"Quicker, damn it!" I whispered, praying that no police car would cruise past and wonder why a vast, flashing truck was depositing a grapevine and a metric tonne of earth into a pub's beer garden at gone midnight.

The hydraulic arm hummed, lifting the spade-claw and its grim, muddy load to an upright position. In an exact reversal of its movements in Little Chalfont, the hydraulic arm extended, pushing the spade-claw out over the rear of the truck until the teardrop hung in the middle of the yard, the tip of the claw hovering just a foot above the paving stones.

"It'll make a hell of a bloody mess," called the driver.

"Do it!" I shouted.

The spade-claw shuddered and the four blades separated and rose, revealing the smooth cone of soil inside. As the blades retreated further, cracks appeared in the great scoop of earth and lumps began to drop off, breaking open on the ground. I had a horrible vision of a corpse falling free too, rolling down the pile of earth and coming to rest at my feet, an outstretched skeletal forefinger pointing at me for the benefit of any passing policeman. But the bulk of the soil held together and suddenly, all at once, the muddy mass slipped from the spade-claw's blades, landing with a thump on the paving.

"Careful!" wailed Fistule, from the side of the road.

The claw, now empty, withdrew from the garden and hummed its way back to its sleeping position on the truck's flatbed. The driver climbed into the cab.

"Thanks ever so much," I called.

The driver didn't reply. The truck growled back on to the main road and disappeared into the night. I stared at the great pile of soil, still crowned by the vine, which now pointed, proudly but drunkenly, at the pub wall. Fistule stood at the base of the heap of earth, stretching his arms up towards the vine to comfort it, but the trunk and branches were out of reach and he had to make do with grasping a root protruding from the dirt.

"Hang on in there, my darling," he called.

"Right," I said, "let's lock up. Wodin, tie that old sheet over the gate." *Best to obscure our grave-robbing antics from the curiosity of any late-night pedestrians*, I thought to myself.

"Ok, man."

Now for the dirty work. Earlier that day, I'd visited a DIY store and purchased a large roll of horticultural fleece, some twine and a shovel, which I'd stashed in a shed in the corner of the pub garden. My plan was to extract Rizzo and his companion from the mass of earth and wrap them in the fleece, ready for collection the next morning by Poletti & Sons, Funeral Directors. It was a plan, however, that I was yet to share with my friends.

I poked at the pile of earth with my spade.

"I have a confession to make, chaps," I said.

I wondered how my dear flatmates would take the news that we were not just vine thieves but grave robbers too. I suspected Wodin would take it in his stride but Fistule was undoubtedly at the more sensitive end of the spectrum.

"Oh, wow. Sounds like we need to stoke the pipe, man." Fistule crouched, clasped his bong between his knees, and crumbled a large pinch of hashish on to the gauze.

"What's up, Felix?" said Wodin.

"You remember when we dug that composting toilet for our trafficked Somali friends, all those years ago?"

"Of course," replied Wodin, "it was a triumph of engineering, until you collapsed it."

"Indeed. I wasn't completely honest with you about how it collapsed, actually."

Fistule exhaled a lungful of sweet smoke. "You broke the toilet, man. No need to beat yourself up about it."

"I didn't break it. I was ambushed by two members of the Calabrian mafia and they fell into the composting pit."

"The mafia?" whispered Fistule. He paused for a minute. "Wow. That must have stunk, man. I bet they were pissed off."

"Yes, Fistule, they were pretty pissed off."

"How long were they pissed off for, Felix?" said Wodin. He took the bong from Fistule and inhaled deeply.

"A couple of minutes."

"Oh," said Fistule. "I thought they'd be pissed off for much, much longer. The mafia know how to keep a grudge, man."

"Yep, it was all over pretty quickly."

There was a pause as Wodin exhaled a long jet of smoke. Fistule looked puzzled.

"They saw the funny side then?" said Wodin.

"Yes. They were hysterical."

Wodin considered the pile of earth for a moment. "That's pretty heavy, Felix. So, what's the plan?"

"They're being collected in the morning."

Fistule held out his hand for the bong. "What's being collected? I thought we were planting the vine here?"

"We are, Fistule. I've bought a big pot and we'll plant her right here, in the corner of the beer garden."

"Cool, man. So... what's being collected?"

"The rest of Felix's mess, Fistule," said Wodin. "Am I right, Felix?"

"Yes. The rest of my mess." I pushed the spade, gently, into the pile of earth. "It's my responsibility, so I'll do the donkey work. But I might need a bit of help at the end. Hope that's ok?"

"What are friends for?" said Wodin, lighting up a large spliff.

"Yeah, man. Whatever you need," said Fistule, holding the bong. He blew a tender plume of smoke up at the vine.

I slowly removed a spade-load of dirt and peered at it, checking for decayed pieces of Mafiosi.

"Well, you're going to have to work faster than that," said Wodin.

He was right. A dose of performance-enhancement was required. I emptied a sachet of *Madame Joubert's Lekker Medisyne Trommel* into a bottle of water, gave it a shake and downed half the liquid.

"When you get to the difficult bit, let us know," said Wodin. "We're in this together."

"Thank you," I said, genuinely touched. *We're not quite all in it together to the same depth*, I thought, observing Fistule as he whispered encouragement up to the vine. But we soon would be.

I felt *Madame Joubert's* warming tingle and, removing my shirt, set to work, hacking at the great mound of earth and shovelling the loose soil and rocks to the far end of the beer garden.

"Careful, man. Mind the roots," warned Fistule. He pulled *The Sayings of The Buddha* from his belt and began to read to himself by the light of a street lamp.

After half an hour's heaving, my spade pushed against something soft. Carefully, I scraped away the mud, revealing a patch of shiny pink fabric. As I removed more soil, a drawing revealed itself, a cartoon face with flowing golden hair, a pink dress, a pair of wings. Finally, an entire fairy princess, complete with sparkling wand, smiled back at me from the mound.

"Oh man, that's the little Wendy house that covered our toilet!" cried Fistule.

It was indeed. I cast my mind back to that terrible night and recalled Rizzo's companion grabbing the tent as he sank into the mire, dragging it with him as he was consumed by the foul fermenting pit. The bodies probably lay just beneath the fabric. I'm not a squeamish chap, but I wasn't much looking forward to unearthing those two again. I was glad I'd fortified myself with a dose of *Madame Joubert's*; the venerable lady's medicine was always good for a little Dutch courage.

I dug around the tent, but for every shovel-load I removed, more dirt cascaded down from the top of the pile. It was another hot and sweaty hour before I'd removed sufficient soil to expose a large enough section of fabric. I pulled on a pair of gardening gloves and yanked the material from side to side, trying to dislodge it further. Then something else caught my eye. More fabric. But not plastic, this was dark wool or cotton. Someone's clothing. Very gingerly, I dug around it with the corner of my spade. The soil fell away and there, looking rather the worse for wear, was a human hand. The skin was black and shrunken but it was still looking very hand-like. It hadn't decomposed anything like as much as I'd expected. A gold ring glinted from one of the fingers. I shivered.

"I've found one of them."

"So you have," said Wodin, peering at the grisly limb. "Well done. Do you need some whisky?" He pulled out his hip flask and waved it at me.

I did and took a hearty swig. The peaty Islay purred down my throat, adding a little Scots backbone to *Madame Joubert's* buzz.

"Found what, man? Oh, man!" Fistule grimaced and pointed.

"Yes, I'm afraid it's a corpse, Fistule. We're here to give them a proper burial."

"Who is it, man?"

"It's the Mafiosi, Fistule. I mentioned they fell into the compostable toilet, remember? Well, they never got out."

"Oh, man! This is bad karma."

"We're improving the karma, Fistule, by giving them a Christian burial."

But Fistule shook his head. "Bad, bad karma," he muttered.

"*They* had bad karma, Fistule. The bad guys," I assured him. "That's why they ended up in the toilet."

"But now we're practising bad karma too, man!"

"No, I planted the vine over them, as a symbol of *good* karma, and to remind us to bury them respectfully when the heat had died down."

Fistule took a long breath from the bong and held it. He was thinking, very deeply.

"We're definitely practising good karma here, Fistule," said Wodin. "You know it makes sense."

Perhaps half a minute went by. Then, finally, Fistule exhaled a long, smokeless sigh. He nodded, slowly. "Yes. We must complete the circle, man. Make things right."

I placed a hand on Fistule's shoulder. "Spoken like the Buddha himself, my friend."

Whether it was karma playing up or not, I definitely had a problem. The vine's roots had grown throughout the mound of soil and completely imprisoned the bodies. Some were slender and could be severed with a few stabs from the shovel, accompanied by pained wails from Fistule, but others were far thicker. It was another grubby couple of hours before I'd chiselled the entirety of the pink tent and the two bodies free of the vine's roots. In the end, I climbed up the pile of earth and grabbed the vine's thick trunk with both hands, dragging it free of the mess. I swear the bloody thing fought back, the remaining canes whipping against my face and the sharp pruned ends digging into my neck. With a huge heave, I dragged the entire vine, from its branched top to the great bolus of mud and roots beneath, free from the pile, and laid it on its side. Fistule flung himself over the vine and embraced it, tearfully, while I paused, panting like an overworked ox, and took another swig of *Madame Joubert's*.

While I'd been working up a fine old sweat, Wodin and Fistule hadn't been entirely idle. They'd unrolled the horticultural fleece and cut it into two large mats, several layers thick, ready to receive the bodies of the unvirtuous gangsters. Both corpses were resting face down, thank God, and I tossed a respectful layer of fleece over each man's head to avoid any accidental ghoulish eye contact. I didn't want my abiding memory of the evening to be a zombie Mafioso grinning up at me in the middle of the night – it would have quite spoiled my enthusiasm for further summer evenings in the Balladeer's beer garden.

Through some clever spadework, I gently cajoled each of the blackened, soil-caked bodies onto the matting. Fistule turned his back and covered his eyes, while Wodin looked on, sombrely. I folded the horticultural fleece over each corpse and, grimacing, rolled them so each was enclosed in a thick layer of fabric. Wodin helped tie the end of each sausage, very tightly, with twine, and together we dragged them to the gate. I was surprised how light the corpses were, barely half the weight of a living body. Other than a rather rich and pervasive earthiness, I was pleased they didn't smell too bad either. *Not a million miles from the aroma of a fine Pinot*, I mused. *There's a tasting note to remember*.

"You're filthy," said Wodin.

I was indeed. My chest and arms were smeared in mud, the rivulets of sweat from my face carving pale lines between the patches of brown. My jeans were caked in earth and I had scratches on my neck from the vine's branches. And now, the sky was lightening in the east. Just an hour or so until sunrise. Poletti & Sons would be here soon.

I'd never had much to do with funeral directors, long-estranged as I was from any elderly or ailing relatives, so I hadn't known what to expect from Mr Poletti or his sons. I'd called the day before, explaining who I was and that I'd been advised Poletti & Sons were the right firm for my needs. I'd been prepared for a degree of surprise, if not downright incredulity, as I sketched out the peculiarities of the job, but the gentleman on the phone was a credit to his profession and couldn't have been more accommodating. Nor did he seem at all surprised when I explained the bodies would require collection at the crack of dawn. It was clear my mysterious Italian friend had briefed them well.

"We understand, sir."

"And, there may be some… soiling. I mean, mud. On the bodies. They're very muddy bodies."

"We've been expecting your call, sir."

"And the bodies are a bit old, too."

"Yes, sir. We're aware."

I suppose funeral directors take possession of soil-coated bodies all the time, when you think about it. There must be thousands every year who die in muddy conditions, whether motorcyclists dismembered on cross-country rallies, people falling drunkenly into silted-up canals, or just old farmers dropping dead in their fields. I was still a little embarrassed, however, at the state of the two I was presenting for collection.

"Do you need any kind of paperwork?" The last thing I'd wanted was an awkward stand-off while the undertaker demanded some bloody medical certificate.

"The paperwork is all in order, sir. We just require the bodies."

"Do I need to… package them up?"

"Just ensure they are enclosed and able to be transported with safety and dignity please, sir."

I looked at the two sausages of netting, tied at each end. They looked pretty safe, though I wasn't so sure about dignified. They looked, in fact, like a pair of giant Christmas crackers. Never mind, too late to worry about that now.

The cost had been eye-watering – three thousand pounds per body. When I protested, the funeral director explained that the fees for Brompton Cemetery were amongst the highest in England and that the state of the bodies required specialist treatment. Did Sir understand the situation?

I suppose Sir did understand the situation, even if Sir suspected he wasn't quite in full control of it. Between the bribe for the Truck Spade operator and the cost of the funeral, I'd cleared out my entire savings. But what choice did I have?

At 5 a.m. on the dot, a vehicle pulled up outside the gate. I peered round the side of the sheet. I'd been expecting a long black hearse, but this was a white van, unmarked. *They must reserve the posh cars for the actual funeral service*, I thought to myself. Two men climbed out and I unlocked the gate. The men looked at the two giant Christmas crackers, at Wodin and Fistule, then back at me. Without a word, they lifted the first body and placed it in the back of the van, followed by the second.

"When's the service?" I asked, feebly.

"Tomorrow, 8 a.m.," said one of the men. "No flowers."

They drove away and I locked the gate.

"Thanks for your help, both of you. I owe you," I said to Fistule and Wodin.

"No worries, that's what friends are for. Good job," said Wodin.

"I hope they show better karma in their next life, man," muttered Fistule, shaking his head. He took a long draw from the bong and returned to his copy of *The Sayings of The Buddha*.

"What a bloody mess!"

The voice made me jump. The manager of the Balladeer stood on the back doorstep, arms folded, and surveyed the mass of earth disfiguring his beer garden. Thank God we'd got the bodies away before the staff arrived.

"Look at the state of you! What the hell are you playing at?"

"We've brought you a present," I said, pointing at the vine, lying on its side like a drunken brawler.

"You've brought me a ton of bloody filth. We open in an hour. I hope you're intending to clear all that up."

"Don't worry, we've got a skip coming at eight. We'll shovel all the muck away, I promise."

"What's so special about this vine, then?"

"Aha!" I said. "Just you wait and see. This will have the punters flooding in. We've bought you a nice big pot too. Next summer, your customers will be dining beneath a canopy of fine Pinot Noir."

"And it will bring you good karma, man," added Fistule.

The manager scowled at Fistule and looked down at the vine, giving the great gob of earth and roots a kick. The vine replied with a dull chime, like a bell under water. A piece of mud fell away, revealing a patch of white porcelain.

"What's that?"

I wasn't sure. I crouched and tried to prize it from the lump of earth. More soil fell away, revealing a larger expanse of ceramic and a curved edge. I hooked my fingers over it and pulled. The object came away in my hand and clanged to the ground. It was, quite clearly, a toilet bowl. The manager looked at me.

"Why is there a lavatory bowl embedded in the vine's roots?"

I thought back to that horrible night, Rizzo's bloodcurdling threats, his accomplice holding a knife to my belly, then their slow, gurgling death in the composting toilet. I remembered Rizzo pulling the ceramic bowl down with him as he floundered, attempting to keep his head above the filthy morass.

"I have absolutely no idea."

"Well, get rid of it please, you've made this place enough of a crap-house already." The manager frowned at a smear of mud on his shoe and stomped back inside.

"Oh, man. Our old toilet, back from the grave," said Fistule. "I don't know if that's good or bad karma."

"I'm sure it's good, Fistule. Right, I need some coffee and I'm going to clean myself up a little. Least I can do is buy you some bacon sarnies."

I placed my order with the scowling manager and headed to the bathroom to wash some of the soil off my body. When I returned outside, my blood froze. In the centre of the garden, hands on hips, stood Sow-Thistle and Cranesbill, frowning at the pile of earth, disinterred vine and marooned toilet bowl. They studiously ignored Wodin and Fistule, who were seated in the corner, busy sharing a ferociously billowing bong.

"Ah, Hart," said Sow-Thistle. "Would you like to explain what you and your peculiar friends are doing here?"

"You should chill out, lads," said Wodin. "We are simply indulging in a little urban viticulture." He held out the smoking bong for Cranesbill, who screwed up his face and twitched. "Suit yourself," shrugged Wodin, passing the hashish bonfire back to Fistule.

"The manager called us," said Cranesbill, "asking why a fellow member of House Terroirist was converting his beer garden into a filthy allotment."

"I'm not sure why I have to explain myself to you two," I said, "but since you ask, I can reveal that the Little Chalfont vine is no longer in Little Chalfont. It is now here, right in front of you, on House Terroirist premises!"

The two men looked at the drunken vine. Sow-Thistle sniffed. "So what?"

"So, the story you're intending to spread, regarding me being involved with Hawkins's Pinot Noir and an alleged vine in Little Chalfont, has been rather undermined, hasn't it?"

"Not really," said Sow-Thistle. "We'll just point out that you've moved the vine here."

"I don't have to remind you that the Brompton Balladeer is House Terroirist premises, do I?" I said. "Surely you wouldn't drag the Minstrels of Wine into this? What about your responsibility to the Institute?"

"You're the one who conspired with Paris-Blois to subvert the Judgement of Basildon," said Sow-Thistle. "It's not our problem that you're also a Minstrel. It makes it even more newsworthy, frankly."

At that, a wave of self-righteous anger swelled in my breast.

"You're a disgrace to the Institute and you're no better than Paris-Blois!" I shouted. It *had* been a bit of a long shot, hoping the *Malherbes* would just drop the story, but after disposing of the bodies, I'd felt as though I was on a winning streak.

"We're wasting our time here," said Cranesbill. He placed his foot against the toilet bowl and pushed it over. It fell on to its side and, with a sad clang, broke in two.

"That's definitely bad karma, man," said Fistule.

Sow-Thistle had been midway through a particularly unpleasant sneer, but his jaw suddenly dropped, as did Cranesbill's.

I looked over at Fistule, who was now standing, and my own jaw slackened too. In one hand he held his smouldering bong, but in the other he held a corroded, gold-coloured pistol, which he was waving vaguely at Cranesbill's head. I'd seen that gun once before, several years ago. It was Rizzo's. The last time it had been wielded in anger, it had been pointed at yours truly, before the good Lord saw fit to plunge it into the composting toilet along with its owner.

"There's no need to be silly," said Cranesbill, raising his hands and twitching. Sow-Thistle raised his too.

"As the Buddha says, if a man speaks or acts with a pure thought," said Fistule, "happiness follows him, like a shadow that never leaves him." He traced a large circle in the air with the pistol, by way of illustration. Cranesbill flinched.

"Fistule makes a very good point," said Wodin.

"But if a man speaks or acts with an evil thought," continued Fistule, "pain follows him. That is the essence of karma, man."

"You really should put that gun down. You're only making things worse," said Sow-Thistle, looking even paler and waxier.

Fistule stretched his arms before him, pointing both gun and bong at the *Malherbes*. Cranesbill flinched again.

"Relax, man. If we act virtuously, the seed we plant will result in happiness." Fistule brought the bong to his lips and, with a gentle underarm lob, tossed the gun at the two men's feet.

The pistol exploded with a sharp crack, smoke and particles of mud spraying from both ends. My ears sang and I clapped my hands to my head. When I removed them, I could hear a persistent, high-pitched sound. *Oh God*, I thought, *I've burst an eardrum*. Then I saw Sow-Thistle clutching his foot and realised the racket was coming from him.

"You shot me!" he squealed, eyes bulging.

"Oh, wow. Sorry, man," said Fistule, the hashish smoke from his lungs merging with the mist of spent gunpowder drifting from the shattered pistol.

But my attention had moved to the clump of earth that had tumbled out of the broken toilet bowl. It had a strange yet familiar shape and was topped with muddy weeds and moss. I lifted it for a closer look. It was much less heavy than I expected, far lighter than a lump of soil.

Sow-Thistle's wail rose to a horrified scream, while Cranesbill just pointed and whimpered, "Oh, Mother of God…"

I was holding Rizzo's head. In pretty bad condition it was too, what with the sunken cheeks and black, dried-out eye sockets. What I'd thought was moss was, in fact, his hair. Revolted, I flung my arm out before me and tried to shake it free, but the hair was entwined in my fingers and the foul bloody thing just jumped around, stuck to my hand.

"Stop! Stop! It's horrible," screamed Sow-Thistle.

"What… what… *is it*?" gibbered Cranesbill.

"It's the head of the last person who crossed us," said Wodin, deadpan.

"Karma, karma, karma," warbled Fistule, in a very unsettling manner.

The two men goggled at Rizzo's mummified skull, terror bleaching their faces white. Their concern was quite understandable, my own face had contorted into a mask of horror and, with hindsight, I've realised my mask-of-horror face looks quite similar to my murderer-about-to-do-some-murdering face. Cranesbill turned and ran, shrieking, from the garden, followed by Sow-Thistle, who hopped after him on his un-shot foot like a drunken wallaby.

As they careered back into the pub, they knocked over the Balladeer's manager, whose curiosity, no doubt, had been aroused by the sounds of shouting, screaming and gunfire.

"What the bloody hell's going on?" he bellowed at the retreating *Malherbes*, who had already flung themselves out of the front door and were putting as much distance between themselves and the pub as their limbs permitted.

"Nothing," I said, holding Rizzo's head behind my back.

"What was that bang? And all the shouting?"

"A car backfiring," I said. "And a disagreement about who was paying for breakfast."

"Well, they've just scarpered, so it looks like *you're* paying," he said, climbing to his feet.

"Yes, of course," I said. "Any chance of those bacon sandwiches?"

The manager glared at me and returned inside. I slipped Rizzo's head into a carrier bag and called Poletti & Sons.

"Ah, hello. This is a little embarrassing, but we missed a bit."

"Missed a bit, sir?"

"Some of the deceased is still here. It became separated from the rest of the body.

There was a pause.

"How much of the deceased, sir?"

"A head's worth. A head."

"A head, sir?"

"Yes, one head. It must have fallen off. Apologies, my fault, very careless. Would you be able to pop back and pick it up please?"

There was a longer pause.

"We'll be right round, sir."

Chapter Twenty Three

Grave Misgivings

The handover of Rizzo's head involved even less conversation than the transfer of the bodies. I suppose all parties were somewhat embarrassed by the situation. Wodin and I had spent a frantic hour, before Poletti & Sons' reappearance, sifting through as much of the earth as possible, checking for any further unsecured skulls, limbs or recognisable organs, while Fistule calmed himself with a series of extra-strong bongs. To my relief, Rizzo's head appeared to be the only noteworthy item to have parted company with its host body.

As the working day began, the skip arrived and we wheeled barrow after barrow of earth through the gate, up a plank and dumped it within. With a mammoth effort, we wrestled the root-bulb of the vine into the big clay planter I'd bought from the garden centre and heaved it upright. The manager pointed to his chosen spot and we rolled the pot into position before filling it with spare soil.

"Your final home, hopefully," I muttered.

The vine didn't reply but she stood proud once more in her new pot, her three arms thrusting upward, like a victorious athlete.

"Safe at last, my darling," said Fistule, stroking the branches.

"It's been a long night," said Wodin. "You coming back to Little Chalfont?"

"No, I have business to take care of in town." The truth was that I didn't dare return to Little Chalfont, not now that the countdown to my execution was ticking. The best plan was to lay low for a couple of days, until I'd formulated my escape plan, then leave the country. I returned to my room at Minstrels Hall and collapsed into bed, fully clothed.

I awoke early evening and phoned Little Chalfont to lay down a false trail and check on any developments since the visit of the Truck Spade.

"Hi, Fistule. I wanted to let you know I'm leaving the country."

"Oh, wow. Where are you going, man?"

"I'm off to the Philippines. I've had enough of the rat race. I'm training to become a diving instructor on the Tubbataha Reef."

"Cool, man. Did you know we're famous again?"

"Famous for what?"

"For aliens, man."

I had a feeling this might be a complicated and incoherent story, so I congratulated Fistule on his renewed celebrity before forcing him to write down the address of a scuba diving centre in Puerto Princesa under the headline 'Felix's forwarding address', read it back to me, correct the spelling, then pin the note prominently to the kitchen wall for the attention of any visiting murderers. In total, the task took around three-quarters of an hour, including several pauses for Fistule to refresh himself from his gurgling bong.

The next morning, I caught the bus to Brompton Cemetery. I wanted to see the two Italians laid to rest with my own eyes. I made my way to the chapel office.

"I'm here for the eight o'clock funeral," I said, tapping on the little booth's window.

The woman didn't look up from her newspaper. "There are three funerals at eight. What name?"

"Rizz… I mean… Rob… Roberto," I mumbled, idiotically.

The woman scowled. "What *surname*?"

"Ah, I'm not sure. Sorry. I only knew him as Roberto. There are two of them. Roberto and… Tim… Timato. They're Italian. They died together. In an accident. Terrible tragedy."

The woman continued to scowl. "There are four burials at the eight o'clock slot. Plots 465a, 476c and 590f."

"Oh, thank you. Could you just repeat those numbers please?"

"465a, 476c, 590f," she spat, before I could fish my pen from my pocket. "Hasn't the funeral company told you which one?"

"Sorry, no. I lost the invitation."

"You'll have to stand by the gate and wait for the cortege to arrive."

She lifted the newspaper in front of her face. For a moment, I thought she was showing me the headline, then I realised it meant the conversation was over.

'Space Oddity' shouted the front page.

And, beneath it:

UFO booze cruisers stole my grapes!

To my astonishment, there was a picture of Fistule, looking like an orphan who'd had his Christmas presents stolen, pointing to the hole left by the Truck Spade in our Little Chalfont garden. I pressed my face against the glass and read on.

The sleepy village of Little Chalfont woke yesterday to find their prize-winning grapevine beamed up by an alien spaceship! Neighbours reported terrifying noises and flashing lights during the night, followed by an explosion. A local hero, who bravely confronted the aliens, was hurled through the window of a neighbour's house by the force of the blast.

Buckinghamshire police raced to the scene, but the extraterrestrials had scarpered, leaving a strange, perfectly smooth hole in the ground. "It was over in seconds," said a witness. "They must have used some kind of tractor beam."

"I've never seen anything like it," said PC Trevor Fladgate of the Buckinghamshire Burglary Squad. "We're completely stumped." Police confirmed there had been some damage to a telegraph pole and some fencing. A local man has been cautioned for possession of cannabis.

"Muslims, pagans and now aliens! We're England's most invaded village!" complains local pensioner. See page 5 for an exclusive eye-witness interview.

Slowly, the newspaper lowered, revealing the chapel administrator's face.

"The first service is due to start in five minutes," she said. "You're going to miss it if you don't get a move on."

As I reached the main gate, I was confronted by two horses pulling a glass-sided carriage, their white plumes bobbing.

I leapt aside and the carriage rolled past, followed by a black limousine and a line of mourners. *Good God,* I thought, *no wonder it had cost three grand per body.* Had they hired all these people specially?

I read the wreaths propped against the coffin, 'Grandad', 'Champ', and 'Undefeated', spelled out in white flowers. Not my funeral, I decided. The next cortege was similarly well-attended, four vehicles in a line, each full of sombre persons of African heritage. That meant the next one was mine.

Sure enough, a minute later, a hearse with opaque panels nosed through the main gate. It turned off the central avenue and bumped down a side track, with me in pursuit. After a minute, the vehicle came to a stop near the perimeter wall.

By the time I'd caught them up, I was out of breath and the two undertakers had already manhandled the coffin out of the hearse. It looked like a very cheap casket indeed, just a few pieces of unpolished plywood knocked together, with no gold knobs or handles to be seen. I started to suspect Poletti & Sons had done rather well out of this little episode. I glanced into the back of the hearse but it was empty.

"Isn't there another coffin?" I asked one of the men.

"We tend to use just one," he replied.

"Even for two people?"

He ignored me.

"Are you family?" asked the other man.

"No… just a friend," I said.

"Did you visit him, then?"

"Visit him?"

"When he was inside."

The man watched my blank face for a few seconds.

"This is George Berkmann of HMP Wandsworth, guest of Her Majesty for the past twenty-five years. Murdered someone in a pub back in the seventies. And now the cancer's got him. Are you sure you're his friend?"

"No," I said, "my friend appears to be missing."

As I walked back to the main gate, I called Poletti & Sons.

"Sorry. The number you have dialled has not been recognised," said an automated voice. "Please check the number and try again."

I suspected I might need to leave the country, very quickly.

***

"Minstrel Hart."

Provost Jordaan didn't turn around. She just stared, serenely, from the tenth-floor balcony, surrounded by her beehives and lavender bushes, watching the twilight fade over the rooftops of central London.

"Hello, Provost," I said.

I'd headed straight back to Minstrels Hall to collect my suitcase and passport, intending to catch a train to Paris that afternoon. But my room had been cleared of all my possessions and the guard posted outside had made quite clear that I was expected in the Top Garden that evening.

"You're not the first person I would have named, when asked to identify the members of a sacrificial death cult residing at the heart of House Terroirist," said Jordaan.

"No. Well, I'm not really in a death cult at all. I can imagine why some people might think I am. I'm not though, I can assure you."

Jordaan turned to me. Behind her, the lights of London's West End caught the silver hairs in her dreadlocks, making them glitter.

"I'm sure you're not. I do, however, have a fellow member of House Terroirist with a bullet wound to the toe – not the most grievous gunshot injury I've seen, granted – and another who claims you brandished a severed head at him."

"I was only trying to scare them. They were blackmailing me."

"You certainly managed to scare them. What were they blackmailing you over?"

"Well… I don't want to compromise myself…"

"You must tell me, Minstrel Hart. I am Provost of your House, and if you wish to retain the privileges and protection of the

Worshipful Institute of the Minstrels of Wine, you are obliged to tell me of anything that threatens the wellbeing of this institution. The penalty for withholding such information is expulsion, as I'm sure you know."

And expulsion from the Minstrels would mean black-balling from any decent wine job on the planet. Oh misery. How the hell had I plunged myself into such a sorry plight? I should have called Sandra's bluff back in Champagne when she first mentioned the Judgement of Basildon. It might have signed my death sentence, but at least it would have saved me the past six months of vicious persecution.

"Don't look so dour, Minstrel Hart. I'm not the police. And I'm not Paris-Blois International either."

I looked up, sharply.

"You wouldn't be the first individual to fall under Paris-Blois's malign influence. Tell me what they've done."

Here we go, I thought. *Washing my filthy laundry in public, yet again.*

"Paris-Blois forced me into a conspiracy to fix the Judgement of Basildon."

"How, exactly, did they force you?"

"They learnt I was involved in the accidental death of a pair of criminals, and they've held that over me for years, threatening to tell the deceased's murderous cronies."

"Go on."

"Then, a group of people within House Terroirist found out about the Judgement of Basildon and my involvement. They're intending to go public with my part in the plot, to embarrass Paris-Blois."

"A group. You mean *Les Malherbes*?"

"You know them?"

"I'm one of them, Minstrel Hart."

My heart sank. Why the hell didn't I buy a flight to Tasmania a week ago, when this nest of vipers first hatched? I'd been within twenty-four hours of escape, only to waltz straight into the arms of the biodynamic lunatics at the final dance. Of course Provost

Jordaan was one of them, she was probably the Grand Dandelion, the Lord High Nettle and Queen of the bloody Daisies all rolled into one.

"I suppose I'm just collateral damage then?"

"No, Minstrel Hart. You're not collateral damage. An attack by a Minstrel on another Minstrel is unacceptable. A member of House Terroirist conspiring against one of their own… that is unforgivable."

I wasn't quite sure whether this meant I was in trouble or not. "Shooting Sow-Thistle was an accident," I mumbled. "The gun went off accidentally."

"Never mind that," said Jordaan. "I'm far more concerned with the dark turn our Judgement of Basildon plan has taken."

"*Your* Judgement of Basildon plan…?"

"Yes, Minstrel. Ours. Or, if we're really assigning credit, hers."

"Who's *her*?"

"We know her as Bittercress."

"Bittercress? You mean Lily… Minstrel Tremaine?"

"Yes. Your lover, I believe?"

For the second time on that rosemary-scented balcony, I blushed as red as a warm Fleurie. "Well, that's rather a strong way of putting it," I mumbled.

"Yes, we're lovers," said a voice. I wheeled round. It was Lily, of course, hidden in the deep shadows that cloaked the rear of the balcony. She stepped forward and the city's glow illuminated her face, complete with knowing smirk.

"Then why would Minstrel Hart deny it?" said Jordaan.

"Maybe he's embarrassed," said Lily.

"I have nothing to be embarrassed about," I declared.

"Oh, I think it's abundantly clear that's untrue," said Jordaan. "But what's more important is that we retake control of the situation, now we all know where we stand."

I didn't have the slightest idea where I stood, to be honest. It sounded like yet another layer of conspiracy in which I was nothing more than an innocent lamb, tethered to a stake in a clearing in some godforsaken jungle.

"What are you even doing here?" I said to Lily. "You're not a member of House Terroirist!"

"The Provost may invite *any* Minstrel into the Terroirists' realm," said Jordaan, sharply. "Bittercress is my guest. She is under my protection."

"Oh. Well, that's good, I suppose. And what did you mean when you said this was Lil... Bittercress's plan?"

"It was hers from the very start," said Jordaan. "Tell him, Bittercress."

"I gave Lord Flashman the idea of a competitive blind tasting a year ago," said Lily. "Back in the seventies, there was a famous tasting in Paris, pitting the top wines of Bordeaux against those of California. It caused quite an upset, as I'm sure you know. I suggested a repeat, featuring Pinot Noir. Flashman loved the idea. In fact, he was quite annoyed he hadn't thought of it himself."

"How did you know Paris-Blois's wine would be included? I thought the French wines were chosen by Sir Francis Walsham."

"I couldn't guarantee it, but as the most expensive wine in the world, Domaine Henri-Leroy was highly likely to be a contender."

"Ex-most expensive," smiled Jordaan. It was true. At last week's Hong Kong fine wine auction, Domaine Henri-Leroy had plummeted to seventy-eighth in the price league table. No wonder Boulle's throat-slitting gesture had been so heartfelt.

"House Terroirist is well aware of the tricks employed by Paris-Blois to inflate the value of their price-gouging wines," continued Jordaan. "We know they pay agents to bid up their own wines at auction, for example. And we've identified at least one famous wine reviewer who has benefitted handsomely from his unadvertised relationship with the company."

"Doesn't surprise me in the slightest," I said.

"So, when Bittercress's impressively conceived plan was presented to the *Malherbes*, we were delighted to help."

"You told me it was Percy Woods, blabbing to his boyfriend about how he'd been blackmailed, that alerted you to the conspiracy," I said.

"That was a slight fib," said Lily. "I wasn't ready to reveal myself to you." I frowned and thought back to that night in the Balladeer's guest room, Lily stripping off her clothes in a matter of seconds and demanding I do the same.

"Originally, we just wanted to embarrass Paris-Blois," continued Lily. "We were confident their wine would lose in a blind tasting against other fine Burgundies or even top Pinots from other countries. Then news reached us of Percy's blackmail and it became clear they intended to subvert the competition. Once *you* turned up in Vougeot, with your transparent attempt to trick me into helping you, we realised there was a full-scale conspiracy afoot. A conspiracy we decided to blow wide open. Can you imagine the damage that would have caused to Paris-Blois? It might have brought down the whole company."

"I imagine that wasn't lost on Paris-Blois," I said. "As Tom Hawkins found to his cost."

"Yes," said Jordaan. "Things got rather out of hand. Your Little Chalfont wine rather inflamed the whole situation; we hadn't planned for that. And, for some reason, Sow-Thistle and Cranesbill took a strong dislike to you, Felix, and became fixated on exposing your part in the conspiracy, to the exclusion of everything else."

"I don't know what their problem was," I muttered. "Sheer jealousy, I expect."

"Actually, Sow-Thistle did make a pass at me when we first met," said Lily. "Which I turned down," she added quickly.

I thought back to yesterday morning at the Balladeer, Sow-Thistle wailing with pain and hopping around, clutching his mangled toe. I smiled to myself. "There you go, then. But why are you telling me all this? A week ago, you were merrily selling me down the river, accusing me of being a cowardly mercenary."

"I thought you were. I didn't believe you about Tom Hawkins's death, not at first. And I hadn't realised you were being blackmailed. Then, you retrieved those photographs of me from Paris-Blois at the Brixton Grand, while you were in danger. And I remembered the phone messages you left, after you had that trouble in the Loire chateau. Those are the actions of a man of principle, not a mercenary."

Lily looked at me, she wasn't smirking now. I was rather lost for words, to be honest. I'm not used to being called a man of principle.

"We know you're with us," said Jordaan, softly. "Bittercress came to see me last weekend, as soon as she realised the gravity of the situation. We're conscious that you're in trouble, and the protection of a member of House Terroirist takes precedence over a campaign, even one as important as bringing down Paris-Blois."

"On balance, you've probably helped us, really," said Lily. "The victory of your Little Chalfont wine was far more humiliating for Paris-Blois than if they'd simply lost against some other fine Burgundies. The story was covered from Shanghai to San Francisco."

This sounded better. And Lily's smirk was back, which was a good sign too. At least she and Jordaan realised I was on the side of the angels. Now I just had to convince the rest of the world.

"What are you going to do about those two fascists you've been hanging around with, then? They're a bloody liability. They're determined to expose me and the Little Chalfont wine story, even if it sucks in you, the Minstrels and House Terroirist. They're obsessed!"

"We appreciate that our colleagues' zeal has overwhelmed their sense of priorities," said Jordaan. "Their methods, in fact, threatened to bring the roof down on our heads. As a result, they have been banished from *Les Malherbes*."

This sounded better still. With a bit of luck, they'd been nailed into a barrel and hurled into the Thames too.

"But they're intending to go public with the Little Chalfont story," I said.

"I don't think they will. For one thing, you've put the fear of God into them. For another, I've told them they'll be disciplined and expelled from the Minstrels if the news gets out. And then I'll be unable to protect them from the attentions of your sacrificial death cult."

"What about Carter, the journalist for *Drinks Digest*? They might have told him already. He wouldn't want to spike such a great scoop."

"I've spoken to the editor-in-chief, who happens to be a Minstrel of Wine. They won't be linking you with the Little Chalfont vine. They have little interest in putting out a highly speculative story that might embarrass Paris-Blois, their main source of advertising income. I understand Paris-Blois have already threatened the magazine with legal action if they so much as hint at a conspiracy."

"Oh, good. Thank you, Provost."

"You're welcome. Congratulations on your membership of *Les Malherbes*. You'll be working with us now, under our protection. You're not much use to us in prison or dead, are you? I have a feeling you'll be very effective in our campaign against malevolent entities like Paris-Blois."

"The pleasure's all mine." *Oh well. Better inside the tent wetting my own mattress than outside being peed on by the rest of the campsite*, I thought.

"You require a *naturae nomine*," said Jordaan. "A name by which you will be addressed by fellow *Malherbes*. I have decided upon Lady's Bedstraw. A low, scrambling weed, sometimes considered invasive, but quite pretty and not without its uses."

"Bedstraw it is. Much obliged."

"Now then. To more serious matters. From the look of your suitcase, you were planning to leave the country. And I don't think it was for a short holiday, was it?"

"I'm in peril, Provost. A hunted man. It's Pierre Boulle. The man's got it in for me. He's completely unhinged."

"You're close to danger, true. But you're safer here for the next couple of days. We've prepared a secret room for you, in the heart of House Terroirist. We'll post a guard outside."

"I'd rather take my chances abroad, I think. There are some peculiar types hanging around Minstrels Hall these days."

"It's not an option, Minstrel. You're staying here. And you'll have to occupy the room alone, I'm afraid. We don't want you two drawing attention to yourselves."

That's a shame, I thought. *A weekend locked in a small room with Lily would have been a lot more enjoyable.*

Lily stepped forward and kissed me. "Good luck, Bedstraw," she whispered, before slipping away into the shadows.

"I'm having lunch with Provost Jägermeister of House Mercantilist tomorrow," said Jordaan. "As you know, House Mercantilist includes, among its membership, employees and operatives of Paris-Blois International. That's not a sin, of course, even if that company's business practices frequently border on the obscene. Provost Jägermeister is a far-sighted man, however, and he won't want any bad apples threatening the whole barrel."

I had the sense of treading water and realising the ocean bottom was not just a few feet down but miles, and that a vast, unknowable depth lay beneath my innocent, paddling legs.

"Can you stop them bumping me off?"

"No. But I understand you're not in danger until Monday."

"How do you know that?"

"We hear things." Jordaan smiled and shook her head. "I can't begin to wonder how you found yourself in so much trouble, Minstrel."

"No, me neither. It's a rum old do, it really is."

"It's time to retire to your new quarters. Take dinner in your room tonight and stay there tomorrow too. Keep a low profile."

Behind me, a guard cleared his throat. I turned to leave.

"Just one more thing, Minstrel. That was a *fake* head you brandished at poor Cranesbill and Sow-Thistle yesterday, wasn't it?"

I laughed, wildly. "Of course!"

Jordaan turned away and stared over the city once more.

Chapter Twenty Four

Restructure

Sunday brought the sharp, familiar tap of staff against door. I peered through the spy-hole and there was my guard, beckoning me to open up. Was it safe? No more likely to be a trap, I judged, than any of the other knocks on the door over the past week. Might there be news following Jordaan's meeting with the Provost of House Mercantilist?

"You'll be wanting lunch," said the guard. "Provost Jordaan suggests the Salon de Dijon."

Why there? It was my favourite, of course, but that was no reason for Jordaan to propose it. I took the service lift down to the third floor.

The moustachioed Italian saw me before I saw him. He was sitting behind a low table, in a corner armchair, facing the door. I froze, teeth clenched, but he just nodded, quite calmly, at the empty chair beside him. I approached, heart fluttering, and eased myself into the seat. The Italian studied the newspaper on his lap.

"I arranged the funeral, as instructed," I said.

"I know," said the Italian, without looking up.

"I waited for the burial but there must have been some confusion. I couldn't find the ceremony and the undertaker's number…"

"I know."

Well, it's wonderful you're so well informed, I thought. *Care to share your inside track? Or are you just going to garrotte me?*

"Do you work for Paris-Blois?" I said, ready to spring away if the man's hand so much as hinted at straying to his jacket pocket.

The Italian didn't answer, just placed his newspaper on the table and pushed it towards me. It was the previous day's copy of *Il Mattino*, folded to an inside page. My knowledge of Italian doesn't stretch much further than menus and wine lists but before I could confess my ignorance, the man tapped an article, halfway down the page.

Corpi scoperti a Reggio.

Reggio is a city in Calabria, a region famous for hearty wine, grilled cheese and spicy 'Nduja paste. It's also the headquarters of the *'Ndràngheta*, the most vicious mafia clan in Christendom. *Corpi*, I was pretty sure, meant bodies. I peered at the picture, a pair of police cars parked outside an office building.

"The burial took place, as planned," said the Italian. "The gentlemen, I'm afraid, enjoyed only one night of peace before they were disturbed again. Perhaps they will find a more permanent resting place soon."

I stared, uncomprehendingly, at the article. There was something familiar about the building. But what? I'd only visited Reggio a couple of times, and then only to fly in or out of the airport. There was a logo above the door. The letters 'P' and 'B', artistically combined. Paris-Blois International.

"You should stay in Minstrels Hall today and tomorrow. Don't be tempted to leave, Minstrel Hart."

He withdrew the newspaper and folded it, then stood up.

"Your girlfriend is very beautiful," he said.

"Thank you," I replied, in utter bewilderment. "I'll pass that on."

***

Monday. The day of my termination. I'd placed a chest of drawers against the door, just in case the *'Ndràngheta* were early risers and did their murdering before breakfast. I phoned Gatesave once more, informing them my body was on the mend following my ham poisoning, but that I'd need a couple more days to recover properly.

"The Director of Commerce is on the warpath, Felix," said Sharon, the departmental secretary. "He keeps calling you Broken Hart."

"I'm sure he's just being affectionate."

"He keeps calling you That Bloody Arsehole as well. He's talking about shaking up the wine department and getting back to basics. I think he's got it in for you."

"Thanks, Sharon, just what I wanted to hear while recovering from a ruptured spleen. Send my regards to the team."

Wonderful, I thought, *I'll add The Dick to the ever-expanding list of people who want to see me in an early grave.*

I was hungry but didn't dare call room service, out of fear my scrambled eggs might be poisoned. I decided to eat upstairs, in the open, at La Terraza Asada. I pulled the chest of drawers back, just enough to open the door a few inches.

"Minstrel Hart, you have a dinner invitation at the Salon de Bordeaux, tonight," said my guard, as I squeezed through the gap.

"Who's invited me?"

"Minstrel Delacourt. He said he'd be delighted to share another bottle of claret with you. Provost Jordaan asked me to tell you the invitation is legitimate."

Legitimacy was the least of my concerns. Safety, security and long life were somewhat higher up the list, particularly where it involved my dear, innocent body. Once on the rooftop, I insisted on watching the chef cook my sausages and bacon, before removing them from the grill myself. I ate slowly, with my back against the wall, scanning my fellow breakfast companions for assassins, then headed back to my room.

Evening arrived and I took the back stairs down to the Salon de Bordeaux, though not before tucking a stolen steak knife in my sock for protection. The *maître d'hôtel* led me to the far corner and there sat Delacourt, at a table laid for two. He stood and shook my hand.

"Here we are again," I said.

"A pleasure, as ever," replied Delacourt.

"What are we drinking tonight then? More Château Nenin?"

"You'll have to ask your host."

"I thought you…"

"Thank you, Charles," said a familiar voice.

I span round. Sandra stepped past me and kissed Delacourt on each cheek. He smiled and gave a little bow in return. Then, with a brief nod to me, he glided away through the tables.

"Have a seat, Felix. We're on a date."

I must have blanched, because Sandra raised her eyebrows.

"Are you feeling all right?"

Was this it then? Was the *coup de grâce* to come from Sandra herself, right here in Minstrels Hall? I suppose this is how it worked at the highest levels of the mafia. It was a question of respect. I raised my foot and tapped my ankle, checking the steak knife was still there. Where was her gun? In the clutch bag, it had to be. I couldn't see any bulges in her figure-hugging dress, except the obvious ones, which distracted me for a second... *Christ, Felix, concentrate! It's a trap!*

"What *is* the matter with you? Are you having some sort of spasm?"

"No," I said, wondering if I should make a grab for her clutch bag before she had a chance to withdraw her pistol.

"Well, sit down then."

Sandra tossed her purse on the table and took her seat. It landed softly, without the momentum a concealed firearm would have given it. No, Sandra would have tucked the murder weapon into a stocking, no doubt, the barrel snug against her inside thigh. I lowered myself into the chair, feeling under the tabletop for the metal tube designed to direct the fatal bullet from her pistol to my stomach.

"I have some sad news," said Sandra.

"There's a lot of it about," I replied, exploring the underside of my seat for limpet mines.

"Pierre Boulle passed away today."

"Oh dear." *That's not sad news*, I thought, cheering up slightly.

"He was on a business trip, in Italy. To our office in Reggio, in fact."

"Reggio," I repeated. The Italian man and his newspaper article. "They found some bodies," I said, attempting to sound informed but feeling even more stupid.

266

"Yes, they did."

A waiter glided in, brandishing a bottle of Champagne. We remained silent as he filled both glasses.

"How did he die?" I asked, once the waiter had departed. I clinked Sandra's outstretched glass and took a large gulp. She smirked as I swallowed the liquid. Of course, poisoned Champagne! What a schoolboy error. I clutched my throat and grimaced.

"You *are* behaving very strangely today, Felix. I understand you've been under a lot of pressure." She took a sip herself. "Do you want some water?"

I nodded and poured myself a glass. It was only after I'd drained it that I realised it might be the water that was poisoned.

"Pierre was in Reggio for a meeting with some business associates. He wished to inform them of the identity of the man who murdered their colleague, Signor Rizzo, several years ago."

Here we go, I thought. I finished the glass of Champagne in one gulp, reasoning it might dilute the effect of the poisoned water.

"He claimed Rizzo had been killed by a double-crossing Englishman, and that the murder took place in a village called Little Chalfont, a few miles from London. He even claimed to know the exact burial site."

"Fancy that," I mumbled.

"Just two days earlier, however, Rizzo's body and that of his associate had been unearthed in Reggio itself, in the grounds of a property owned by Paris-Blois. The bodies were not in good condition, but they were buried in their clothes and with all their possessions, including credit cards, so identification was quite straightforward. It sounds as though you've read about it already."

"Yes. I… spotted it in the paper."

Sandra refilled my glass.

"A nasty business. And one which completely undermined Pierre's story. Can you believe someone had actually *beheaded* the unfortunate Signor Rizzo? He must have become involved with a very unpleasant crowd."

I shook my head, then nodded, attempting to convey simultaneous wonder and disgust.

"I'm not sure what Pierre's involvement was with these Reggio business associates, but they didn't believe his story of Rizzo dying at the hands of an Englishman at all. In fact, with the corpses being unearthed on Paris-Blois premises, they concluded that Pierre was intimately involved in the murder and assumed his story was a cynical attempt to cover up his own guilt. I understand there are rumours that Pierre was involved in a drugs and people-smuggling ring."

"Oh. So what did they do?"

"They shot Pierre dead, Felix. A few hours ago."

Upon hearing this terrible news, my spirits rose and warmth flowed to my tender breast. I felt like a peasant watching the sun peep over the horizon after a long and vicious winter.

"Right. So… that's the end of all that?" I suggested.

"The end of what?"

"The end of… our business difficulties?"

"I don't know what you're talking about, Felix. The reason we're having dinner is that I've been promoted from UK to European Sales Director. I've just got off the phone with our CEO. I thought you might want to congratulate me."

"You got Boulle's job. You must be thrilled."

It occurred to me that Boulle had barely been dead more than a couple of hours and our dinner date had been arranged since this morning, but I didn't want to raise awkward facts on such a happy occasion. I was gratified to be feeling thoroughly un-poisoned too, unless the venom was a particularly slow-acting variety. I took another mouthful.

"Yes, it's nice to receive the recognition. Pierre was being groomed to be Paris-Blois's next CEO but, to be quite honest, I don't think he was good enough."

"Well, I never liked him."

"I'm sure you didn't."

"So, you were next in line?"

"Paris-Blois's UK sales have been very strong over the past year. Champagne was a particular highlight, of course. I probably couldn't have done it without you, Felix."

"Well, I'm delighted I could help. I hope your successor is as rigorous in their attention to our mutual business as you've been."

"Thank you, Felix. I'll be sure to appoint a suitably attentive successor. And just because I'm overseeing Paris-Blois's entire European business doesn't mean I'll neglect the Gatesave relationship. After all, you've always been my favourite account."

"Yes, I've been flattered by the attention." I suspected this was my last opportunity to understand exactly what was going on. "Who was my Italian friend in the Salon de Dijon? The one with a sideline in international funeral logistics."

"It's not important. Just a man representing an organisation whose interests suddenly aligned with ours."

"Ours? You mean yours?"

"I mean ours. And the interests of some members of this Institute."

"Members of House Mercantilist, I suppose?"

Sandra looked around, quite casually, perhaps to check whether anyone was listening.

"You gave me the idea, actually, when you were diving in and out of that barrel at Château Trélazé, claiming to be an assassin hired to liquidate our CEO. You're an unreliable partner, Felix, but you're good under pressure, I'll grant you that."

I didn't really want to relive last month's near-drowning so I remained silent, but I confess to having felt a grim satisfaction with the way things were turning out.

"You haven't congratulated me yet," said Sandra.

"Congratulations." I raised my glass.

She touched hers against it. "Here's to us." Sandra leaned closer and lowered her voice. "I know I promised you a long weekend at Maison Flavigny recently. I suppose I've missed my chance."

"Well, never say never," I said, attempting to hide my surprise.

"I think you're already spoken for."

"Why do you say that?"

"Because she's standing over there."

I followed Sandra's eyes across the room to a small group standing at the bar. One of their number stood slightly apart, unsmiling, staring right at us. It was Lily.

I raised my glass and Lily, without changing her expression, did the same.

"You've done well there." Sandra refilled my glass.

"Just a friend."

Sandra smiled. "I received a phone call last week, very early in the morning, from a young woman. She didn't give her name, but she got straight to the point, which is a quality I admire. She said she knew that someone might have to die. And she expressed a preference that it shouldn't be you."

"Oh. That's good."

"Quite. Then, she asked whether it might have to be me. And, of course, I said no, I didn't want it to be me. And so, she suggested I find someone else."

I took a sip of Champagne and glanced over at Lily. She was still watching.

"You know, Felix, I'm not sure whether she had the means, but I can tell when someone's determined. It might even have helped focus my mind, actually."

"Could have been anyone," I said. "I'm sure there's no shortage of jealous women wishing you harm."

Sandra smiled. "That almost sounds like a compliment."

"It was probably your CEO's wife."

"The call came from your mobile number, Felix."

I paused, mid-sip.

"Which, I imagine," continued Sandra, "was deliberate."

The waiter appeared, noiselessly. "Madame. Monsieur. Are you ready to order?" He lifted the bottle and made to top up Sandra's flute.

"That's enough for me, thank you," said Sandra, holding her hand over her glass. "And I won't be ordering, the gentleman is dining with someone else."

She rose and I, somewhat confusedly, did the same.

"I'll say goodnight now, Felix. Is there anything else I can help with in the meantime?"

"I think that's probably everything. Unless you can get rid of my Director of Commerce? He appears to rather have it in for me."

Sandra raised her eyebrows.

"That's a joke, of course," I added, hastily.

"One good turn deserves another, Felix. Just remember to keep count." Sandra leaned in and kissed me on the lips, for slightly longer than necessary. "Enjoy your dinner."

As Sandra departed, I saw that Lily was already halfway across the restaurant. As she reached me, she kissed me on each cheek.

"Mind if I join you?"

She sat without waiting for an answer. I was conscious that a fair proportion of the restaurant was observing the comings and goings of these two beautiful women and, I have to say, I was rather enjoying being the centre of attention.

"What's the verdict then? Are you in the clear?"

I sat and ran my eye down the wine list, pausing at the superlative end of the Champagne section. I pointed to the Dom Ruinart Rosé and the waiter beamed.

I closed the menu cover with a snap.

"I think a short period of celebration may be in order," I replied.

Chapter Twenty Five

One for the Road

After a week of mafia persecution, medieval torture and midnight grave robbery, my return to the office that Wednesday morning was something of an anti-climax. I fired up the laptop and waited for the cascade of emails to rattle into my inbox.

A woman's hand touched my shoulder. "A word, please, Felix."

The Head of Human Resources. That meant almost certain bad news. She glided to a nearby meeting room, like the angel of death. I followed and she slid the glass door shut behind us.

"I have a sensitive matter to discuss."

This was it then. The Dick had finally got his way. I was out, exiled, about to be sacrificed like a virgin atop an Aztec pyramid.

"I realise my indisposition over the past couple of weeks has been inconvenient for the business," I began, "but I really was erupting from both ends, with shocking vigour."

"I don't doubt it, Felix. We're not here to discuss your alimentary issues." The HR Director opened a folder and removed a photograph.

"Do you recognise this woman?"

I did. It was the pretty concierge at Maison Flavigny, Paris-Blois's magnificent Champagne château, the only bright spot in that otherwise corrupt and dismal trip.

"She has made an allegation of inappropriate behaviour..."

By God, I thought, *that's an outrage!* There I was, nearly naked, and the little minx had barged into my room and absolutely thrown herself at me. I opened my mouth to protest but the Director ignored me.

"...against the Director of Commerce."

I closed my mouth.

"How disappointing," I said.

"Quite. I understand the young woman didn't want to cause a fuss, but her employer operates a zero-tolerance policy regarding such episodes. Quite rightly."

"Yes, I should jolly-well say so."

The HR Director observed me over her glasses.

"I need you to confirm one more thing for me, please."

She extracted another photograph. It was a picture of the château's guest book, open at the page the Director of Commerce had signed.

Manifique! Steve 'The Dick' Pendle.

"The Director of Commerce's host that evening, a lady named Sandra, who I believe you know, stated that he was behaving boorishly that night, boasting of his... physical attributes... amongst other inappropriate comments."

I stared at the photo and my cheeks flushed a little.

"Sandra said she'd shown you this entry in the guest book, when you stayed a week or so later, and expressed her concern at the Director's behaviour. Is that the case?"

"Yes," I whispered.

"I understand why you might have felt awkward reporting such an issue, particularly given the seniority of the colleague involved, but you do understand how important it is to protect the integrity of the Gatesave brand, don't you?"

I nodded.

"Don't worry, Felix. This isn't your fault. Thank you for your help confirming the evidence. The Director of Commerce has been placed on indefinite leave. I don't expect he'll be back. And I trust I can count on your discretion?"

"Discretion is my middle name."

"Good. And, difficult as it is to see a silver lining in such a sorry episode, we've promoted the Head of Charcuterie, Olive Oil and Delicatessen to fill the vacancy left by the Director of Commerce."

I nodded, slowly.

"And that, in turn, leaves a vacancy in Delicatessen. We're under pressure on numbers right now, so we can't afford to recruit. But the remaining directors speak highly of you and we feel it's within your capabilities to perform your current role and this new one simultaneously."

My eyes opened wider.

"The Head of Delicatessen role requires a great deal of travel. In addition to your existing wine role, we will require you to spend even more of your time abroad, meeting suppliers, sourcing product, and representing Gatesave with integrity and pride. By way of support, we will provide you with an executive assistant, and there will be a modest increase in your remuneration, to reflect your greater responsibilities. Do you accept?"

"Madam Director, I do."

"Excellent. And congratulations." The Head of Human Resources shook my hand, gathered her papers and left.

Well, the wheels of natural justice turn slowly, I mused, *but perhaps the righteous do receive their just rewards, after all*. I was lost in reverie for a minute, dreaming of olive oil sourcing trips to the Amalfi coast, dinner tables heaped with fresh pasta and risotto, fabulous desserts of ricotta and pear washed down with Limoncello.

I was brought back to earth by a buzz from my mobile.

A message from Sandra.

You owe me.

The End

CORKSCREW

The highly improbable,
but occasionally true, tale of a professional wine buyer.

Don't miss *Corkscrew*, the first novel in the Felix Hart series and the prequel to *Brut Force*.

Felix Hart, a tragic orphan, is expelled from school, cast on to the British high street and forced to make his way in the cut-throat world of wine retail. Thanks to a positive mental attitude, he is soon forging a promising career, his sensual adventures taking him to the vineyards of Italy, South Africa, Bulgaria and Kent.

His path to the summit, however, is littered with obstacles. Petty office politics, psychotic managers and the British Board of Wine & Liquor prove challenging enough. But when Felix negotiates the world's biggest Asti Spumante deal, he bites off more than he can chew and is plunged into a vicious world of Mafiosi, people smuggling and ruthless multinationals.

Part thriller, part self-help manual and part drinking companion, Corkscrew is a coruscating critique of neo-liberal capitalism, religious intolerance and the perils of blind tasting.

"One of the funniest novels I've ever read. I honestly didn't want this book to end."
The Wine Stalker

"...casual storytelling mastery and the sharp-tongued wit of Tom Robbins..."
John Staughton, Self-Publishing Review

"...if any of it is true, any at all, then Peter himself has truly had a wild ride."
RedWinePlease.com